Return items to **any** Swindon
time on or before the date sta
and Audio Books can be ren
library or visit our website.
www.swindon.gov.uk/libraries

Copying recordings is illegal. All recorded items
are hired entirely at hirer's own risk

6 689 627 000

CONFERENCE INTERPRETING

PRINCIPLES AND PRACTICE

Third Edition

Valerie Taylor-Bouladon

First Published   2000
Revised Reprint 2001
Second Edition   2007
Third Edition 2011

Cover designed by David H. Barrett

National Library of Australia Cataloguing-in-Publication entry
    Taylor-Bouladon, Valerie, 1927 -
        Conference interpreting : principles and practice.
        Bibliography.
        ISBN 1-4196-6069-1
        1.   Communicative competence.
        2.   Translating and interpreting.
        3.   Congresses and conventions. I. Title

    418.02

CONTENTS

The assertiveness of minority languages -
television and dialect - the paradox: Will American-
Asian-English prevail ?- European Language Portfolio -
European Language Council - French National Institute
for Oriental Languages and Civilisation - Intergovern-
mental Agency for French-speaking Communities - The
Linguasphere Register and Observatory –
Terralingua - The very last word.

Further reading

FOREWORD

During its brief history Australia has undergone many political and social changes. From a far-flung outpost of the British Empire, it has become a sovereign nation.

From a country looking, despite geographical distance, towards Britain for economic sustenance and a cultural philosophy, it now asserts its independence as a nation in the Asia-Pacific region, and is coming to terms with its own, as opposed to a borrowed, culture. From a country strongly conscious of its Anglo-Celtic background, and its brief flirtation with the White Australia policy, it has, in the years since the end of World War Two, become a multicultural society in which migrants from all around the world can proudly maintain their own cultural traditions and languages while conscious of the fact that they are Australian. Not all migrants have been able to speak English, Australia's official language, and there grew from this, in the early 70s, a recognition on the part of the Commonwealth Government that provisions should be made for the provision of interpreters and translators to assist them in their dealings with English-speaking government officials, medical practitioners, bank clerks and the like. This led to the establishment of a government body charged with the accreditation and organisation of training of interpreters and translators to work in the local community - community interpreters. For the first time in Australian history, formal and official recognition of the need for, and the value of, the interpreter began to take root. And at the popular level, there was for the first time a faint glimmer of awareness of the role and function of the interpreter.

It is against this background that we need to consider the role of the Australian conference interpreter in contemporary Australia. We need to understand that the conference interpreter, while obviously able to undertake community interpreting, is *not* a community interpreter. The level of skills and expertise required by the conference interpreter to be able to interpret at an international conference, or at a Ministerial Meeting is very much higher than that required of the community interpreter. We need to understand that while the community interpreter works at the *local* level, the conference interpreter works at the *international* level, where there is still no guarantee that diplomats, politicians and conference delegates will have language skills in any other than their native language.

The author of this book is the *doyenne* of the conference interpreting profession of Australia. Much of her long and highly successful career has been spent working for international bodies in multilingual Europe with its proud history and tradition of conference interpreting. She has, however, been able to achieve a great deal for her profession in her adopted country at all levels. Her dedication, her enthusiasm, her generosity with her time, her willingness to help, and her (dare 1 say it?) *implacable* insistence upon the maintenance of the highest professional standards have touched many in this country. Indeed, she may not realise it, but it was these precise qualities of hers that led to the decision to set up a postgraduate conference interpreting training program in my university back in 1980. She has had to fight, and is still fighting, many battles for the profession in Australia, and all Australian interpreters owe her an immense debt of gratitude.

Conference interpreting has come of age. The

skills and techniques of conference interpreters have gained international recognition. These skills are now the subject of research by linguists and cognitive psychologists, as well as interpreters, as they teach us much about the workings of the human brain and the interpreting process. Indeed, the number of books and journal articles being published each year is increasing.

The continuation of research into cognitive and linguistic aspects of simultaneous and other forms of conference interpreting is obviously important. But so, too, is it important to write about conference interpreting from the conference interpreters' point of view. It is thus gratifying to have, at long last, a book about the practical and vocational aspects of conference interpreting written by a practising conference interpreter, for interpreters and would-be interpreters.

Within this book, which has obviously been a labour of love, the author shares with her readers her thoughts on a variety of topics and provides the reader with a distillation of her many years of professional experience - from the "how tos" and the "dos and don'ts" to matters ethical, organisational and mechanical, and everything in between. Herein is to be found a wealth of practical information, coupled with a dynamic and honest insight into the world of the conference interpreter. Not only is this a book that no interpreter or interpreting student will want to be without, but it is also, for the general reader, an excellent introduction to the fascinating and "larger than life" world of the conference interpreter.

Peter Davidson　　　　　*Director, Japanese Language Proficiency Unit*
　　　　　　　　　　　　The University of Queensland.　　July 2000

ACKNOWLEDGEMENTS

I would like to take this opportunity of expressing my gratitude to three brilliant interpreters and excellent colleagues: Eric Simha, Gedda Preisman and Pierre Lambert, prominent conference interpreters in Geneva in the 1950's and 1960's, whose solidarity and encouragement were so precious at the beginning of my career. They even managed to break the tension and make me laugh during difficult moments at medical conferences with silent impressions of animals to help me find the names in English of animal vectors of long-named, difficult-to-pronounce diseases. Thanks to them I shall never forget the difference between a warthog and a groundhog in all the languages.

I would also like to thank George de Modzelewski, who was an outstanding interpreter, a gentleman and a kind, considerate colleague, solid as a rock even in the old days when we worked from 9 in the morning through until 5 o'clock the following morning.

And David Walters for similar comic restoring of my morale during a difficult technical radio conference in Norway, with his fictitious pronouncements as I climbed the rickety wooden steps to reach the booths perched on high in a temporary conference construction. I didn't discover until later, with relief, as I took my seat, that the microphone had not been turned on and the incredible words I had heard as I mounted the stairs were not part of the discussion I was about to start interpreting.

I would also like to express, after all these years, my distaste for the actions of another colleague whose name I shall not divulge, who felt there were enough interpreters and no need for more beginners; who went out for coffee at the beginning of my half-hour in the Finance and Budget Committee of the World Health Assembly, taking all the pencils, pens and writing pads with her as she went...

May I also thank Pat Longley for her endless patience and support from AIIC in Geneva when I first came to Australia in the late 1970s and was struggling throughout the 1980's to put some order in the difficult situation prevailing in this country at that time. There were bitter conflict and endless personality clashes between the two non-AIIC Queen Bees, making the interpreting scene most unpleasant.

I am extremely grateful to Judge Margaret O'Toole for her help with the section of Chapter 14 dealing with court interpretation. She has spent an enormous amount of time checking my drafts, and has done so with great patience. But for her assistance, this limited summary of the complexities of legal and court interpretation would not have been possible.

Finally I would like to express my appreciation to AIIC for all the invaluable texts they have published, which I have used freely, and for which I owe an enormous debt of gratitude to AIIC and to all my colleagues who, over the years, have worked so hard on them.

USEFUL TERMS AND DEFINITIONS

A, B and C languages

These are terms used by professional interpreters to define their different language skills. An A language is the mother tongue or a language of equal proficiency. Interpreters work **into** their A language.

B languages are acquired languages in which an interpreter is absolutely fluent and ideally should be used for working from, into their A language. However, interpreters also work into their B languages in consecutive mode (and in exceptional circumstances in simultaneous interpretation.)

C languages are passive languages of which the interpreter has a thorough knowledge and can work out of into their A language in simultaneous, or into their A or B languages in consecutive.

Consecutive interpretation

This is suitable for meetings where only two, or at the most three languages are being used. The interpreter sits at the conference table taking notes of what the speakers say and then interprets into another language. This method is most suitable for negotiations, drafting groups, arbitrations and other small meetings. "Whispered" interpretation, a form of simultaneous without the use of a microphone, may also be used in such meetings when two or at the most three delegates require interpretation in a particular language.

Simultaneous interpretation

This is the most common form of conference interpreting today because it is virtually instantaneous and thus saves much conference time. Interpreters sit in soundproof booths with a clear view of the meeting room and receive the speakers' statements through headphones while giving a running interpretation in another language to delegates listening by means of headsets.

Translators and Interpreters

Sometimes people confuse interpreters with translators. The difference is that the interpreters deal with spoken language and translators with written texts. These are complementary skills but the processes involved differ.

Interpreting is a means of providing an immediate understanding of the spoken word. Translators have time to read texts and use dictionaries and reference books to provide a definitive version of the original, often required for future reference and for international agreements (where French is generally the reference language because of its precision).

Conference interpreters try to convey the speaker's meaning almost instantaneously and this often includes subtleties like cultural nuances, sarcasm, gestures, body language, facial expressions, the effect of which the interpreter may convey through tone of voice, intonation, emphasis, speed of delivery, and so on.

A.I.I.C.

International Association of Conference Interpreters, 10 avenue de Sécheron, CH 1202, Geneva, Switzerland.

N.A.A.T.I.

National Accreditation Authority for Translators and Interpreters, PO Box 223, Deakin West ACT 2600
Ph: (02) 6260 3035   Hotline: 1300 557 470   Fax: (02) 6260 3036   E-mail: irena@naati.com.au

AUTHOR'S NOTES

1. Each time the word "interpreter" is used please read "conference interpreter", unless another type of interpretation is specified.

2. For the sake of simplicity and because it is shorter, "he" is used throughout this book as a convenient abbreviation for he/she and is not intended to be sexist. The vast majority of interpreters are in fact "she" (language ability like mediumship seems to be a predominantly female characteristic,);"he" is the most common case for delegates.

3. The views expressed in this book are those of the author and the author's responsibility alone. They do not implicate any professional association or other body; no professional association or other body bears any responsibility whatsoever for the contents of this book.

POLONIUS' ADVICE TO INTERPRETERS

If thou dost deem thyself prepared to do
The work of an interpreter - for good or ill -
These precepts let me print upon thy mind.
They are not taught in schools or institutes,
Nor written down in books nor true compiled.
They are the gleanings of the many years
That I have spent behind the darkling glass
That doth divide us from the world beyond:
Know thy place and give thine own ideas no tongue-
Nor any unproportion'd thought his sound.
Be thou respectful but by no means servile.
Be thou e'er present but be unobtrusive
Do not take sides when working on moot questions.
Give every speaker ear - speak not thy views.
Take groundlings' censure: Thy profession's risk.
Decent thy habit as thy purse can buy,
But not expressed in noisy chains - they clang.
Neither a pack-rat nor a shedder be -
Keep all the papers 'til the subject's done
Then neatly dispossess thyself of them.
Do thou thy part, nor poach nor shirk.
Stick to thy language not your colleague's work
Leave not thy booth to strut and roam
Where clients see you, seeming unemployed.
Smoke not if that your booth-mate doth disturb
But be prepared to aid with sorely needed word.
This above all and always bear in mind:
Sound thou convinced that what you speak is true:
Let not an uncompleted sentence live.
Your hearers rest on YOU.
    Now with my blessings, Go!   *Ted Fagan*

(with apologies to our friend from Stratford on Avon)

"The dictionary meaning of a word is no more than a stone in the edifice of sense, no more than a potentiality that finds diversified realization in speech."

L.S.Vygotsky

"Interpreters are not linguists, they are not experts in languages,they are rather experts in comprehension, that is, in hermeneutical penetrating of intentions of saying as it evolves in language communication."

Mariano Garcia-Landa, Doctor in Translation (Sorbonne Paris III)

"If language is not in accordance with the truth of things, affairs cannot be carried on to success."

Confucius

1
INTRODUCTION

This book, apart from Chapter 11, is intended for Australian interpreters, would-be interpreters wondering whether to embark on interpreter training and formally trained beginners. It cannot of course take the place of a training course; however I hope it will be a useful adjunct to training courses and provide some of the information that students find it difficult to obtain in this country.

I also hope that it will succeed in dispelling some of the myths about interpreting: that we don't understand what we are saying, that the act of listening while speaking is the essence of simultaneous interpretation (whereas in fact the essence is understanding), that we all know ten or even seventeen languages (does a good musician play ten instruments?), that spoken language is more difficult for us than texts that are read out (the contrary is true).

Conference interpreting is at least as old as the Book of Genesis in which Joseph outwitted his brothers by, as the book says, speaking "unto them by an interpreter." But it is a new profession in this country. This book is intended as a guide for those interested in this new profession, to give you some idea of how it is practised in the rest of the world. Colleagues will often feel that some of it is obvious whilst newcomers may not fully understand the reasons behind some of the statements.

However, it is based on contributions from many professional interpreters and some delegates, as well as thirty years' experience working at international conferences all over the world both for United Nations and the private business market.

There is an urgent need in this country to maintain quality and standards. Our reputation for quality is only the sum of our individual efforts to create it.

Breaches of simple rules of behaviour affect the delegates' image of the professional interpreter and if we want to be treated like professionals and paid as professionals, we must behave and work like professionals.

Conference interpreting is a highly qualified and demanding profession. In some ways it is like tightrope walking without a safety net. It requires not only an exacting knowledge of languages but also thorough training in interpreting skills and the ability to understand people with all sorts of different accents, of different cultural backgrounds, and in a wide variety of subjects - even the most technical.

There are between five and six thousand languages in the world today to choose from. There is no doubt that learning a foreign language is hard work. Only dieting seems to take up so much human endeavour with so few results and the prosperity of the language industry, like that of the diet business, is founded on failure. Banish the fantasy that one day, by concentrating on language tapes, you will converse fluently and wittily with foreigners and perhaps even eventually become a conference interpreter. Do not tackle Finnish unless you are confident about coping with the sixteen cases including the triple dative. Banish too the thought that a good community interpreter who works hard will one day work his way up through the NAATI levels to become a top level (Level 5) conference interpreter. Conference interpreting is a different kettle of fish. Until your other languages are almost equivalent to a mother tongue, there is no point in studying conference interpretation skills.

To start with, if you must learn a language, choose your own neglected mother-tongue. Dazzle your friends with your clarity of expression, your perfect diction. Your mother tongue is one of your most precious possessions, whichever type of interpreting you eventually take up. It is certainly the most important language for a conference interpreter. Take good care of it, polish it, cosset it and protect it from contamination from other languages and accents (and Australian vowels). Keep it up-to-date by reading newspapers and modern literature, as well as the classics. Keep it clear and authentic and easy to understand. For example, the English booth has to be understood by Indians, Norwegians, Nigerians, Philippinos, Finns ... You cannot expect them to understand a Welsh accent or gallicisms. So, keep your language pure and above all, clear.

There is no point in giving an excellent interpretation if your audience cannot understand what you are saying.

Conference interpreting is a profession which, to the uninitiated, seems either strange and exotic or totally faceless, according to your perception. This book is an attempt to draw back the veil of mystery and explain our profession.

Conference interpreters are to be heard working at large and small international conferences or meetings, where the delegates or participants are using two or more different languages. They are therefore language and communication experts who transmit a message spoken in one language in a different language and hence make trans-lingual communication possible. They do this either "simultaneously" or "consecutively". With simultaneous interpretation, they sit in a booth in the meeting room and, listening through earphones to delegates' speech in one language, transmit the verbal message via the microphone into another language for delegates wishing to listen to that second language. With consecutive interpretation, they sit in the meeting room, listen to and take notes on a speech or intervention and, when it is completed, re-create that speech or intervention in the second language.

Consecutive interpretation is more time-consuming, and is more suitable for small meetings, using two or at most three languages, whereas simultaneous interpretation can be used for an almost unlimited number of languages and participants - all you need is one booth per language, a sufficient number of interpreters to understand all the languages being used and a sufficient number of receivers for the delegates. Some interpreters may prefer one method over another but a professional conference/court interpreter is expected to work in either mode.

Conference interpreting today - as opposed to interpreting as it has existed from time immemorial and which has often been called the second oldest profession - started with the foundation of the League of Nations, where everything was interpreted consecutively. Simultaneous interpretation was introduced for the Nuremberg trials after the second World War, by which time the necessary technology was available. The old hands of the League of Nations said disparagingly at the time that it was a crazy idea, would probably not work and would certainly be impossible to keep up. Today, however, the overwhelming majority of our work is done simultaneously.

Who are the people who spend their lives engaged in these high-speed mental gymnastics? In the "old days" they tended to be people who could speak several languages naturally because they had "naturally" grown up in a multi-lingual family environment or because, for various reasons, they had moved around from country to country. Today's young interpreters tend to have acquired their languages "artificially" via school, university and interpreters' school - with, of course, visits to the countries where their languages are spoken.

In either case, the basic *sine qua non* is a deep and thorough knowledge of one's own and one or more foreign languages and, obviously, some are more useful than others - English, French, Spanish, Russian, Japanese and Chinese, for instance, are heard more frequently at international meetings than, say, Korean, Turkish or Finnish. Then, the interpreter needs training and experience in conference interpreting techniques - how to create English that sounds like English out of a message say, in Russian or German where the verb often comes late in the sentence. How to cope with differences of cultural background between, say, Arabic and English, how to use a microphone without coughing and rustling into it, how to pitch the voice so that it is pleasant to listen to.

But over and above linguistic skills, a conference interpreter needs a wide general knowledge, an adequate understanding of an enormous range of subjects; obviously we have to know about the structure and activities of the international organisations where we work; we have to have a deep understanding of all aspects of current affairs; we have to understand the political, legal and financial systems not only in our own countries but in many others as well. In addition, to cope with the many varied working environments in which we find ourselves, we have to be able to speak the language of heads of state, of nurses, surgeons, fishermen, lawyers, nuclear physicists, of computer experts, aircraft designers, foresters, animal protectionists... the list is literally endless, but these are all worlds with which we have to familiarize ourselves, whose subject matter we have to understand before we can interpret at their international meetings. So, in view of the increasing complexity and technical sophistication of today's world, in addition to languages a university level of education or its equivalent is becoming increasingly important, and a law, engineering, medical or economic degree is preferable to a degree in languages.

Having acquired our skills, we like any other profession try to practise them to the best of our ability and according to a strict code of ethics which lays down absolute confidentiality and professional standards.

So all the prerequisites are there but, like so many other people today, we are also heavily dependent on technology - in our case, the sound system through which the message enters our earphones. These days it can be a wire, radio or infra-red based system, but only if we receive the message not too loudly or quietly and very clearly can we process it and communicate it to our listeners. They in turn need to hear us clearly. So the sound system with which we work is one of our key concerns.

The demands are great, but so are the rewards for, coming as we do from an enormous variety of cultural backgrounds, we conference interpreters have one very important thing in common - an enormous enthusiasm for our job. We are all fascinated by language, how it works, how it can be used to promote understanding. We want to use all our linguistic and general knowledge to enable our listeners to overcome the barriers of language and to communicate fully and without restriction, and this our profession gives us the opportunity to do. It also gives us the satisfaction of having contributed to the advancement of science, the conquest of disease and efforts to achieve world peace. Interpretation is a fascinating subject that has close links with politics, diplomacy, science, human rights, declarations of war and peace and the development and dissemination of knowledge throughout the ages.

Now, if you still want to be a conference interpreter, read on ....

2

A LITTLE WORLD HISTORY

According to Greek mythology, Hermes was the first interpreter for he interpreted messages from the Gods for mankind. In Greek interpreters were called "*hermeneuties.*" "Hermes transmitted the messages of the gods to the mortals, that is to say, he not only announced them verbatim but acted as an "interpreter" to render their words intelligible - and meaningful - which may require some point of clarification or other, additional, commentary." (Bleicher 1980)

Hermes, interpreter of the Gods, also accompanied travellers and souls passing over into the other world, Hades, where he was their guide. In Greece, when there is a moment of silence in a conversation, the Greeks say that Hermes, the popular God of the everyday, is "entering the room."

Olympian gods were rational (Garcia-Landa 1985) but Hermes was not one of them because he was a God with magic powers - his magic hat made him invisible. In "*Le Petit Prince*", Saint-Exupéry says: "What is important is invisible." The sign of a good interpreter is that participants in the discussion forget he is there. Speakers carry on their negotiations, their discussions, or even their arguments, each in his own language, naturally and uninhibitedly, forgetting the presence of the interpreter. So Hermes with his magic hat is certainly still applicable today.

But let us get down to the more tangible aspects of our profession. It is certainly one of the oldest (Andronikof 1968) and at the same time, one of the most modern. Herodotus, an early Greek writer, was the first to mention interpreters; he wrote of the interpreters beside the pharaohs and the Kings of Persia, receiving ambassadors.

There must always have been interpreters for people, in spite of their differences, their rivalries and perhaps because of these, have always experienced the need to communicate and there have always been many languages. Greek and Latin texts mention interpreters. They march with conquerors into foreign lands. Before the rise of Rome, the traders and armies of Carthage used interpreters with parrots tattooed on their breasts or arms.

The word *interpreter* goes back to ancient Roman times, to the Latin *interpres* and *interpretari*, which were used with reference to both written and spoken translation processes alike. From the Latin the words passed via Old French into Anglo-French and so into the modern English language.

Needless to say, the activity of interpreting is as old as the word for it and one has to go back a long way in history to find the first reports of interpreting as a recognized profession. There are, for example, records of the official status of interpreters in Carthage (that is, between the fifth and the first centuries B.C.), where the ethnic composition of the empire, comprising more than a dozen distinct races, each speaking its own language, necessitated the use of interpreters, who could be identified by means of a parrot motif tattooed on their forearms. Theirs was a highly respected occupation; the interpreters of Carthage were excused military service and exempted from taxation. Moses was the interpreter for Jehova and used the voice of Aaron to speak in Hebrew which was a language he did not speak.

Caius Julius Caeser in his *De Bello Gallico* mentioned the Roman military interpreters, and some princes of ancient Egypt conferred upon themselves the title of Chief Interpreter in 3,000 B.C. Then there is the Levites' oral translation of the Holy Scriptures (Nehemia 8:8) and a thousand more examples, in every era and every place following the collapse of the legendary Tower of Babel: someone helping people to understand one another, people divided from one another by the most insuperable barrier one could imagine: the barrier of language.

Ancient Egyptian stone carvings in the Nile Valley show a small figure with two faces interceding between an Egyptian overlord and a Nubian group. In 538 BC Ezra the Scribe read the Torah in Hebrew and then translated it into the vernacular. St. Mark interpreted for Saint Paul from Aramaic into Greek.

Luther translated the Bible into German from Hebrew and Greek texts. His translation was criticized and he defended it by writing his famous *Sendbrief des Dolmetchens (The Translator's Mission*) where he explains that one should translate the meaning and not the words.

Spinoza introduced, for the first time in the history of translation and interpretation, the concept of "situation" (context) in the seventh chapter of his *Tractatus theologicus-politicus*, saying that the historical situation of the text and author had to be taken into account.

An interpreter was also described by Saladin in 1192 in a letter to Richard the Lion-Heart.

When the Americas were discovered, interpreters made possible the first contacts between Europeans and

American tribes. They accompanied conquerors and colons from Genoa, Portugal, Spain, France, Holland and England. Christopher Columbus had a yellow parrot tattooed on the forearm of his interpreters in order to identify them.

The first interpreter of the New World was the Spaniard, Cristobal Rodriguez, called "The Tongue" (*La Lengua*). (In the Spanish spoken at that time, interpreters were referred to as *tongues - lenguaraz, faraúte* or *lengua.*)

Cristobal Rodriguez probably travelled with Colombus and remained in his favourite island called "Hispaniola" at that time (today Saint Domingo, Dominican Republic). He must have lived there for some time because when he appears in history he had been living with the Taino people and is familiar with their culture and language, which enabled him to interpret for Spaniards and the Tainos and defend the latter against the cruelty of the Spaniards of that time - well before the Dominican Bartolome de las Casas, who was the best known of their defenders.

Here then is one of the essential ingredients for an interpreter: to have lived in another country and assimilated its culture, its values and been culturally transformed in such a way that he felt "one of them" and ready to defend them and explain them to others.

In her article entitled "Luis de Torres", Irene Kurz (1992) explains:

> *When they set out on their voyages and expeditions they generally enlisted "interpreters", i.e. people who had picked up Arabic or other foreign languages by living in the respective foreign countries. References can be found in a great variety of*

archives of the late Middle Ages and the Renaissance. From the writings of Marco Polo and the reports of other traders who had been to the Far East, Christopher Colombus knew that Arab traders had reached his expected goal - Cathay (China) and Cipango (Japan) - before him by sailing eastward. Thus, when in August 1492 he set out on the expedition that led to the discovery of America, he, too, "was careful to include a few men in his crew who would be able to converse in Arabic"... As it turned out, however, they were of no use in the New World... Colombus's logbook contains several entries referring to the use of interpretation and the overcoming of language problems, with specific mention of an interpreter by the name of Luis de Torres.

When a small mutiny had to be quelled on 10 October, Colombus reports: "I was not alone. Chachu, de Harana, the two Royal officers and the interpreter stood next to me, willing to sacrifice their lives."

It became the custom to capture a few natives and take them back to Spain to be converted to Christianity and taught Spanish so they could be used as interpreters for future expeditions. Their wives were also taken to ensure they would not try to escape. One of the captured natives taken back to Spain was later christened Diego Colón and learnt to speak Castilian: he returned with Colombus on subsequent voyages as an interpreter.

The works of V. Arnaud, L.V. Mansilla (1890, 1966) and Hernán Cortés give us some idea of what happened in the nineteenth century. The *lenguaraz* was always placed at the right hand of the most important person present. Military chiefs frequently asked the "lenguaraz" for his opinion and even took his moods into account (Bertone 1985). As Laura Bertone explains, three centuries earlier, in Mexico, Fernando Cortés was saved by his Indian interpreter, the famous Doña Marina[1].

In his second letter to Emperor Charles V in 1519, Cortés tells of the ambush he almost fell into in Churultecal. The last stage of their journey before arriving in Temixtitán, the Aztec capital, and meeting with the Great Montezuma, could have been a massacre for the Spaniards, were it not for the warning Marina passed on to another interpreter (Spanish) who in turn warned Cortés.

Doña Marina was called "Malintzin" by the Indians, or "Malinche" and her mother tongue was nahuatl, the language of the Aztecs. She was sold as a slave to the Mayas, so also spoke their language. Doña Marina must have had the gift of languages because she soon learnt Spanish too, which increased her usefulness even more. Cortés considered her to be an indispensable ally. Looked at with the eyes of today, her role as interpreter gave her access to power, yet she did not give away any professional secrets nor use information obtained in the course of her work.

Even after the fall of Mexico, she was still a very important person and Bernal Diaz says: "Without her, Cortés could not handle any dealings with the Indians." She was present in all the pictures and written accounts. The first meeting between Cortés and Montezuma depicted in the *Codex Florentin* shows the two military chiefs on one side of the picture while the figure in the centre is that of Malinche.

In the 16th century the role of the interpreter was particularly important as is shown by Indian legislation.

---

[1] This native princess called Malintzin lived from 1501 to 1550. She was sold as a slave to Cortés. When she converted to Christianity, she changed her name to Marina and was the conquistador's guide and mistress. She also bore him a child. She died in Spain after marrying Juán de Jaramillo.

No. XXIX of the *Recopilación* of the Laws of the Indies, promulgated in 1680, refers to the status of interpreters and the first of the 14 laws stipulates that the authorities must pay great care to the moral qualities of the interpreter because serious harm may result if he is not faithful, Christian and generous, since it is through him that justice is done, the native peoples are governed and wrongs can be righted.

It is specified that interpreters must take oath before hearings, must interpret clearly and openly, hiding nothing and adding nothing, and be impartial. For this reason, they must have no interest in the affair apart from receiving their salary. They were not allowed to receive gifts or promises from the Spaniards or the Indians nor from anyone else concerned by the dispute "even in the case of food or drink that they have not asked for." If they failed to respect these conditions, they would be deemed guilty of perjury, lose their jobs and have to pay costs and interest. Programmes and hours of work are set forth in the greatest detail as well as their remuneration and fines in case of absence.

The number of interpreters and their working conditions were also specified - at first there was only one interpreter but because of errors, the presence of two interpreters was required later when Indians were making statements. Today, too, the presence of two interpreters also guarantees some degree of control.

In their annual reports or *Cartas Anuas* the Jesuits tell of their problems when administering the sacraments (including confessions and the last sacrament or extreme unction) through interpreters. Father Burges "accuses interpreters of disguising the fact that there were words they did not know by saying the "mocobies" had no such words in their vocabulary." According to the Royal Decree of 9 October 1556, the accused, in accordance with

Spanish tradition, had the right to the assistance of at least one lawyer and one interpreter (Arnaud 1950).

The edicts of Louis XIV of France (1643 -1715) refer to the training of dragomans at the Lycée Louis Le Grand in Paris; the translators at mediaeval courts were invested with the title of *Maistre latinier* and there were monk-interpreters at the Lateran Councils.

The Jesuit missionaries of the 17th Century were notable linguists and interpreters (Arnaud 1950:59). One of the most successful of these was Ferdinand Verbiest (l623 - l688) who was born in Flanders and educated at the University of Leuven where he studied Greek, Latin, philosophy and mathematics which at that time embraced virtually all scientific knowledge from astronomy to engineering. At the age of forty, Verbiest was sent to China to take over from an elderly Jesuit who had risen to become Imperial Astronomer and advisor to Emperor Kang-Xi. Apart from designing instruments for the Imperial Observatory, constructing over 300 canons and a self-propelled vehicle, Verbiest found time to learn Manchu and publish the first Manchu grammar written in Latin.

In 1678, Verbiest played a vital role as interpreter in historic negotiations with Russia - the first time China concluded a treaty with another country. Russian seems to have been one of the few languages Verbiest did not speak, but he was able to communicate in Latin with a member of the Russian delegation, possibly an A language as far as Verbiest was concerned. Unscrupulous interpreters who misinterpreted for their own gain were imprisoned or executed in China at this time and a punishment decreed against wilful misinterpretation was a form of bamboo torture.

In the 18th and 19th centuries, international business and particularly diplomacy was most often conducted in French, the language of the cultured at the time. Moving on to the 20th century, between the two World Wars, the League of Nations held its meetings in French and English with consecutive interpretation. The interpreter would take notes of a speech, often very lengthy, then re-deliver it from the rostrum in the other language, thus doubling its duration.

At the Geneva Peace Conference in 1919, conference room seating was arranged in a semi-circle with aisles going from the back to a central point in the front, dividing the audience up like pieces of a semi-circular cake. The interpreters stood at the central point, side by side, each responsible for a different language: the language of his slice of the cake. You can imagine how difficult it was to be heard - each interpreter had to shout louder than his colleagues so that his slice of audience could hear him.

The International Labour Conference takes place in Geneva each year and is composed of representatives of governments, employers and workers. One of the employer delegates at the 1926 session, Mr. E.E. Filene, a rich businessman owning department stores in Boston, asked an ILO staffmember, A.G. Finlay, to see if he could work out a system so that the delegates could listen to a translation of the speeches by means of something similar to a telephone. This was done: the interpreters had microphones but no booths and no headphones, while the delegates wore headphones. Thus on Saturday 4 June 1927 at 10.30 a.m. the very first meeting with simultaneous interpretation opened at the International Labour Conference in Geneva. The invention was patented in 1926 by Mr. Finlay and Mr. Filene had it manufactured by IBM. It was called the Filene-Finlay Hushaphone (Bourgain 1991).

In 1928 a type of simultaneous interpretation was used in the U.S.S.R. for the VIth Congress of Komintern (Chernov 1978). Simultaneous interpretation was used at a number of meetings such as the Scientific Organisation Committee in 1929 (Geneva), International Chamber of Commerce (Amsterdam, 1929) and the XVth International Physiology Congress (Leningrad, 1935), which was called the "Pavlov Congress" and was quadrilingual, i.e. Russian, German, English and French. The first booths were used in 1933 at a meeting of the Komintern.

André Kaminker, a great interpreter of that time and a founding member of AIIC (International Association of Conference Interpreters), invented his own "simultaneous translation system" for French radio and interpreted the first major speech by Adolf Hitler at Nuremberg in 1934 (Paneth 1956, 1958; van Emde Boas 1957, 1958). The interpreters must have used large, heavy headphones made of black bakelite and those old-fashioned microphones hung in a cradle that we see in old Hollywood films.

After World War II, there was an immediate and urgent need for interpretation in English, French, Russian and German at the Nuremberg Trials of Nazi war criminals. To rely on consecutive interpretation would have been lengthy and cumbersome. The job of organizing this was given to General Eisenhower's former interpreter, Colonel Léon Dostert, who was completely bilingual.

Simultaneous interpretation was the answer; Dostert was convinced that it was possible to listen to a speaker and convey his message in another language at the same time, and that a satisfactory technical solution could be found. He also understood the importance for interpreters to be able to see the speakers and follow the whole proceedings so as to understand what was going on, while working in as soundproof an environment as possible.

At the Trials, presided over by Lord Justice Geoffrey Lawrence, resplendent in wig and clumsy earphones, the interpreters were placed next to the defendants in their "aquarium" to give them a view of the proceedings.

Needless to say, exact, faithful interpretation was of capital importance for the defendants, in the true sense of the word 'capital'. The necessary disciplines imposed on the interpretation services at Nuremberg demonstrated the advantages of simultaneous interpretation, which has since greatly increased both in use and number of languages.

Ann and John Tusa (1983) describe the proceedings in their book *The Nuremberg Trial*:

What outsiders noticed and marvelled at was the vital cog in the machinery - the simultaneous translation system. It was truly simultaneous. As long as speakers maintained a steady hundred words a minute, the translators in their glass booths could provide an almost current version of the trial in any language. Given documents in advance so that there was time to prepare, the translators could be synchronized even more exactly with the speakers. It was an extraordinary achievement and it staggered all visitors to Nuremberg. The art of simultaneous translation was virtually unknown at the time. Of the teams of interpreters at Nuremberg possibly only two members - Haakon Chevalier and Eduard Roditi - had ever practised it before on the new IBM equipment. The others had scarcely any time to learn: the equipment went astray and only turned up five days before the start of the trial. This allowed

*merely five days of rehearsal: reading documents to
each other to see if it was going to be possible to talk
in one language while listening through headphones
to the court proceedings in another. Exciting times!*

*Colonel Dostert, the head of the translation sec-
tion, had grouped his simultaneous translators into
three teams of twelve: one team had to sit in court
and work a shift of one and a half hours; another to
sit in a separate room, relatively relaxed, but still
wearing headphones and following the proceedings
closely so as to ensure continuity and standard vocabulary when they took over; the third having a
well-earned half-day off. The work was exacting. It
needed great linguistic skill and total concentration.
For many of those involved the subject matter imposed a further emotional strain. Working conditions were uncomfortable: the translators were
cramped in their booths, which were even hotter than
the courtroom. They spoke through a lip microphone
to try to dampen their sound (the booth was not enclosed at the top) but not even the use of the microphone nor the huge headphones they wore could
deaden the noise made by their colleagues. As they
worked they had to fight the distractions of other versions and other languages ...*

*Colonel Dostert was a hard taskmaster - woe be-
tide anyone he found in the rest room without headphones. He imposed high linguistic standards; everyone had to acquire the jargon and technical terms required by the evidence. But Dostert was universally
respected. Though he demanded more than most
people would have believed they could give, he always estimated exactly how much strain they could
bear. The efficiency and accuracy of the translations
owed everything to his planning and expectations.
Accuracy was essential both to avoid confusion in*

court and to provide an impeccable record of the trial. Each team had three monitors and a chief interpreter attached to supervise its version. The monitor sat outside the booth, maintaining the flow of documents to the translators and controlling the speed of speakers with the red and yellow buttons...

Another reference to the "IBM system for multilingual interpretation" is to be found in the article by David and Margareta Bowen (1985) who explain that Justice Jackson had it brought from Geneva to Nuremberg.

Colonel Dostert, Eisenhower's interpreter, assembled a group of linguists to provide simultaneous interpretation. Although the system had been used before in Geneva and in the United States, it was still in its experimental stages. The equipment was what we call today a "wired" one, but the cables were exposed in the courtroom and got periodically disconnected whenever someone stumbled over them ...The equipment had a floor channel and four language channels, headphones for all participants in the trial for listening to any one of the channels, and six microphones in the courtroom (one for each judge, one for the witness box and one at the speaker's podium). One extra feature, which is hardly ever provided today, was the warning light by which the interpreters could request the speaker to slow down or to repeat what he said. The booths for the interpreters were placed in such a way that the accused were sitting directly in front of them (in profile); the speaker's lectern and the prosecutor's tables were also in their direct field of vision; the judges were at the far end, at right angles from the row of booths, and the screen and the witness box could not be seen at all. The working schedule for the interpreters provided for fewer hours in the booth than does the Charter for Permanent Interpreters today, and each interpreter was expected to interpret from one language into his own only. The most striking feature is the concern for speed: an all-out effort was made to hold the speakers to almost dictation speed, approximately 60 words per minute. The record shows that interpreters were given copies of documents even if the distribution to all participants was limited...

Modern day conference interpreters cannot fail to experience a surge of deep admiration and respect for the colleagues who were able to withstand the pressures and horror of what they heard at Nuremberg in order to help the course of natural justice. Most interpreters there had no formal training of any kind - they were there because they happened to be fluent in more than one language, often because they were refugees who had been forced to leave their native country. Mechanical arrangements were cumbersome and awkward in the extreme,the floor of the court-room was strewn with loose wiring and if anyone tripped over it this could send the whole sound system crashing down. The content they were interpreting was laden with unimaginable horrors and in many cases deep personal trauma. Some coped by having a frenetic social life when off duty, others say they had never, before or since, been to so many bars! Others could only deal with the experience by suppressing it and most found that while they managed not to think about it at the time, it came back to them in nightmares.

Technically, the basic things haven't changed. "The separation of your technique and your reaction to the material, the division of your mind into parts, is just as true now as it was then," was a comment made by a colleague at a ceremony marking the beginning of the AIIC Extraordinary Assembly in Brussels on 28 August 1992.

Although the League of Nations made an attempt in 1931 to use the simultaneous system, their "parliamentary interpreters" continued in the main to operate in consecutive mode. The interpreter waited until the speaker had finished and then strode up to the podium and delivered his interpretation from his notes (Coleman-Holmes 1971). The speech might have lasted 45 minutes or even an hour ... The audience waited to hear the interpreter who was much like an actor taking centre stage. He had had time to assimilate the speech and could polish it up in his own words and find flowery expressions to equal the most eloquent rhetoric. The interpreters were all known by name and were even consulted by speakers and by Editorial Committees as to the best wording for an Agreement, i.e. words that could be translated into the other conference languages most unambiguously. There were few interpreters on the world stage at that time and they were all famous: Jean Herbert, Antoine Belleman, Robert Confino, André and Georges Kaminker, Georges Mathieu, Evans and Lloyd. I must also mention Ted Pilley, the well-known English interpreter who worked before World War II, inter alia for the Non-Intervention Committee in the Spanish Civil War (1936-1939), who was one of the founders of AIIC and the father of interpretation in the British Isles.

After the Nuremberg Trial, Col. Dostert gave several public demonstrations of simultaneous interpretation in the United States of America but the United Nations continued to use consecutive interpretation in the main, especially for the Security Council. It is only in the 1950's that simultaneous interpretation was put into general use at the United Nations in New York. The interpreters working in the English booth at the Security Council then became national celebrities because their interpretation was broadcast over the radio.

Simultaneous interpretation changed the structure of international conferences because instead of a series of statements and speeches, discussions could now take place, with questions and answers, and debates. But it also meant that interpreters became invisible, anonymous voices, heard in headsets but rarely seen, relegated to the wings in their glass boxes, instead of being centre stage.

After some ten years during which wired installations were the only means available, it became technically possible also to use wireless (radio) systems and then, more recently, infra-red.

The wired system requires the listener to remain in his seat but does have a degree of security from the point of view of unauthorized listening-in. In general, the wireless (radio) system lacks this security. As for the infra-red system, its security is certainly better than that of a radio system and in a window-less environment may be very secure.

After the Second World War, there was an enormous demand for information. H.Kolmer says in his article "Interpretation at Scientific Meetings: is it efficient?" (1987) that earlier practised methods of literature study and correspondence between scientists and personal contact were no longer sufficient to allow a researcher to remain up-to-date in a given field:

> *This was the background for the rising demand for meetings between researchers on a national and international level to allow them to keep abreast and assess developments, exchange experiences and plan future projects in cooperation. World War II brought a general development in the use of communication engineering, and components which enabled a larger number of listeners to hear simultaneously through headphones side by side, without disturbing one another, in a number of languages. This wirebound or wireless radio equipment made technically supported simultaneous interpretation*

possible for the first time. This was a great improvement in listening comfort and time-sharing, resulting in more efficient and widespread dissemination of information through international conferences during postwar years and up to the present day.

The worldwide availability of this new technical equipment and developments in the field of electronics and computerization have resulted in the internationalisation of science, thus creating an enormous demand for expert linguists with a number of languages and at the same time a high level of scientific and technical vocabulary, with the ability to gain sufficient understanding of a scientific matter within a short period of time, so that they could interpret meaningfully. Without such a minimum understanding, interpretation would remain mechanical and meaningless. During the fifties therefore a number of West and Central European universities created training institutes for the new profession of simultaneous interpretation to enable future interpreters to transmit scientific content from language to language. During past decades several thousands of highly qualified experts in interpretation have graduated from these university institutes.

The first modern School of Conference Interpretation, ETI (Keiser 1992) was set up at Geneva University in 1942. The HEC School of Interpreting was created in Paris in 1948, attached to the Paris Chamber of Commerce, and set many of the standards still in force today. It was replaced in 1954 by the Sorbonne School of Interpreting and Translating (ESIT), attached to the Sorbonne University in Paris. In both cases the teachers are practising conference interpreters themselves, as is also the case in Spain where the universities have grouped together to form EUTI (University School of Translation and Interpretation), one of which has already started in Barcelona,

23

and here again all the teachers of interpretation are practising conference interpreters. In this way, students are kept up to date with the latest events in the conference world, and are given texts fresh from real live conferences to work on so that they feel closer to reality rather than learning theory from teachers who have never themselves felt what it is like to be working in the booth. Unfortunately this is not true for many of the 100 or so schools of interpretation/translation in existence.

Various attempts were made to form conference interpreters' associations. In 1945 there was AIT (Anciens de la Société des Nations) (interpreters who had worked at the League of Nations), AAEEI (Association des Anciens Elèves de l'Ecole d'Interprètes de l'Université de Genève)(former students of ETI, Geneva). AMICI (Association Mondiale des Interprètes de Conférences Internationales)(World Association of International Conference Interpreters) was short lived.

After the failure of international associations to survive, local groups were set up such as FLIG (Free Lance Interpreters of Geneva), IACIT (International Association of Conference Interpreters and Translators) based in Paris and London with three or four German colleagues and LACI (pronounced "lacey") which was the London Association of Conference Interpreters, founded and presided over by Thadé (naturally known as "Teddy") Pilley who had also established the Linguists' Club in London (of which I was an associate member and later a fellow), principally as an interpreters' training school, in a charming house with lacy curtains (very appropriate) in Grosvenor Place, Mayfair.

Teddy belonged originally to the theatrical school of great consecutive interpreters and in spite of the "Thadé" was thoroughly English in education and style, portly, warm and generous. He did a great deal for the interpreting profession. LACI co-existed with AIIC (International Association of Conference Interpreters) until 1970.

Very active in Geneva was Jean Herbert (see Herbert 1952), an affable man who, like Pilley, was a brilliant exponent of the theatrical consecutive style. (Jean Herbert said he used interpreting effectively as a travel ticket in the pursuit of his studies in oriental religions and philosophies. He wrote widely on Hinduism and studied Shinto in Japan for a number of years (Kerr 1988).)

Various national associations of translators and interpreters were also set up at that time, most of which subsequently joined FIT (Fédération internationale des traducteurs)(International Federation of Translators).

By 1951, the number of conferences had grown enormously and with it the number of conference interpreters had grown from a handful of prestigious amateurs into a profession. The number of languages used had also increased and at United Nations New York the Big Five were debating in four languages. With the increased use of simultaneous, interpreters found themselves relegated to anonymity in their booths.

Three colleagues got together to organize the profession over lunch at the Château de la Muette. The three founders of AIIC were Constantin Andronikoff, Chief Interpreter of the OECD, Russian, André Kaminker, also Russian and Chief Interpreter of the Council of Europe, and the German Hans Jacob, Chief Interpreter of UNESCO, who became the first President of AIIC. André Kaminker (father of the actress Simone Signoret) had joined the Free French Forces during the war and been an interpreter at United Nations headquarters before taking up his post at the Council of Europe. Hans Jacob was a magnificent interpreter of the spoken word and also a remarkable translator (the written word), two talents not generally found in one person. His German translations of Proust and Colette are famous and much admired.

After two years of contacts and planning, a Constitutive Assembly was held at the Maison de l'UNESCO in Paris on 11 November 1953 and the International Association of Conference Interpreters (AIIC) was born. There were 35 Founding Members.

Two important principles that were decided upon then and are still valid today are:

1: Unity of the profession (permanent and free-lance interpreters carrying out the same task, with the same responsibility as to quality, integrity and professionalism should belong to the same association and respect the same rules) and
2: Universality of the profession: since quality and professional responsibility criteria apply to all members, whatever country they may be domiciled or working in, it is essential to avoid geographical separations. (Keiser 1992)

Membership is therefore on an individual basis so that the association can not become a federation of national associations.

Soon there were 150 members of AIIC who monopolised the market and insisted upon

- at least two interpreters per booth;
- acceptable booths;
- direct contract with the organizer so that the interpreter does not have to pay a "middle-man";
- first class travel;
- a universal fee which remained universal until the devaluation of the dollar by Nixon in 1971;
- a fee for travel days to compensate for loss of earnings on that day;

- a *per diem* which in those days amply covered all accommodation, meals and out of pocket expenses;
- most important of all, a Code of Ethics and the promise to respect professional secrecy.

These rules defined professional practice which is today the reference standard all over the world (Keiser 1992). AIIC can be said to have created our profession and made it the liberal profession it is today rather than the uncoordinated, disparate and perhaps unprincipled profession it might have been.

AIIC also set up administrative structures which still exist today. It is a highly centralized professional organisation run by a secretariat now in Geneva (previously in Paris), with a Council which meets once or twice a year, composed of representatives of all Regions. The organization defends the interests of interpreters in all countries of the world.

Ever since its creation, AIIC has continued to evolve. Perhaps this is proof of its vitality. It also reflects the vicissitudes of international affairs. At the 1992 Brussels Extraordinary Assembly, decisions were taken regarding deregulation and increased regionalisation (Skunke 1993). The aim behind all of these activities has always been the same: to improve and maintain quality.

Between 1945 and 1970 the number of international conferences using simultaneous interpretation increased in spectacular fashion. In 1969 the Secretariat of AIIC moved from Paris to Geneva.

Simultaneous interpretation in Japan

Sen Nishiyama, explaining the history of interpretation in Japan, tells how in 1861 the British Foreign Office (which had staff diplomatic interpreters stationed in China at that time) announced a competition for student interpreterships in Japanese. One of the successful candidates was a young student at University College, London, named Ernest Satow (see Satow 1968). He later advanced in the diplomatic service to the rank of ambassador and a knighthood and wrote a handbook of protocol which is still a standard reference work for diplomats.

He explains the low status given in Japan to interpreters, whereas translators enjoyed high esteem, by the fact that translating has always been assimilated to scholarship, whereas interpreting was associated with trade. "The language reflects the discrepancy :"to translate" = *honyaku-tsuru*, "to interpret" = *tsuyaku-tsuru* (where *tsuru* is the verbal suffix); but "translator" = *honyaku-ka* whereas "interpreter" = *tsuyaku,* where *ka* is an agentive suffix, and its absence after *tsuyaku* marks lack of respect.

The turning point in the interpreting profession in Japan came about in 1957 when the US Embassy sent a party of Japanese interpreters to Washington for training at the State Department, where simultaneous was by then the rule. Since then, simultaneous interpreters have been in constant demand in Japan. The profession is organized differently in Japan, however, as compared with the rest of the world because Japanese interpreters work through agencies and because there are different grades of interpreter, the fee varying according to the grade.

Interpretation and Translation Machines

Satisfactory and widespread use of voice- and speech- recognition translation/interpretation machines is still some years away. Users of speech recognition software find their main problem is not the words so much as the way they say them; accents, hesitations, ungrammatical constructions, intonation and rhythm all add to the problems. We all know that delegates at conferences frequently speak unclearly, often their pronunciation is unusual especially if they are not speaking their

28

own language. Sometimes they have accents which are difficult to understand, and accentuate the wrong syllable of a word. However progress is being made and while in 1984 a one thousand word vocabulary was available and it took two minutes for each word to be recognized, there is now a 30,000 word vocabulary and it takes a quarter of a second for the recognition of each word. One firm of lawyers installed a speech recognition application as part of their computer system two years ago, thinking the lawyers would be able to dictate directly into it, thus leaving the secretaries free to do other jobs. The system was a failure because it required a period of "training" for the computer to get accustomed to the user's voice and the lawyers felt this was a waste of time that could not be charged to the client.

Spoken English is often vague and imprecise and does not lend itself to this type of application as much as a more precise language such as French.

"Speech recognition" is about what is being said, whereas "voice recognition" is concerned with the voice saying it, analysing key aspects of the voice pattern. Speech recognition relies on the training of the user who has to repeat different words and phrases which are then recorded, analysed and used to build a voice profile.

Speaker independent programmes are more complicated; they require analysis of a wide variety of different speakers whose speaking patterns have to be recorded and built into the programme. In the case of discrete speech input, users have to pause after each spoken word so that the speech recogniser can tell where one word ends and the next begins. Continuous speech input is still many years away, that is to say where users speak at normal speed with words running into one another. Programmes generally have a limited vocabulary - unlimited vocabulary is still somewhere in the future. Even the latest Voice Type programme, which looks at the contextual meaning of a word within three words either side of it, is said to maintain only 97% accuracy at a dictation speed of 150 words per minute, requiring a training time of between 40 and 60 minutes. This is just recognizing the spoken word, without any attempt at translation.

It seems that what Jacques Ellul, the French sociologist and philosopher, wrote in 1964 in his *The Technological Society* is still true today, that is instead of technology being subservient to humanity, the reality is that "human beings have to adapt to it and accept total change."

Martin Heidegger, the German philosopher and father of existentialism was also deeply concerned with technology's potential for dehumanising society and wrote:

> *The language machine ("sprachmaschine") regulates and adjusts in advance the mode of our possible usage of language through mechanical energies and functions. The language machine is - and above all, is still becoming - one way in which modern technology controls the mode and the world of language as such. Meanwhile, the impression is still maintained that man is the master of the language machine. But the truth of the matter might well be that the language machine takes language into its management and thus masters the essence of the human being.*

Computers have not yet been able to understand and render the subtleties and nuances of spoken language into other languages. A language is the living expression of a culture, a social context, the traditions and history of people, the mood and whims of speakers, their social class and profession, their personal character and above all their intent. Only the human brain of the professional interpreter can grasp and transform the many manifestations of the combination of such features into another language and its appropriate cultural context. Experiments have been made with machine translation and some say that this helps by translating the key words, to enable the reader to know whether or not the article or speech is of interest. For this purpose I believe machine translation may be of use. However it can also be considered dangerous because it may give the reader an entirely erroneous interpretation of a text or speech. In many cases, if you look a word up in a dictionary you will be given four or five possible translations in the other language and only the human brain can select the most likely one, based on context, intuition, general knowledge, knowledge of the subject matter, and so on. Before a computer can do this it needs to be fed the living knowledge in the brain of the human interpreter.

It would seem that although computers can be used for providing a rough translation of a written text, they cannot provide real-time translation such as provided by a human simultaneous interpreter; machine translations also require a great deal of pre- and post-editing. Also, interpretation requires sensitivity to the speaker's mood, gestures and body language in order to provide a fair understanding of what is being conveyed, and this is not within the capability of the machine.

I am sure you have heard of the time when "Out of sight, out of mind" and "The spirit's willing but the flesh is weak" were translated into Russian at United Nations in the course of an experiment with a translation machine. The translations were then re-translated by the same means from Russian back into English, with the following results: "Invisible idiot" and "The vodka is good but the meat is off."

Through the ages, interpreters of all languages have made contact possible between peoples and assisted in the transfer of knowledge, the propagation of religions, the dissemination of science, the exchange of goods and property, the drawing up of agreements and declarations of war and peace.

In the old days, before the times of interpreter/translator training courses (the AIIC Schools Committee was set up in 1957), especially in the days of consecutive when interpreters were the élite globe-trotting jet-set, the distinguished, elegant, witty actors on the world stage, interpreters and translators were self-taught. Their table manners were impeccable, their command of five or six languages perfect and their dazzling wit in all languages as sophisticated as their knowledge of wines. They were extremely well-educated and much-travelled aristocrats, Russian princes and princesses, barons and baronesses, counts and countesses, diplomats who had lived in different countries and learnt not only the languages but also the cultures behind them. Their endless repertoire of humorous anecdotes made them highly desirable dinner guests. How could I ever forget the dazzling humour of the heel-clicking, hand-kissing Prince Sviatopolk Mirsky, the gentle Prince Galitzin, and the regal baroness who had escaped from Poland with a diamond the size of a walnut taped into her navel and the rest of her family jewels hidden in her chignon?   Although they spoke Polish or Russian to their servants and in their families before becoming refugees, on formal occasions they spoke French which was the elegant language and also the language of diplomacy for some 200 years until the Second World War when economic power and the technological prowess of the Anglo-saxon world imposed the English language.

I have indelible memories of Marcela de Juan (1977), who was still interpreting in her eighties, as tall and straight as ever, a Chinese princess whose father, a real pig-tailed Mandarin and Chinese poet, later became a diplomat. Marcela was a writer in her own right; she wrote in Spanish and worked mainly in the Spanish booth (sometimes in the French, even in the most difficult telegraphy and telephony conferences), yet she was a member of the fifth branch of the line of Emperor Wang-Li, thirteenth emperor of the Ming dynasty (l620). This is the Emperor who was famous for inviting the Italian jesuit Mateo Ricci to the Imperial Court of China and giving him a pension in exchange for teaching all he knew to the Emperor's son. In addition to working as a conference interpreter, Marcela de Juan (Spanish version of her Chinese name: Huan) was an eminent translator of classical and modern Chinese poetry into Spanish and a diplomat. When I visited her in Hong Kong, she was there as Cultural Attaché to the Spanish Embassy and I well remember her regal posture as we sat on the ferry boat, her white rice-powdered face protected from the sun by her parasol for fear of suntan. I could never forget the tales of her childhood when her amah bound her feet every day and her Belgian mother crept into her nursery every night to unbind them in secret.

Sadly, perhaps, the impressive figures I have mentioned are all dead now and conference interpretation has changed. It is no longer merely a matter of diplomacy and has fallen into the hands - or rather mouths - of ordinary mortals who need to study to be able to provide quality simultaneous or consecutive interpretation in the present-day scientific context. It has become the domain of the earnest, hardworking student with a hunger for learning and the ability to grasp medical and scientific explanations rapidly.

But there is a secret, the key to success, that links like a silver thread all the famous simultaneous interpreters of the past with the successful ones of the present. Remembering Hermes' magic hat of invisibility and the words of St.Exupéry's *Little Prince*, we need to be discreet, humble and modest. Our greatest triumph is when our audience forgets we are there.

3

MEANWHILE, BACK IN AUSTRALIA...

At the time of the First Fleet, boats were sent to capture some of the natives to act as interpreters. Many of them, like Arabanoo, later jumped overboard, swam ashore and had to be recaptured several times. Arabanoo was the first to be a useful interpreter but later died of measles.

Australia's first serious interpreter was the aborigine, Bennelong or Baneelon (c.1764 - c. 1815), who eased the way between the early white settlers and the aboriginal population of Sydney. In 1789, Governor Arthur Phillip met Bennelong, then aged 25, and decided to include him in the Governor's household to be trained as an interpreter.

Bennelong applied himself to the task and his constant involvement with the whites, as well as a highly developed sense of mimicry, improved his command of English in a short time. Governor Phillip had a house built for Bennelong on what is now the site of the Sydney Opera House - Bennelong Point. Apparently Bennelong "towered above the others" (at 5ft. 8 inches), was muscular and fit: the first thing the government officials did was to measure his girth of chest, belly, thigh, leg at calf and so on.

According to Watkin Tench (1966), he was a "mercurial character, fearless and never slow to grasp an opportunity"; he "acquired knowledge, both of our manners and language, faster than his predecessor had done. He willingly communicated information, sang, danced and capered, told us all the customs of his country and all the details of his family economy." He too, however, jumped overboard many times and had to be recaptured until it was realized that the only way to keep him was to clamp him in leg-irons. Even then he escaped and disappeared for several months, proudly showing his captors how his leg-iron had been removed when later voluntarily resuming his interpreting duties.

The first conference with interpretation in Australia (consecutive) on record was probably the South Seas Conference, Canberra, January 1947. Anne Robson, who later became Lady Kerr when she married Sir John in 1975 (Kerr 1988), was the only professional conference interpreter in Australia at that time, and she was the French/English interpreter on that occasion. The first United Nations meeting to be held in Australia was the fourth session of ECAFE (Economic Commission for Asia and the Far East), operating under ECOSOC (United Nations' Economic and Social Council), which took place in Lapstone (in the foothills of the Blue Mountains) in November 1948. ECAFE later became ESCAP as we know it today (Economic and Social Commission for Asia and the Pacific, now located in Bangkok, Thailand).

In 1956, Geneviève Barrau came to the Region, and frequently worked with Anne Robson, for example at meetings of the Human Rights Division of the United Nations in Canberra, the International Office of Epizooties, also in Canberra, the Board of Governors of the Asian Development Bank in Sydney, the Indo-Pacific Fisheries Board in Brisbane. When teams of interpreters were needed, they brought colleagues out from Europe with the required language combinations; Philips (Melbourne) provided the simultaneous interpretation equipment including mobile booths and a technician.

Anne Robson was Regional Secretary of AIIC for many years and it is thanks to her that international standards were implanted in Australia and the Asia-

Pacific Region, with the help of Geneviève Barrau, also working free-lance at that time. By 1970, AIIC rates were charged and AIIC rules and working conditions applied throughout Australia and the Region.

When Anne Robson left the profession in 1975 and Geneviève Barrau moved to Nouméa, New Caledonia, to become Chief of the Linguistic Division of the South Pacific Commission, the situation in Australia returned to its former disorder. Two rival businesses in Sydney tried to commercialize interpreting services in this country and an "interpreter training group" - perhaps the best that could be done in the circumstances and at that time but not of international standard - was set up in 1974. Companies offering interpreters and translators appeared in Perth, Adelaide, Melbourne and Canberra, as well as others in Sydney, some professing to provide "in-house training programmes" for interpreters, unfortunately based on local rather than international standards and of insufficient duration to be acceptable. It is not possible to train a conference interpreter in four weeks even if the course were full time, every day. Sorbonne University in Paris , Geneva University (Switzerland) and most training courses all over the world, including the Japanese/English course at the University of Queensland, take two years to train a conference interpreter. The Training/Schools Committee of AIIC sets international standards for training courses, vets those that exist all over the world and classifies them. At the time of writing there is only one course in Australia meeting international standards and this is at the University of Queensland, St. Lucia, Brisbane.

From the point of view of the Australian government, the first recognition of our profession came in March 1976 when the Commonwealth Government established an Interdepartmental Working Party on Interpreters/Translators, whose task it was to report to the Prime Minister and make recommendations for the improvement of the interpreting and translating services available to the Australian community. The Working Party reported in February 1977, recommending the establishment of an accreditation body. Thus on 14 September 1977 the National Accreditation Authority for Translators and Interpreters (NAATI) was established, headquartered in Canberra with branches in all States. On 1 July 1983, NAATI was re-established as an independent body jointly subsidised by the Commonwealth, State and Territory Governments, and is now incorporated as a public company, limited by guarantee, under the *Companies Act, 1981*. The major objectives of NAATI were and are to establish professional standards for interpreters and translators, to develop the means by which practitioners can be accredited at various levels, and to develop and implement a national system of registration and licensing. For further information about NAATI, see Chapter 16.

In 1977 NAATI began testing candidates for accreditation at levels 1, 2, 3 and 4. Levels 4 and 5 come within the framework of this book. The nomenclature of these levels has now been changed as follows: Level 4 is now designated "Advanced Translator" or "Conference Interpreter" and Level 5: "Advanced Translator (Senior)" or "Conference Interpreter (Senior)". NAATI also assesses standards and advises on the content of courses in Australian institutions and accredits not only interpreters and translators with Australian or overseas qualifications but also those working in Australia without academic qualifications, and the translation/interpretation courses themselves.

Most accreditations so far have been for community interpreters, that is, former Levels 3 and 2 now known as "Translator/Interpreter" and "Paraprofessional Translator/Interpreter". However, tests are also being held for Level 4 translation and soon, it is hoped, will be held for Level 4 interpretation in certain European languages. The University of Queensland has been running a

NAATI-accredited Level 4 translation/interpretation Japanese/English course for a number of years.

Over recent years, there has been an increase in the demand in this country for Japanese-English and English-Japanese. According to *Forum* (June 1991):

> *One characteristic of the Australian market seems to be that there is more demand for interpreting than for translating, at least J-E translating. At the moment the main demand for interpretation seems to be for consecutive at business meetings, technological exchanges, study visits etc. rather than for simultaneous conference interpreting.*

Over the years, various interpreters' and translators' associations were set up such as ATIACT (Canberra, 1982), AACI (Sydney, 1984), AICIA (Sydney, 1984) and, more recently, on 5 September 1987 in Canberra, The Australian Institute of Translators and Interpreters (AUSIT) was created by the Professional Development Committee of NAATI (see Chapter 16).

The first AIIC member (since 1966) in this country was, as I have explained, Anne Robson. Lucía Bibolini (who retired from the profession shortly afterwards) was the second, and I was the third. I came here in 1978 and for the first five years I was professionally domiciled six months of the year in Canberra and six months in Geneva, Switzerland, having been a member of AIIC since 1971. When I arrived in Australia, teams were still being brought in from Europe for all top-level international conferences.

My first task therefore was to travel all over Australia, to New Caledonia (South Pacific Commission) and to New Zealand to ascertain what local skills were available, listening to as many interpreters at work as I could. I was encouraged to find there were many potential conference interpreters, but discouraged that no training of international standard was available in the Region. It was difficult to recommend would-be interpreters to go to train in Europe or America when they had families in Australia and the cost would no doubt be beyond their means, although three, to the best of my knowledge, did so.

My first meeting with local conference interpreters took place in a private home in Sydney in 1983. The seven local interpreters present, who worked mainly as community or court interpreters, gave me a picture of the interpreting scene that showed the enormous gulf existing between status, standards and pay in Australia as compared with Europe and America. I have been working ever since to raise these, and to improve professionalism in Australia, whenever possible recruiting mixed teams of local and overseas professional interpreters to enable the former to learn from their colleagues and give the latter a better understanding of the problems facing interpreters in this country.

The earlier practice of bringing entire teams over from Europe was extremely costly because, apart from air fares and subsistence allowances, interpreters required a number of paid rest days to compensate for the fatigue of long-distance travel. It was therefore not only in the interests of Australian would-be interpreters, but also in the interest of conference organizers who could save large sums of money by using local interpreters when they became available with the right language combinations and the appropriate level of expertise.

Through the good offices of Pat Longley, Secretary-General of AIIC in Geneva at that time, and the Schools Committee, I was put in touch with the Japanese/English interpretation course at the University of Queensland, which proved to be the first course in this country applying international standards and, at the time of writing, is still the only post-graduate school of translation and interpretation in Australia (NAATI former Level 4 - conference interpreter).

In 1983 I was appointed by AIIC Council to negotiate with NAATI concerning the status of conference interpreters in Australia; this appointment was confirmed by the new AIIC Council in 1986. I was then elected to AIIC Council, representing the Asia-Pacific Region, in 1985 (for three years).

One person who played a prominent part in the development of the interpreting/translating profession in Australia was Jill Blewett, Coordinator of the Interpretation/Translation Department of the School of Languages at the South Australian College of Advanced Education in Adelaide. She later became a member of the Board of Directors of NAATI and went so far as to attend a conference interpretation course at the EEC (European Economic Community) in Brussels as an observer in order to gain as much knowledge as possible on the subject of interpreting and translating. She was one of the few prominent people in Australia at that time who understood the problems the profession was encountering and was always willing to help in any way she could. Her death in October 1988 was a great loss to the profession.

In March 1988, the International Congress of Free Trade Unions, headquartered in Brussels, met in Melbourne with a team of sixteen interpreters from Australia covering English, French, Spanish and German. All Australian AIIC members were on the team as well as a large number of pre-candidates - a higher proportion of pre-candidates than there should have been according to normally acceptable standards. Interpreters were brought in from overseas for the language combinations that were not available here at that time: Japanese (in sufficient number) and Scandinavian languages. It was extremely difficult to find sixteen interpreters of the required standard and three were actually from Europe but had changed their professional address to Australia in order to help us, i.e. for the sake of their Australian colleagues - otherwise the whole team would have been imported from Brussels.

In November and December 1988 the International Telecommunication Union, headquartered in Geneva, Switzerland (a specialized agency of the United Nations) held a meeting of its International Consultative Committee on Telephony and Telegraphy and the World Administrative Telegraph and Telephone Conference in Melbourne, lasting a total of five weeks. More than 1000 delegates from 114 countries attended the conference. There were 41 interpreters covering English, French, Spanish, Russian, Chinese and Arabic,i.e. the six languages of United Nations. Thirteen interpreters were recruited from Australia which was the maximum that could be found of the required standard at that time - all AIIC members, pre-candidates and/or NAATI Levels 4 or 5. The others had to be brought over at great expense from the Region (eight) and from Europe (twenty).

Another interesting detail concerning these conferences, both of which took place in Melbourne, is that in both cases formal complaints were received from local interpreters' professional associations that it was unfair to bring interpreters from Sydney and Canberra to Melbourne, i.e. that it was unfair not to have recruited local interpreters ! This shows that even the local interpreters' association itself seemed to be unaware of the difference between community and conference interpretation and the fact that conference interpretation requires NAATI Level 4 or 5 accreditation. In fact there was only one Level 4 interpreter domiciled in Melbourne at that time, also an AIIC member, who was recruited for the Chinese booth. Obviously community/court interpreters at NAATI

Level 3 could not be expected to provide conference interpretation (at Level 4) of United Nations standard.

Four more large international conferences have taken place in Australia:

1) The Government-Industry Conference Against Chemical Weapons, Canberra, September 1989, where the entire team of l6 interpreters came from Australia and included six AIIC members and seven pre-candidates. Languages: English, French, Spanish and Russian.

2) Metropolis '90, Melbourne, October 1990, where there were 21 interpreters (13 local, 6 from the Region, and 2 from USA). Languages: English, French and Spanish.

3) The Seventh General Assembly of the World Council of Churches held in Canberra in February 1991, where there were 46 translators, 32 interpreters (7 local, the rest from Europe) and the languages were: English, French, Spanish, German, Russian, Greek and Indonesian. There were more than 4,000 participants.

4) The World Congress and associated meetings of the International Federation of Employees and Technicians, held in Sydney Town Hall in March 1999, with 1500 delegates and some forty interpreters, working in English, French, Spanish, Portuguese, Italian, German, Dutch, Japanese, Swedish, Norwegian and Danish. Of these, fourteen came from Sydney itself, eight from elsewhere in Australia, one from New Zealand, eight from Europe and the remainder from the Asia-Pacific Region. In Australia the only languages available were English, French, Spanish, Italian, German and Japanese which meant that interpreters for the remaining five languages had to be brought in from overseas.

We can conclude from all this that when large international conferences are held in this country, there is a shortage of interpreters with the required language combinations.

It is rather a chicken-and-egg situation because clearly there is not enough conference work here to provide a livelihood for free-lance interpreters. Even for those now in Australia this is true and for those who might wish to come here the prospect is bleak. They all have to earn a living doing something else in between conferences.

If you have read *The Age of Unreason* by Professor Charles Handy (1989), you will see that this lifestyle fits in very well with his "portfolio" people, that is, professionals who, in the future, will not work every day, such as writers, actors, composers and musicians, and who will run two or more careers in parallel. In Professor Handy's view, this is the way employment will develop in the years to come: available work will be shared by more people and all will have more leisure.

Most conference interpreters have a second job as a translator, sub-titler or something quite different such as running a business of their own. Often they have to obtain leave without pay in order to work on a conference. On the other hand, perhaps if there were more professional qualified conference interpreters of the right standard and with the missing language combinations available in this country, there might be more conferences.

Now we have international standard convention centres in Canberra, Adelaide, Melbourne, Sydney, Hobart, Brisbane, and Cairns, not to mention the built-in interpretation booths in Parliament House, Canberra, there is no reason why there should not be more international conferences held here. If this happens we will be short of qualified interpreters to man the booths. After doing all we can to train the best of the candidates by recruiting them and working with them, it is disappointing (though understandable) when they promptly leave for Europe where they can get more work.

There seems to be a world-wide shortage of English-booth - that is, English mother-tongue - interpreters, amazing though it may seem, especially in Washington and New York, and the demand in Brussels and Strasbourg is enormous at the moment for all European languages. Already there are hundreds of free-lance conference interpreters earning a good livelihood there from full-time conference interpretation. In Europe, an interpreter who works less than 60 days a year is not considered a true professional, whereas in Australia, 50 days is considered a good year. But we must maintain high standards in this country so that our interpreters and translators are on a par with those of the rest of the world. That is why NAATI cannot accredit people only because they have been "doing the work for 20 years", or they "speak" the language concerned. That is not good enough. Our standards must be the same as those of other countries so that free circulation of interpreters and translators is possible. It is no good producing inferior grade interpreters/translators who are "good enough for this country" but are not good enough for "export". The only way our interpreters will gain the polish they sometimes lack, however good their skills may be, is by working with other professional interpreters from other countries, whether the conference they are working on is in Australia or elsewhere. Most beginners say they learn more from working one week with experienced professionals than from months of training. If Australian interpreters are of international standard, they can expect to be recruited to work in Japan, Indonesia, Fiji, the Pacific Islands, China, New Zealand, New Caledonia, Polynesia, Manila, Singapore and Thailand.

It must not be forgotten however that this works both ways - they must also expect to work with experienced colleagues from overseas on conferences in Australia. Our profession is ever-evolving. Interpreting is not a static skill; it is a profession where you learn something new each day - new vocabulary, new short cuts, new expressions - and working in a closed circuit always with the same people teaches you nothing.

There must be freedom of movement across frontiers if we are to maintain the same standards here as prevail internationally, and give ourselves a chance of measuring up against international colleagues. Australia is not different. The more one travels professionally the more one realizes the commonality of problems and situations. Just as there is a world-wide movement to remove tariff barriers and government subsidies in trade, so we must have freedom of movement for interpreters and translators and our standards must be on a par with those of the rest of the world.

We have a big battle on our hands to implant our profession in this country and combat the ignorance that still prevails. We have all heard the comment : "Why pay for an interpreter from outside when the tea-lady speaks Italian?"

I am frequently asked by government department officials over the telephone what is needed for interpretation at a forthcoming conference - mostly by people who have never organized an international conference before or never even attended one. Sometimes they seem to think all they need is a phone number where they can hire the "translation equipment", not realizing that human beings are also required. You just push the right knobs and the languages you require come pouring out.

One conference organizer rang me and after forty-five laborious minutes of explanation said in a resigned voice: "O.K. I'll take ten." "Ten what?" "Ten interpreters, of course.""Fine," I said, "what languages do you require?" The reply was full of contempt. "How can I tell what languages are required until they speak?"

I hope that my book will help clear up some of these misunderstandings.

4

Sine qua nons
PRE-REQUISITES FOR A
CONFERENCE INTERPRETER

Although both translators and interpreters belong to the family of language communicators, translators and interpreters are not interchangeable, their techniques are different and they generally also differ in temperament. It has been said that interpreters are extrovert while translators are introvert. Also, the factor of sheer physical stress has prevented many otherwise gifted translator-interpreter candidates from becoming conference interpreters (Keiser 1975).

Translators and interpreters have one thing in common: a knowledge of languages, but the psychomotor component is very different and this is why excellent translators are often unable to handle simultaneous interpretation.

Conference interpreting (formerly NAATI levels 4 and 5) is quite different from community and court interpreting (formerly NAATI levels 2 and 3) and is not just a step up from Level 3. The skills are not the same, nor are the prerequisites.

Community interpreters play an essential part in Australia and although their tasks may sometimes seem to lack prestige, the role of the community interpreter should not be underestimated. Community interpreters are often required to work in three-way interview situations involving a professional, an interpreter and a client and sometimes through the use of a telephone rather than in person. Interpreting is usually done in the consecutive mode which permits timely breaks in the conversation and opportunities to seek clarification when necessary. It is not an easy job and has emotional aspects which can be exhausting; in the case of court and medical work it has daunting life-and-death aspects. Furthermore, we must not forget that simultaneous interpreting began with court interpreting at the Nuremberg trials.

A conference interpreter plays quite a different role, more anonymous and at a different intellectual level. The primary mode of interpretation is simultaneous, that is, the interpreter is expected to listen, interpret and speak all at the same time. However, the conference interpreter may also be required to work in consecutive mode at high level negotiations, at ministerial meetings, for visits from foreign Heads of State etc. and to provide whispered simultaneous interpretation when there are only two or three delegates speaking a given language.

At conferences, simultaneous interpreters are removed from the action by a pane of glass as they operate from an enclosed booth, well removed from the speaker. They must be able to speak like a doctor, a scientist, a lawyer or a physicist - this is called *register*. They must sound plausible when they are interpreting radio-astronomy, cardiology or anaesthesiology and be able to pronounce all types of scientific vocabulary with ease and fluency. As well as a good all-round education, they must have perfect mastery of their active languages (into which they interpret) and an in-depth knowledge of their passive languages (from which they interpret) as well as a sound general knowledge (university level or equivalent).

This will help them in their first task, which is to understand. "To interpret is first and foremost to understand" is one of the fundamental maxims of our profession. The interpreter must be able to put himself at the intellectual level of the speaker he is interpreting and since most conference delegates are specialists in a given field, they are more often than not, university-trained.

That is why Interpreters' Schools place their interpreters' training section at post-graduate level.

The importance of one's mother tongue

It is essential that conference interpreters maintain the purity of their mother tongue, which must not be tainted by the influence of another language. For example, if your mother tongue is not English, it is difficult to maintain its purity without conscious effort when you are living in an English-speaking environment. Interpreters who say *el reporte* instead of *el informe* or *injures* for *injuries* (and I have heard both) are not likely to succeed. Once they have overcome the initial difficulty of speaking and listening at the same time, they need to learn microphone technique, how much volume to use, etc. They need to know how to prepare for a meeting and how to interpret for relay. Too many students yearn to become conference interpreters because the perceived advantages and prestige of the profession appeal to them but they are unaware of the difficulties and uncertainties involved as well as the high standards required. You must be quick-thinking and alert because in simultaneous there is no time to stop and think, no time to cast about in your mind for the appropriate expression as there is with consecutive or escort interpreting. If you stop to think you will have missed the next sentence which may be the key to the argument.

"Take care of the Sense and the Sounds will take care of themselves" as Danica Seleskovitch says (1977).

Modesty

Modesty is essential if you are to convey other people's thoughts without interjecting your own views on the subject - epecially if you happen to disagree with the views you are articulating! However, a certain degree of maturity and self-confidence is an asset. No-one wants to hear a hesitant, uncertain voice which corrects itself all the time, even if the actual words are correct.

The proficiency of an interpreter does not remain static - it improves with the years; the same is true of the knowledge of languages. This is an area where experience really counts.

The interpreter must be capable of concentration to a degree not required by many other professions. This effort of high-level concentration can only be maintained for a limited period of time, which explains why meetings cannot last longer than three hours or three-and-a-half at the most. After this period of time the interpreter's efficiency decreases rapidly, fatigue takes over, there are hesitations and then errors. Somehow the filter that checks what you are saying seems to become blurred after an excessive period of concentration (more than 45 minutes) so that you don't care what you are saying after a while! This is particularly true towards the end of the working day.

Experience also helps the interpreter cope with the problems of diversity of accents and stress-patterns in speakers particularly in the case of those using a language which is not their own, and problems of microphone voice distortion particularly if the speaker is too close or too far from the microphone.

A conference interpreter's language combination is of paramount importance if he wants to work in the field of international conferences (Keiser 1975). All European Interpreters' Schools have made the mastery of at least three languages a prerequisite - now the tendency is to make that requirement four languages. Among them there must be at least one 'A' language and one 'B' language. This is because interpreters are required to work in both directions in consecutive interpretation which means that only one' A' and the rest' C' would not be sufficient.

In consecutive interpretation, note-taking is the key to success but voice projection, pronunciation and intonation are also important, as well as appearance, posture and professionalism.

From what I have said, you will see that, in addition to perfect mastery of the active language or languages, candidate interpreters need full understanding of their passive languages, a solid general background of university level or equivalent professional experience, and certain mental and physical qualities (such as those listed below), in order to become a successful conference interpreter:

- analytical mind and intuition
- quick thinking and ability to adapt immediately to different speakers, accents, situations and subjects
- power of concentration
- rapid grasp of meaning
- above-average physical and nervous stamina
- excellent memory
- art of public speaking, pleasant voice
- great intellectual curiosity
- absolute intellectual integrity
- tact and diplomacy.

These qualities are not used individually as the need arises, but rather they blend together in the complex operation which constitutes simultaneous interpretation.

Karla Déjean le Féal (ESIT, AIIC) has carried out considerable research into the way in which the brain operates during simultaneous and consecutive interpretation and has written extensively on the prerequisites for a conference interpreter.

Do not embark upon this career if you are a slow speaker, if you are a hesitant, painstaking perfectionist, if you have the slightest speech problem or speak unclearly, if you are nervous and easily upset or if you get carried away by emotions and feelings. Speakers at conferences talk at anything between 100 and 250 words a minute and for a three-hour session this could mean 40,000 words, equivalent to some 150 typed pages. No wonder that physical resistance and good nerves are a must.

Conference interpreters work in a variety of fields particularly when they work free-lance. Study in any particular scientific field or law, medicine or engineering for example is therefore an asset, in addition to mastery of the languages.

Conference interpretation in summary is a difficult, stressful occupation where in the course of a few months you may be talking about the standardization of synthetic fibres, sexual abnormalities in the new-born child, radio communications, cancer research, metallurgy, radio-astronomy, tick-borne encephalitis, hydrology, orthopaedic surgery, the calibration of eggs for the Egg Marketing Board, telephony and automatic switching systems, the safety of life at sea, economics and countervailing duties, space communications or legal matters - sometimes at top speed - and all of this has to be done as if you are speaking your own words. Your audience expects correct terminology that has been thoroughly prepared beforehand, and prefers a lively, interested tone of voice. Just as a good translation must read like an original text, so the words of the interpreter must sound natural, like the words of a speaker voicing his own thoughts.

That is the challenge. It is true that conference interpreting and translating is a glamorous highly-paid profession with plenty of travel, staying in luxury hotels and going to the best restaurants, enjoying prestige and admiration, jet-setting all over the world, cocktail parties and official receptions, buying one's clothes in Paris, one's shoes and handbags in Rome, one's silks in China and Thailand. The vitality of the scene goes to your head, you meet people, go to places and enjoy occasions beyond the reach of the general public, as Anne Kerr (1988) said:

> *The profession offers these in the context of working in and with the countries concerned, a totally different feeling from tourism, however*

delightful that can be... Interpreting enables minds to meet; and further, makes possible the interpenetration of differing mentalities and of differing cultures. There is an intense pleasure in this. Interpreters of course have preferences as to subject matter (I enjoyed less, for instance, talking about the inside of a gas turbine than about the novels of Mishima), but the work is deeply satisfying in its nature at any time. Conference interpreting must surely be one of the most absorbing professions of the present era.

Jean Herbert referred to it as an "itinerant international university." He also observed (Kerr 1988) that:

while for interpreting it is indispensable to be bilingual, just as in order to play the violin one must first have a violin, the fact of having a violin does not make one a violinist, and similarly knowledge of languages is no more than an instrument in the hands of someone wishing to become an interpreter.

Most of the 2,500 or so professional conference interpreters in the world are free-lance, working partly for the private market and partly for international organizations and the United Nations family of specialized agencies. Most of us prefer the free-lance way of life, the independence it gives us and the possibility of saying "no" to a conference offer that does not appeal for one reason or another. Most of us feel we would not be happy in a regular nine-to-five job seeing the same people every day, dealing with the same subject every day, knowing where we will most probably be next month or next year at the same time. We enjoy the unexpectedness and the unpredictability of the lifestyle. But it must not be forgotten that conference interpreting and translating is hard work. The unpaid study time to prepare for a conference should also not be forgotten - sometimes two weeks of study may be required for a difficult two-day conference.

But the trust people like Fidel Castro, Marshall Tito and Pandit Nehru in the past, and Prime Ministers, research scientists and eminent thinkers of all countries today place in their interpreters, in their integrity and professionalism, is a reward for the effort and sacrifices one makes to achieve the standard required.

5

WHAT CONFERENCE INTER-PRETERS DO

Mother tongue and the brain

In 1874 the German neurologist Carl Wernicke located the area of the left hemisphere of the brain concerned with comprehension of spoken and written language. Recently even more refined experiments have shown that in about 95% of people, in addition to language, the left hemisphere controls such logical processes as mathematics, while the right hemisphere is involved in non-verbal activities of a more artistic or emotional nature. There are three centres of the left hemisphere of the brain involved in language skills.

Professor Tadanobu Tsunoda (1981) of the Medical Research Institute of the Medical and Dental University, Tokyo, conducted a series of experiments on a group of Japanese subjects aimed at determining ear-dominance for a group of vowel sounds and spoken syllables in Japanese. Left ear dominance for a particular sound indicates right brain dominance while right ear dominance indicates left brain dominance because the auditory nerves of each ear mainly connect with the opposite side of the brain.

In 1972 by pure chance Professor Tsunoda applied his tests to his first non-Japanese subject, a Frenchman. To his surprise he found that the French subject showed marked differences from his Japanese subjects in the patterns of cerebral dominance in response to the same auditory stimuli. After this he tested fifty-seven speakers of West European languages such as English, French, Spanish, Italian, German and Swedish, fifteen Chinese speakers, seventeen speakers of Korean, as well as speakers from Vietnam, Cambodia, Thailand, Indonesia, Israel and Africa. The results clearly indicated that "steady-state" vowel sounds as well as pure tones induced left ear (right brain) dominance while syllables ellicited right ear (left brain) dominance. Only native speakers of Polynesian languages (Tonganese, Eastern Samoan and Maori) showed the same dominance patterns as the Japanese, displaying right ear (left brain) dominance for both vowels and syllables and left ear (right brain) dominance for pure tone sounds. It would therefore seem that the left hemisphere is the "verbal brain" in both groups because the left hemispheres in both cases are dominant for syllable sounds. But Japanese and Polynesian people exhibit left brain dominance for both vowel and syllable sounds, whereas other people show right brain dominance for vowel sounds and left brain dominance for syllable sounds.

The rustle of the wind, the sound of running water and the breaking of waves, human non-verbal sounds such as sighing that convey emotion are all similar to vowel sound structures and are processed in the left or verbal hemisphere of the brain in people of Japanese or Polynesian mother tongue, whereas they are processed in the right brain hemisphere in people of non-Japanese or non-Polynesian mother tongue. This, says Professor Tsunoda, is because, unlike most of the world's languages, in which consonant-vowel-consonant syllables predominate, the Japanese and Polynesian languages are marked by the presence of many vowel-only and vowel-consonant-vowel words. This may in part account for a marked characteristic of written Japanese, its poetry, literature and art - the many references to nature and natural sounds.

In conclusion, Professor Tsunoda states:

> *The dominance patterns of the Japanese people for various sounds suggest that their function of emotion, together with the language and language-based logical function, is based in the verbal brain. In contrast, the brain of the Western*

person clearly specializes the language and related logical functions in the verbal hemisphere and separates the function of emotion in the nonverbal hemisphere.

In the Japanese people, sounds related to emotion are processed in the left brain, and this left brain dominance becomes firmly established as speech ability is developed. Then the left brain also becomes dominant for emotional functions as a result of the established link between emotion-related sounds and emotion-related experiences.

The same processes apply to non-Japanese people with respect to their right brain dominance for emotion-related sounds and functions. It can therefore be said that the laterality of emotion is acquired through the mother tongue.

I believe that the mother tongue differentiates the way in which people receive, process, feel and understand sounds from the external environment. The mother tongue is closely related to the development of the emotional mechanism in the brain. I conjecture that the mother tongue acquired in childhood is closely linked with the formation of the unique culture and mentality of each ethnic group.

Studies and research continue to make a valuable contribution to the growing understanding of the mental mechanisms and psychophysical aspects of interpreting, i.e. what happens in our brain when we listen in one language and speak in another. It is difficult enough to understand how a child learns to talk in the first place.

Interpreters are not linguists, nor are they experts in languages, or translators, they are really experts in comprehension and transcultural communication.

Conference interpretation is a specialized technique whereby people with different languages and backgrounds can communicate with one another. It plays a key role in the modern world which relies on communication in its many and varied forms. It would be inconceivable today to hold international congresses, symposia, negotiations or formal meetings of any kind without interpreters.

The interpreter is the mediator between two cultures, two ways of being. He is an ambiguous creature belonging to two worlds, who has lived here but also there, who is both part of his own people and a foreigner at the same time. Like the bird of Evtuchenko, he knows no boundaries (Garcia-Landa 1975). Perhaps he is more like a chameleon because he says different things depending on the language he is speaking. It is not just the words, it is also the gestures, the facial expressions and even the mannerisms and behaviour that change according to the language.

There is magic in it too. Imagine a meeting room where groups of diplomats or scientists are trying to prove a point, arguing, even accusing one another, or defending their views. Sometimes they throw questions and answers at one another at high speed, interrupting one another - yet they have no common language. They are quite oblivious of the anonymous faces behind the microphones up there in the glass boxes just under the ceiling.

You will notice some of the gestures are the same: the speaker down in the hall rises and waves an arm in the air - and so does the interpreter up in the booth. He is experiencing the feelings behind the words he is saying and his gestures and body language naturally follow suit. At the end of the day, he is exhausted by his emotions. Yet the thoughts he has been expressing, the pleas he has been voicing for his country to be given the right to vote, for example, may have nothing to do with him. He may not even agree with the views he is expressing. But during the debate he is inside the mind of the speaker, so engrossed in what he is saying he may finish the sentence before the speaker. He has entered the speaker's thought processes. An interesting detail is that he can only do this properly if he can see the speaker in the flesh (a television screen is not enough).

The interpreter *must* be able to see the speaker because he needs to know when he is about to start, he needs to see the body language and gestures all of which give a social context and contribute to the understanding of what is being said.

When a speaker is expressing his opinion he is thinking as he speaks and the words and phrases come out naturally with pauses and repetitions reflecting the close thought processes, and helping the listener to understand. If the delegate reads a written text aloud he is reading mechanically and the words are empty of the thought behind them. This is why it is so much more difficult to interpret a written text read out than a spontaneous speech or natural dialogue. In fact what the interpreter is being asked to do in the first instance is provide an oral translation that would normally take a translator some time to perfect, finding the right words and constructing the sentences correctly.

Contrary to a widely held belief, conference interpretation is not simply a word-for-word translation of a speech. It is the transmission of all the semantic, emotive and aesthetic content into a language which may use a totally different means of expression. In fact the interpreter is using his own words to reproduce the meaning of the speaker's words. What the interpreter says is distinct linguistically and philologically from what the speaker says . As Danica Seleskovitch (1968) points out, "To be or not to be: that is the question" is best translated as "Etre ou ne pas être: TOUT EST LÀ".

To be a good conference interpreter, you need to become "English" to understand what is meant by English understatements, how reluctant they are to express feelings, what it is "done" to say and not to say. What can

59

be taken for granted. You have to understand the different ways of proving a point, depending on whether you are Russian, Indian or French for example. English is the language of diplomacy and compromise, but underneath the understatements their position is firm and they are very determined to achieve their objectives.

The French approach is probably like a Cartesian staircase. Often the Indian delegation starts by describing the ideal situation and works down to reality from there. The Italians, Spanish and Mexicans seem to feel the need for a large number of words and repetitions to prove a point, while the Russians often present opposite proposals for you to weigh up. You have to understand silences. And tones of voice. The intonations of a Cuban speaker as compared to those of a Chilean or a Paraguayan. You need to recognize irony or sarcasm and know when a speaker is being deliberately vague because he does not intend to give a precise answer.

Sometimes you have to resist the temptation to "improve" on what the speaker is saying. Your job is to give a faithful mirror reflection of what you hear and no more. Perhaps the delegate is playing for time until the phone call comes through from his capital with instructions from his government and he is just trying to keep the discussion going until then. Or he may have received instructions to be deliberately vague and not commit his government in any way. It is the interpreter's job to understand and reflect all this faithfully and accurately. And however difficult the subject-matter or the understanding of a particular speaker may be, it is part of the interpreters' image to give the impression that what they are doing is easy, no effort at all ! In fact that is how delegates see us: they consider what we are doing is easy, every-day and purely mechanical.

To get some idea of what the interpreter is doing, try "shadowing" - that is to say, repeating for a period of thirty minutes what is being said by a speaker, in the same language. You might try this: "As to the interdependence of the specific and non-specific immune mechanism, antigen-triggered "T" and "B" lymphocytes recruit non-specific effector mechanisms to eliminate the antigen. These mechanisms include complement-dependent lysis and enhanced phagocytosis of antigen by polymorphs and macrophages."

Now try the same thing with the speaker having a strong Indian, Viennese, Scottish or Lancashire accent, and try putting it into another language. You are beginning to get some idea of what conference interpreters are doing - more or less instantaneously. What is more, the interpreter has to speak at the same speed as the speaker or he will miss the next phrase or sentence.

It is easier to be vague in English than in French for example which is the reference language of many international organizations. This is because French is unambiguous due to its masculine or feminine and single or plural nouns and adjectives which ensure that the listener or reader knows precisely to which noun each adjective and verb refers.

For a message to be interpreted it must first be perfectly understood so that it can be removed with all its shades of meaning from its verbal wrapping and reconstituted intact in another language. So, in addition to his knowledge of his passive and active languages, he must therefore also understand the subject, which he has prepared beforehand, and the speaker's mentality. He must be aware of different cultures, political and economic systems, parliamentary systems perhaps, cultural and social values and various nations' positions on the subject under discussion (by reading the newspapers). One of the big challenges is the unpredictability of the signals received. He must be able to adapt to different situations and subjects and understand very quickly another person's reasoning as well as the objectives of the debate and the various delegations' agendas.

Another problem for the simultaneous interpreter is proverbs. You have to search around in your brain for an equivalent proverb in the other language giving the same end-meaning - often the subject or the whole wording may be completely different because proverbs reflect the way of life of a people through the ages. And you have only a split second in which to do this. If an English speaker says "Absence makes the heart grow fonder" for example, the first French proverb containing the word "absence" that springs to mind is "*Les absents ont toujours tort*", which means "Those who are absent are always wrong." Nothing to do with it. Quite different. Beginner interpreters might well spend some time before they start their career preparing a list of the most widely used proverbs and equivalents in their various languages, just in case. Remember, it is not the words you are aiming for but the meaning of the proverb, so the words in the equivalent may be quite different.

Jokes are also a problem. If a delegate tells a joke you do not understand it is difficult to make it funny. Yet it is imperative for your listeners to laugh at the right moment or the speaker will lose face. Some interpreters admit defeat without even trying and say "The speaker is cracking a joke. Would you please laugh." I have a small repertoire of jokes of my own, of varying length, which have saved a few delicate situations. It is of course better to understand the joke and interpret it brilliantly so everyone laughs at the right moment and no-one loses face - not even the interpreter. Most of the audience are listening to the English channel so much depends on the presence of mind of those in the English booth. When a joke begins, you lean forward, close your eyes and intensify your concentration and somehow with the help of an extra flow of adrenalin you generally manage to get the point, even if you have to adapt the punchline to make it funnier for your particular language (culture) audience. As well as jokes and proverbs, quotations (from the Bible, for example) and poems are difficult and so are names of films, books and plays - you may not always recognize them in another language. The answer is to read in all of your languages, novels, newspapers and magazines, to keep up to date. Languages too evolve. A language is a living thing. Reading is the only way to follow the evolution of your passive as well as your active languages. A professional interpreter must read continuously, as well as visiting countries where your languages are spoken regularly.

At one meeting where I was working in consecutive, the American delegate took the floor to say: "The delegate of the UK is pussyfooting with a red herring!" Try putting that into French, Spanish, Japanese or Russian in a few seconds and without hesitation.

Perhaps you are beginning to understand why we love the challenge of our profession so much, why so many would-be interpreters are waiting in the wings, hoping for their big chance when someone will need to be replaced at the last minute and at last they will have an opportunity to prove themselves... When you are on the air you are in a special heightened mental state, the adrenalin is pumping and as you look down at the rows of ear-phoned heads listening to your words, you are suddenly capable of using words you never thought you knew. It is an amazing experience to listen to tapes of yourself, years later, and hear your own voice talking convincingly about things you know nothing of, using scientific terminology with ease. As if you really understood....

But because interpreters participate in conferences on a variety of subjects they are at the forefront of what is happening in the world politically, scientifically and culturally which means that they are constantly enriched. Conference interpreters are impartial, discreet witnesses contributing to scientific and medical research as well as to peace in the international world.

6

Modus Operandi
HOW IT IS DONE

There are two modes of conference interpretation:

Simultaneous

Here the interpreter sits in a sound-proof booth behind a large glass window enabling him to see the speaker, hears a message in one language through his headphones and transmits it simultaneously into another language through a microphone to the listener. In other words, simultaneous interpreting is a kind of speech processing whereby, over a six-hour conference day, up to 36,000 words can be processed which is roughly equivalent to 120 pages of typescript. The interpreter has a volume control to adjust the level of sound he hears through his earphones and in front of him is a box containing the on-off button for the microphone he sometimes shares with his booth-mate, a "cough" button and a device to show on which channel delegates hear him.

Delegates also wear lightweight earphones and have a microphone in front of them, as well as a volume-control and a switch to enable them to choose the channel, that is the language, they wish to listen to. They may also listen to the "floor" if they wish, that is, the speaker in the original language.

There are generally two interpreters in each booth, that is to say for each language, in order to ensure the quality of the interpretation and to cover the various language combinations. In cases where the workload is particularly heavy, however - for example, in two-way booths such as Japanese, Chinese and Arabic - there are generally three interpreters.

In a four-language conference (say English, French, Spanish and Russian which is the most widely used language combination at United Nations) both interpreters in the English booth will work into English from French, at least one works from Spanish and the other from Russian . In the French booth, both interpreters work into French from English, at least one also from Spanish and the other from Russian. In the Spanish booth both work from English and French into Spanish and at least one works also from Russian. In the Russian booth, both interpreters work into Russian from English, at least one also from French and one from Spanish. This is the ideal situation where "relay" is cut down to a minimum. If a Russian-speaker takes the floor, for example, there will always be one interpreter in each of the English and French booths to take it *direct*, that is, without using relay. (The use of relay is explained later in this Chapter). The International Labour Organization has the following booths at its June Conference each year: Japanese, Chinese, Arabic, Russian, German, Spanish, French and English.

The simultaneous technique is very stressful for the interpreter, involving intense concentration. This is why the work is usually shared by two interpreters per booth, each working for short periods interspersed with rest breaks. Generally interpreters work alternate half-hours, but even during the interpreter's half-hour "off the air", he follows the discussion, and is ready to jump into action if necessary (particularly if interpretation is required from one of his languages that his booth-mate does not have).

"Whispering" is also simultaneous interpretation but does not require a booth or electronic equipment. The interpreter sits with the delegation, consisting of one or two delegates (exceptionally three, but no more), speaking that particular language. It is generally combined with "consecutive" interpretation when one of "his" delegates takes the floor and the interpreter then gives a consecutive interpretation of the statement into English or French, using the delegates' microphone. Two interpreters, working both ways, are assigned to this type of interpretation and they take it in turn to work approximately half-hour periods. Today, use of this type of interpretation is comparatively rare except for speeches by visiting Statesmen, businessmen and at press conferences.

You will note that each interpreter has a glass of water in front of him, together with a notepad and pencil. It is important for simultaneous interpreters to note down all figures, dates, percentages, key words and acronyms that may be repeated, titles etc. Figures are very easily forgotten by the time you reach the end of the sentence, especially in cases where the word order is different in the target language. An order of magnitude is not good enough - figures must be absolutely correct. If you are working into English, take your time to finish your interpretation properly. Do not rush the final words because the delegate has finished speaking. Most delegates are listening to the English channel and they will more often than not wait for you to finish.

If the speaker is reading from slides that you cannot see, say so. "The interpreter apologises but he cannot see the slides." There is no point in "soldiering on", running the risk of getting something wrong, especially figures. It is better to cause an upheaval while the screen is moved or some lights turned off and then get it right, rather than give the meeting erroneous information. Obviously it is better to ascertain before the meeting begins that the screen is placed where it is clearly visible to all booths. If necessary, explain firmly but courteously that if you cannot see, you cannot do your job properly. If a film is to be shown, do not attempt to interpret the soundtrack unless you have a direct feed to your headset and have preferably had a chance to study the script in advance. Film and TV commentaries are generally spoken too fast to be interpreted correctly without a prepared script to hand. If the screen is very far away, opera glasses may be useful.

Consecutive

In this case the interpreter sits with the delegates in the room, sometimes with no electronic equipment, although there may be an amplification system with earphones and microphones. At other times, the interpreter may accompany the delegate to a meeting or a function where speeches are to be interpreted. He listens to the speaker's message in one language while taking notes, and reproduces it in full immediately afterwards (consecutively) in another language as if he were delivering his own speech. This may be done for the whole speech if it does not last more than 20 minutes or so; if longer it may be divided up into sections.

Two consecutive interpreters are assigned for two languages. They work both ways, that is, English into Spanish when the speaker uses English, and Spanish into English when Spanish is used. They take it in turn to work approximately half an hour at a time, adopting a convenient break between speakers to change over. During his half-hour "off", the second interpreter follows the discussion in order to understand the situation when he takes over again and familiarize himself with expressions used that may be referred to again later. He may also help his colleague find references in relevant texts.

In the context of a conference, be sure you are seated at the table and within comfortable hearing distance of all speakers. If you cannot hear what is being said there is no point in trying to interpret it. Where you are seated is therefore of the utmost importance and you must get this organized before the meeting starts. When you enter the room, ascertain whether the Chairman wants you to sit next to him, or whether it is better for you to sit next to the delegation most in need of interpretation.

Many books have been written about note-taking but basically this is a very personal matter. The aim is to take notes which represent ideas and concepts rather than words, so that they may serve as memory-joggers. It is a good idea to write at the top of your notepad the subject and title of the meeting and any acronyms, the first time they occur - as the speech progresses you can refer to these by an abbreviation of your own invention, a "ditto" sign, or by means of an arrow, for example, rather than writing them out again each time. You wouldn't write out in full "King's Cross" for example, but rather "KX" - it is clearly much quicker to write a cross than write out the word "Cross". For "King" you could draw a crown but that would take too long unless it is a very simplified, stylized version. Personally I would write a "K" because that would be enough to remind me. Rather than write out the word "stop" it would be quicker to put a full stop. But that might get lost in your notes so I would put a circle or square round it. If a speaker says they like or love something you could draw a heart, if they say they don't you could draw a heart with a line through it. (Unfortunately a heart can take too long to draw if you do it properly because it involves two movements of the hand in different directions so practice a quick version that can be drawn in one movement.) Crossing something out is a good way of expressing a negative.

Some mathematical symbols may also be used if these come to mind easily (equal sign, not-equal being an equal sign crossed through, bigger than, smaller than, therefore, because, plus and minus, question-mark, circle, and so on.) But the interpreter must devise his own system of notation. He is subject to considerable stress when reading back his notes in front of an attentive audience and the symbols used must be immediately understandable. The aim is not to write down every word, but rather symbols, keys, and link words to indicate the logical thread. The notes must be able to be read back in any language so that the interpreter can concentrate on expressing the message he has to convey. Names, for example, can be shortened and written phonetically (*Shoncy* instead of *Shaughnessy*). The symbols used vary enormously from one person to another and are based on intuition and memory association, sometimes going back to one's primary school days and childhood memories.

As Walter Keiser says in his "Memorandum on the selection and training of conference interpreters and interpretation services at scientific meetings"(1975):

> *a consecutive note system must never become a substitute for shorthand. It only serves as a sort of almost optical frame helping the memory to reproduce a speech. Each interpreter will develop his own note-system.*

Shorthand cannot be used because this adds a step to the process - the shorthand has first to be deciphered. It is not easy for the brain to cope with this extra deciphering step as well as concentrating on translation from one language to the other - quite apart from the time element. Also, shorthand writing includes every sound uttered, all prepositions and many words that are unnecessary. All you need is the skeleton. Shorthand is too detailed and too long. He also explains:

> *The less a consecutive interpreter notes, the more he memorizes, the better his rendering of the speech. So do not use too many symbols. Choose them preferably among those already in international use, for example in mathematics, biology, etc. Create some new ones fitting typical conference expressions. Every interpreter has his own system of notes and symbols.*

Most beginners tend to write down too much but with experience you will see that your memory is better than you think and a few clear notes are infinitely preferable to a whole page of notes written so fast you can't read them back.

As to what you should note, W. Keiser suggests the following:

1. Always ideas, arguments, never just words. But write down all proper names, figures, titles, quotes.
2. Who speaks, and about whom or what.
3. Tense of the action i.e. present, past or future.
4. Whether the statement is negative, positive, interrogative or exclamatory.
5. Connections between ideas and arguments.
6. Emphasis and stress.

Notes should arranged vertically on the page, with indentations such as for new paragraphs to indicate new thoughts and a system of arrows and connecting signs.

> *Moreover, in each meeting there will be (sometimes rather long and complicated) typical expressions, titles, etc. The interpreter will form an ad hoc abbreviation thereof to be used systematically during that session. Example:*
> *Le produit national brut aux prix de facteurs: PNBPF*
> *Gesamtwirtschaftliche Kontenrechnung: CN = comptabilité nationale = national accounting*
> *Centres Communs de Recherche : Centres (For centre, I put a dot in the middle of a circle)*
> *Comité Scientifique et Technique: CST*

Also, World Weather Watch : WWW or W3 which is quicker to write.

By far the best symbols for substantive expressions are just abbreviations of the corresponding words, such as *del* for delegate, *Ch* for Chairman, *mtg* for meeting, *Cttee* for "Committee", *Com* for Commission, *SG* for Secretary-General, *Pres* for President, *Gen Ass* for General Assembly or even *GA*.

K. Dejean Le Féal (1981) says, for example, that rather than confining oneself to a rigid system of note-taking learnt once and for all beforehand, it is preferable to remain open to the inspiration of the moment. "Beware of the trees hiding the forest", she says. "Too researched and detailed notes can prevent you from the overall picture of the views the delegate has expressed." At the time of reading back you will find that you actually use only a fraction of your notes, because your memory takes over. The fewer notes you take, the less you will tend to rely upon them. Nowadays, when interpreters read them back in only one language, it is a good idea to write them in the target language, and if there is anything you can't think of as you write, then put the problem word in the original language. By the time you come to read it back, your brain will have worked out what it is without you realizing it.

Make your notes as small as possible and write them clearly. The smaller they are, the smaller (and therefore quicker) the hand movements required. It is a good idea to separate your page into two columns in order to fit as much into one page as possible. Make sure you have two or three sharp pencils or pens with you in case one of them lets you down. I prefer a large A4 notepad (lined) because this means wasting less time turning over pages. I have developed my own system with very small symbols which are faster to write. Do not accept someone else's note-taking system - it is far better to develop your own; you will read them back much more rapidly because they will mean something to you personally, instantly. A French or Spanish person's note-taking system, for example, would be different from an English or Australian person because of different teaching methods at primary school. You can practise doing this from radio or television news bulletins. In Australia the foreign language programmes broadcast and televised by S.B.S. (the Special Broadcasting Service of the Australian Radio and

Television Broadcasting Corporation) are a godsend to would-be interpreters in need of practice.

Be sure to cross out each paragraph as you finish reading it back, to avoid any hesitations or duplication. Valuable tips for note-taking will be found in the writings of Walter Keiser (1975), Jean Herbert (1952), Danica Seleskovitch (1974) and Karla Dejean Le Féal (1981).

The best training for note-taking is working as a précis-writer. In United Nations and all international organizations, English and French précis-writers are in great demand. They summarize the discussions so that only the salient points are given with the threads linking them to produce the skeleton of the statement. Précis-writers learn to analyze what they are hearing **as they write their notes**, which are thus concise, containing no unnecessary words or details. Reading them back afterwards and writing the précis is then a simple matter because the main task of analysis has been done during the note-taking. The same applies to consecutive interpretation. It is no good desperately trying to write everything down, thinking you will analyze the notes afterwards because this becomes a Herculean task after the event when your recollection is no longer fresh. One misreading of your notes can distort the whole statement as was the case recently at Parliament House, when I saw an earnest beginner mis-read a name at the very beginning of a statement (she confused the name of a person for the name of a country), and then valiantly and desperately try to adapt the rest to fit in with what she had already said. The puzzled expressions on the faces of the listeners were quite amusing to watch.

Most important of all is the strict necessity to note down all numbers and dates. If there is a succession of numbers for example in a financial discussion, budget committee, etc. you must write down all the figures as they are uttered, even at the expense of keeping your listeners waiting. It is better to hold up a meeting a few seconds and give correct figures rather than trying to be fast and giving incorrect information. Consecutive interpretation is not a memory test. Your audience doesn't care whether you have performed a feat of memory. All they want is reliable information. Good note-taking is therefore essential. Be sure that your symbols or abbreviations are quick to write; avoid curves that require the hand to move backwards and so take up more time.

In the "bad old days" before our profession was regulated we generally had to read the same notes back in two different languages which meant that the notes we took could not be language specific. Well do I remember the strain of having to do this on difficult technical radio conferences in the 1960's. Sometimes an over enthusiastic speaker would not stop after thirty minutes, particularly if he was a world expert on radioastronomy at last given an opportunity to deliver the results of his lifelong research. Today it is customary to indicate (politely) to the speaker after fifteen to twenty minutes that you wish to interrupt him to give the interpretation of what he has said so far.

Accuracy is of course the most important factor. However, it is also important that the consecutive interpreter raise his head and speak slowly and distinctly, placing his voice so as to be heard right to the back of the room if there is no electronic equipment to amplify his speech. It is no good doing a wonderful job if you cannot be heard! Eye-to-eye contact with your listeners will enhance your work. I find that this happens quite naturally, the interpreter tends to look at the person with whom he is communicating to read on his face whether he has understood or whether further explanation is required. K. Dejean Le Feal (1981) also stresses the importance of self-monitoring when reading back one's notes. By this she means listening carefully to one's words to check that they mean exactly what one wants to say. This seems a wise precaution because interpretation is always improvisation, running the risk of defects of expression which may occur in spontaneous speaking.

Professional appearance and behaviour are also important. Try to avoid irritating mannerisms and hide your nervousness so that you appear confident and reliable, and the tone of your voice is pleasant to listen to. This applies to both simultaneous and consecutive interpretation. All professional conference interpreters must be able to work in both simultaneous and consecutive modes.

Generally speaking, simultaneous interpretation is used for meetings with several languages where there are a large number of participants because it is so much faster. Consecutive interpretation is more suitable for smaller meetings of a technical or confidential nature, and for drafting in editorial committees (when compromise agreements are reached they are later ratified in plenary meetings with simultaneous interpretation) and for ministerial negotiations. In Australia (*Forum*, June 1991) most Japanese interpreting is done consecutively for business meetings and negotiations, as well as for visiting officials where speeches have to be interpreted from and into Japanese and English. As explained earlier, when simultaneous is used in conferences there are generally three interpreters in the Japanese and Chinese booths because the interpreters work both ways, that is, into Japanese, and into English (or French sometimes) when the Japanese or Chinese delegation takes the floor.

Perhaps I should explain the half-hour "on", half-hour "off" system of working, which applies to all types of interpreting. Because ours is a highly demanding, specialized profession (even excellent linguists are not necessarily able to do it well) and because of the high level of stress involved, largely due to the unpredictability of what a speaker may say, interpreters do not normally work for more than approximately half an hour at a time, each in turn. The stress experienced by a simultaneous interpreter has been measured scientifically and has been found to be similar to that of an air traffic controller. Great mental flexibility and speed of thought, decisiveness and rapid understanding are required. (For further details of the mental processes involved in simultaneous and consecutive interpretation, see the writings of Keiser, Dejean Le Féal and Garcia-Landa).

Perhaps the most demanding simultaneous conference interpretation is when amendments to texts are being drafted. The help of the booth-mate who is "off the air" is indispensable in this situation because he can find the place in the other language versions of the text. When a delegate proposes an amendment, one cannot merely translate it without first finding the original text in both, all three, or all four languages, understanding the change and only then interpreting the new wording after re-reading the sentence. It is no good merely translating the words because different wording may have been used in the original translation.

Difficulty arises when the speaker refers to "line 2 on page 3" because this will no doubt be a different line on a different page in the other languages (English is generally the shortest version). He may say "amend the text after the comma in the third line of the French text" but there may well be no comma in the third line of the English text and the phrase to which he refers may not be on the same page anyway. You therefore have to refer to the actual words of the text, remembering that your sole objective is to make the delegates listening to you understand unequivocally. It is better to keep the meeting waiting while you find the place of the amendment in both language texts and make sure you have understood before you start to translate, rather than start translation without having first understood. Otherwise you could lead the whole meeting into confusion and misunderstandings which might well take an hour to sort out. (The cost per minute of an international four-language meeting is quite astronomical.)

No interpreter has the right to cause confusion - our task is to provide clarity and understanding. So you may find it necessary to say, while you are sorting out the texts, something on the lines of: "The interpreter apologises for the delay but is finding the appropriate place in the Russian text", for example. If the amendment is proposed in English and you are interpreting into another language, it may be a good idea to repeat the proposal first in English, to give delegates a chance to write it down in English too if they wish, and to give yourself time to think about what you are going to say.

When drafting, remember that there is a difference between "brackets" (round brackets - *parenthèses - parentesis*) and "square brackets" (*crochets - crochetes*). The latter designate a word or words the meeting has been unable to agree upon - a decision will be taken later.

When the meeting decides to set up a working group to sort out a particular problem and refer back to the main meeting later, someone will probably propose terms of reference for the group. It is important that your colleague write these down for you, whether they are in your language or not, because they will probably be amended in the course of the discussion, and it is difficult to remember what you said earlier unless you have the text in writing in front of you.

If you are working in the French, Spanish, Russian or Arabic booth and you think the delegates listening to you are looking at the English text, or if there is no text in your language, then the best thing to do is to repeat the amendment in English and then give a translation and explanation of it. Whatever you do, however, you must not re-translate something which already has an official translation. If you re-translate something that has already been translated, the delegates will not recognize the text, and seeing that some of the words are different they may well think an amendment is being proposed. The golden rule is that you must always respect original texts, quickly find the text of the Constitution, Rules of Procedure, or whatever is being referred to, and read out the official version - never, never re-translate a *sacred text* or you will cause endless confusion.

While one of the two interpreters in the booth is working, the other follows the discussion, jotting down any useful words that may come up again. During this time it is also very useful to switch over to listen to the other booths to see how any doubtful or contentious terms are being translated, so that you are sure to recognize them if the delegate speaking that language takes the floor later. You must also be ready to help your colleague find a new document, or find the place in the document before him, search for any other texts that are being referred to, and jot down any dates or figures that may be mentioned.

If you hear your colleague is searching for a word and you have it, write it down on your pad in front of you where he can see it if he wishes, but do not disturb him by making signs or speaking or thrusting maybe unwanted scraps of paper in front of him. He may have found the expression himself already, and be endeavouring to turn the phrase differently.

You must at all costs avoid disturbing your colleague while he is working by rustling documents, opening or closing the door of the booth noisily, moving your chair or talking to colleagues passing by outside. Also, it is much more difficult to do a good job if you are suddenly plunged into a discussion without having followed what has been happening. This is why it is so important for the interpreter not "on the air" to concentrate on the discussion rather than allow himself to be distracted.

Simultaneous interpretation is less tiring for the interpreter and is sometimes taught to the exclusion of consecutive. (This is not so, however, at ETI (Geneva University), ESIT (Sorbonne, Paris), the University of Queensland Japanese Course or any of the better schools of interpretation). It is a great pity that some new generation interpreters are often unable to provide consecutive interpretation; even when they have learnt they are reluctant to do it, a) because it is more difficult and b) because they are not hidden by the anonymity of the booth but are sitting at the conference table in full view of the delegates who will recognize them if they make mistakes and may ask for a repetition or clarification if the interpretation is not clear.

Because accuracy is the main concern if you are doubtful about something and your colleague, sitting nearby, cannot help you, it is better to ask for the delegate to repeat it, if you are working in consecutive. It happened to me once, when I could not understand what the Japanese delegate was saying (there was no Japanese interpretation because the delegate thought his English was excellent). I passed a note to the Chairman explaining what had happened and he very kindly said: "Perhaps the Japanese delegate would repeat that to be sure we have it correctly." So no-one lost face. If, however, you are working in simultaneous, you think you have missed something important and your colleague can't help you, then the only thing to do is to say "The interpreter apologises. Could the Chairman please ask the speaker to repeat the last sentence?" It could happen to anyone and you must provide an accurate interpretation particularly if you feel the point being made is important.

Active and passive languages

The time has come for me to explain what is meant by A, B and C languages, and what we mean by *active* and *passive* languages.

Active languages:

A: The interpreter's native tongue, or another language strictly equivalent to a native language, into which the interpreter works from all of his other languages in both simultaneous and consecutive interpretation. All professional conference interpreters must have at least one A language but may have more than one.

B: A language other than the interpreter's native tongue, of which he has a perfect command and into which he may work from one or more of his other languages. Some interpreters work into their B language only in consecutive interpretation, and some only at certain conferences on a subject with which they are particularly familiar. A conference organizer generally asks the interpreter beforehand whether he is willing to work into his B language at a specific conference on a given subject.

Passive languages:

C: Languages of which the interpreter has a complete understanding and from which he works. Sometimes an interpreter will downgrade a B to a C as languages can lose their cutting edge from disuse or prolonged absence from that language community. Rarely used C's may also be dropped to avoid disasters.

If you do not live in a country where your A language is spoken, make every effort to keep abreast of linguistic, cultural, political and social developments. Listen carefully to how the langauge is used by native speakers from countries other than yours and note their use of words and expressions. Language is constantly changing and usage varies over time and over distance so we can never relax our linguistic vigilance.

Asian languages

Karla Déjean Le Féal, professor at ESIT (Sorbonne, University of Paris) for many years, maintains that "there is nothing special" about simultaneous interpretation from and into Asian languages, as compared with from one Western language to another:

> *Interpretation means comprehension of the speaker's meaning and re-expressing that meaning in the target language. Thus it is the message*

on which the whole process is hinged, not the language in which this message is conveyed by the speaker nor the language in which it will be re-stated by the interpreter. As long as the source and target languages are appropriate tools for the respective native speakers to express their ideas, the same principle of interpretation applies. (1981)

When teaching at ESIT in Paris, she trained Asian students who were taught the same methodology as the others and performed just as well. She believes that it is gross exaggeration to say that, because the cultural setting and pattern of life in Europe and Asia are so different, the languages cannot be translated into one another in the same way. There may be instances when a concept has to be paraphrased to make it more understandable; sometimes an explanation has to be given but this does not justify the assertion that translation/interpretation is especially difficult because of cultural differences.

Take for instance a Korean writer who has been living in France for such a long time that he has become completely familiar with the French way of life. Now imagine that he writes a novel set in France. Do you really think that he will find it impossible to do so in Korean because the language is inadequate to convey a picture of the French setting? Certainly not. There are many examples in literature that are proof to the contrary: Bodard, Segalen, Malraux, Yourcenar, Conrad, Kipling, Senghor, Pearl S. Buck, Somerset Maugham and Doris Lessing, to name but a few. In simultaneous interpretation conference situations where the subject matter is generally scientific or technical, cultural differences do not surface very often. Those present share the same background knowledge whatever their nationality; the fact that they talk about the subject in their own languages proves that these languages

80

are adequate tools of communication in that specialized field. If they are adequate for the delegates, they must also be for the interpreters. If the interpreters have the impression that they are not, the only possible explanation is that they are not conversant enough with the subject matter and the relevant jargon.

It is often claimed that as tenses are marked more loosely in many Asian languages, it is difficult for the interpreter to choose the right tense in the Western target language. In fact, the problem has nothing to do with the source language; it is solely a question of mastery of the target language. If the interpreter has full command of the target language, he will use its tenses correctly. If he has not, he should refrain from interpreting into it.

In some Asian languages the verb or another important semantic element is put at the end of the sentence. This is also true of German. However, when Germans talk to each other they are not at all forced to wait until the end of the sentence in order to understand its meaning. The listener knows from the start what verb the speaker intends to put at the end of his sentence and whether it will be an affirmative or a negative. He gathers it from clues provided by syntax and prosody as well as from the context, long before the words are actually uttered by the speaker. The simultaneous interpreter does exactly the same. For scientific proof, Karla Déjean Le Féal recommends M. Lederer's doctoral thesis (1981) which clearly demonstrates this phenomenon of anticipation by the interpreter.

When listening to a speaker who suddenly stops in the middle of a sentence in search of a word, we can usually provide the missing word. This is because we are familiar with the referent of the speech and reason along with the speaker. Because we also have full command of the language, we can anticipate the words he is likely to utter.

> *The Japanese, for instance, have a more emotional approach to communication even when dealing with technical matters, while the French approach is a more analytical one. If this difference is not taken into account by the interpreter, the message of the Japanese speaker will seem insufficiently structured and rather verbose to the French listener. This is not at all the impression another Japanese listener would have of the same speech. Thus it is the interpreter's task to adopt the communicative approach that will render the French listener's comprehension and overall impression identical to that of the Japanese, each one receiving the same message in a form that corresponds to the specific rules of communication in their respective languages.*

In Japanese it is highly uncommon to answer a question with a clear cut "yes" or "no". "Instead of the black and white of Western languages, there is a grey zone in Japanese." When asked whether the Japanese, when communicating with each other, know whether it is "yes" or "no", the answer is invariably: "Yes, most of the time they gather it from discrete hints given by the speaker."

> *If Japanese people can do it when talking to each other, the interpreter must be able to do it too. Translation from Japanese into a Western language would thus imply that these positive or negative clues have to be sent through a kind of loudspeaker, so as to make them audible to a Western ear, just as a clearcut "yes" or "no" uttered by a Westerner must be tuned down to a mere hint for the Japanese listener, as it would otherwise be too harsh*

Such differences also exist between Western languages.

If a Spanish-French interpreter does not adopt the French approach to communication, the Spaniard's speech would seem baroque to a French listener although it would not to his Spanish counterpart. If a German-French interpreter does not heed the French rules of communication, the German's speech will appear muddled to a French listener whereas it would not to his German counterpart. A French speech - even a very plain and factual one - would sound stilted and highly abstract if put into English without concern for the English mode of communication.

Karla Déjean Le Féal goes on to say that the interpreter "can only find the right approach if he is translating into his mother tongue. It is the target language that dictates the right communicative approach to be adopted by the interpreter."

Simultaneous interpretation from and into Asian languages is as feasible as from and into any other language; failure or success do not depend on the nature of the language concerned but on the professional and linguistic qualifications of the interpreter.

Working into your B language

Anyone who is not truly bilingual, i.e. is not able to think absolutely automatically, without effort, in his non-native tongue (Seleskovitch 1968) will suffer an unconscionable handicap having to formulate laboriously when translating from his mother-tongue into another language. When formulating in one's mother tongue one's lingual ability is limited only by one's train of thought. An educated person who has prepared for the conference will scarcely be handicapped by a lack of native vocabulary. Formulating however in a non-native language he is automatically at risk: much of his brilliance will be lost, he is forced to sell below true value. The trained interpreter is a true bilingual or multilingual which most scientists or technicians cannot be. His training and his lifelong work with languages enable him to transmit the brilliance of an original speaker, formulating in his own language. His training for precision and succinctness sometimes even allow a better and clearer formulation than the original. However, a great deal of this brilliance is lost if he is working into an acquired language.

It is safer to be modest. Once you have accepted to work into your "B" language, you may find yourself having to draft a new text in that language, which will be published as you have dictated it into the microphone, and live on to haunt you with its imperfections. If you have not done a perfect job, you may find you do not get recruited again by that particular conference organizer.

Professionals must be honest with themselves about their working languages. You can always upgrade your C language to a B or your B to an A later when you have more experience and confidence. You are more likely to find colleagues willing to sponsor your language claims if they are modest. Experienced colleagues will know when they can safely work into their B language - they also know they should not accept work into a C unless it is in the process of being upgraded into a B and the qualifying period for the change has not yet been completed. It is always safer to check beforehand that one member of the team agrees to be "pivot"[2] out of a C language.

French and Spanish booth interpreters occasionally complain that they work harder than the interpreters in the English booth. It is true that they generally work for a much greater percentage of the time. But it is also

---

[2] Pivot: To act as a pivot means that one or more booths will be taking relay from that person's interpretation for the particular language concerned.

true that the English booth has a larger audience. Often the Chair and Secretariat are listening to the English and writing their reports based on the English interpretation, which increases the responsibility, the stress, and the number of people likely to criticise. This is why the growing practice of eliminating the English booth (to save money) is dangerous because the majority of listeners are listening to the English, maybe 95% are therefore listening to an English B (or even C) and not an English A which is not going to give them a good impression. It would be preferable to do away with the French or Spanish booths and let someone from the English booth work into their French or Spanish B language because there may be only 3 or 4 delegates listening to them in the auditorium.

One of our profession's most eminent personalities, Danica Seleskovitch wrote a book in 1968 entitled *L'interprète dans les Conférences Internationales* which is still just as valid today. On the subject of interpreters working in their B language or languages, Danica advises prudence. While it is essential that the interpreter receive the message in the best possible manner, enabling the best possible comprehension and analysis i.e. that he not be confronted with the reading out of a written text, or with bad acoustic conditions, it is just as important that he be able to convey the message effectively. The worldwide shortage of English mother-tongue interpreters - which was the case in 1968 just as it is today - sometimes means that colleagues whose mother tongue is French, German, Spanish or Japanese find themselves working into English, which means that the simultaneous interpretation is not being practised in the best possible conditions. Clearly, an interpreter working into his A language or mother tongue will provide better quality than when working into a B or acquired language. When working into his B language the interpreter understands perfectly the message from the speaker to the interpreter. But it is the retransmission from the interpreter to the listener which will not be perfect. The effect of the linguistic interference of the mother tongue on the acquired language will be much greater than the other way round. The intuition that is present in the mother tongue will be missing, and expression will not have the natural spontaneity which governs the structuring and shaping of sentences, he will not have the ease of expression or the choices of vocabulary that are available in one's mother tongue.

Let us take for example a French listener hearing the interpretation from German: "*faute d'esthétique*". The interpreter has given the first meaning that comes to mind for "*Schönheitsfehler*" but the listener will not understand as quickly or as well as if he had heard "imperfection". The unusual expression would require an extra effort to integrate it into the context and would thus draw attention to itself, acquiring more value than it had in the original. The effort of reflection it called for would also prevent the listener from paying full attention to the words immediately following, the understanding of which might therefore be impaired.

Beginners who feel that it is easier to work into an acquired language forget that interpretation does not stop with the interpreter's understanding. The process is only complete when the message reaches the listener. It is much easier to express one's own ideas in a foreign language at one's own rhythm than to interpret the ideas of someone else. It should be pointed out, says Danica Seleskovitch, that the need for perfect idiomatic expression is not always the same - it is indispensable for rhetoric speeches, but less important for technical work. Professional interpreters who work in their B language or languages choose their conferences carefully: technical or administrative meetings in simultaneous where more direct transposition is possible or consecutive meetings because linguistic interference is less of a problem in consecutive than in simultaneous.

Marianne Lederer, Director of ESIT (Sorbonne, Paris), speaking at the Conference on the Place of French in Interpreting and Translating in Australia (August 1990) at the University of Queensland (French Department) said that one's language is not a matter of choice. The language learnt as a child, the mother tongue, is so intimately linked to all early events in life, its command is so intuitive that it obeys the mind's slightest move. A language learnt at a later age will always bear traces both of the awareness that accompanied its learning, and of the mother tongue acting as a screen during the learning process of the second language. Feelings and ideas will never be expressed as finely in a second or third language as in the mother tongue. Hence the struggle for the preservation of "feeling at home" in one's language and using a language that is part of oneself and not a tool. A tool, however skilfully handled, will always remain a tool and never become a hand.

Our B languages are merely tools. It is important to remember this distinction. When speaking your own language, you adapt your words to your thoughts. When speaking an acquired language you have to adapt your thoughts to your words. But interpreting does not leave any room for this because you are restricted to the expression of someone else's thoughts, leaving you no leeway.

Relay

Relay is the term used when an interpreter does not have the target language and listens to the interpretation of a colleague, which he then, in turn, interprets, so the delegates are hearing a second-hand rendering. Ambiguities in the original interpretation may be magnified and turn into serious mistakes. I have known misunderstandings hold up the debate for half-an-hour until it became apparent that the cause of the problem was an ambiguity in the original interpretation.

Unfortunately over the years conference organizers in Australia have got into bad habits and used relay systematically so that today it is almost the norm. This is because of the paucity of language combinations in this country where so many interpreters have only two languages: their mother-tongue and English. In Europe and America many English-booth interpreters work from the other three languages (French, Spanish and Russian) thus avoiding relay in the booth with the greatest number of listeners and ensuring accuracy.

Bilingual interpreters should be used only for bilingual meetings. In Europe a student needs at least four languages to gain admission to most Interpreters' Schools (at least one A(active) and three C's (passive) languages). Using relay makes it much easier for a conference organizer to recruit a team but the quality of the interpretation is inevitably impaired and the responsibility on the pivot (that is, the interpreter from whom the relay is being taken) is enormous and quite unfair. You can imagine that if there is only one person working from Russian in a team of eight (English, French, Spanish and Russian booths) there is an enormous risk of error if the pivot uses an ambiguous expression or her enunciation of figures is unclear - or if someone nearby coughs when the key word is being uttered. The two other booths are entirely dependent on his/her every word. Instead of the delegates listening to one booth, they will be listening to three booths, who may be missing something and receiving erroneous information (that is, the vast majority of the audience).

I remember a party-game we used to play as children, standing in a line. The first child would whisper something to the second, who would whisper it to the third and so on down the line. The last child in the line had to say aloud what he or she had heard, and that was the big joke because it rarely had anything at all to do with the original message. This is what can happen with relay.

Laboratory studies and surveys clearly show the negative effects relay has upon the quality of interpretation. Jennifer Mackintosh, AIIC, who teaches conference interpretation in London, carried out a study (Mackintosh 1983) of relay interpretation based on a laboratory comparison of information fidelity in direct and relay interpretation. Four French and English speeches made at the European Parliament were read out in a conference room and interpreted by ten professional interpreters, five of whom had an A in French and five an A in English, the other language being a B or a C. The equipment was set up so that for each team of two interpreters, a French speech was interpreted direct into English, then into French over the relay, or an English speech was interpreted into French direct, then into English from the relay. The interpretations were recorded, transcribed, studied and compared with a view to ascertaining the type of informational losses and studying the processes involved. Sentences were split up into units of meaning based on semantic, intuitive and practical judgements. The results of these laboratory studies are to be found in her thesis - Relay Interpretation: An Exploratory Study. It was found that relay interpreters had recourse to three strategies in case of difficulty:

1) generalisation when it was not possible to be precise
2) sticking to the original words as much as possible, that is, word-for-word translation rather than interpretation
3) adding in "padding" to fill gaps.

The difficulty of reproducing numbers accurately was apparent, and the fact that in case of difficulty, unclear pronunciation or unusual words or expressions forcing the interpreter to make a special effort, the interpretation of the following segment suffered.

Janet Altman, AIIC, also studied the use of relay and carried out a survey (Altman 1989). She says the
> *interpreters canvassed were practically unanimous in their distaste for relay interpreting and when asked for their opinion of the effect of relay on the communication process not a single re-*

spondent described it as either positive or very positive.

Some stated that it depended entirely on the quality of the relay interpreter. If, as she has shown, "the involvement of interpreters can in some cases hamper the communication process," the risk of breakdowns must double when the message passes through two intermediaries. If relay interpreting is taken to extremes:

> *Should the English booth interpreter seek relief, a situation can arise whereby an interpreter with an English B (who has probably just completed 30 minutes work in his/her A language) stands in and, when Spanish or Russian is spoken, takes relay from a C language (French), interprets into a B language (English), and is in turn taken on relay by the Chinese and also the Russian or Spanish booths.*

There are situations where the use of relay cannot be avoided. It has always been used extensively for Chinese, Arabic and Japanese and also for Russian for many years because Soviet interpreters generally had two languages: Russian and English or Russian and French and so relay sometimes had to be used for Spanish. In all four-language teams where relay is used there should be at least two pivots per language.

Janet Altman concludes that interpreters strive to improve the service they provide when they know that other interpreters are relying on them as a relay. They take greater pains to simplify and clarify the message, "editing" it as they go along. As pivot you should avoid running speakers together, one after the other. It is important to separate them by announcing each speaker before beginning his statement, for example: "The Chairman says ..." Many professional interpreters believe that special training is required for pivot interpreters, including instruction in the culture of the language from which they interpret. Relay interpreting is gaining importance particularly in view of the further enlargement of the European Parliament and European Union. For example, with a view to the addition of Greek, many colleagues followed intensive language courses in Corfu to enable them to act as pivots as soon as Greek became the seventh Community language. Similar training has been made available for the other languages as they have been added to those used at the European Union.

If you are working in a team where you will be taking relay from the Chinese and Arabic booths, for example, you would be well advised, before the meeting starts, to find out whether they will be interpreting those languages into English or into French, so that you know which channel to switch to when the time comes. Make sure, too, that you know how to switch to the desired channel before the start of the meeting: relay systems vary from one installation to another.

In the absence of the chief interpreter, the team leader is responsible for coordinating inter-booth arrangements regarding relay and must be kept informed of what is proposed. So if you are going to leave the booth for a moment, check first with your colleague that this is agreable (having made sure beforehand that your colleagues in the other booths are willing to work from that interpreter's relay) and always let them know when you leave and when you return.

After the meeting, if the pivot did a good job, say so. If it was not very good do not rush into the booth to complain. Try to be constructive, making it clear that you understand the difficulties and make some helpful suggestions.

No-one with the slightest speech defect should aspire to be a conference interpreter. I remember an excellent interpreter, some years back, working at a conference in Africa in the English booth from Russian and French. We were together one Monday morning, after the government authorities had taken the whole conference on a weekend safari. We had seen gazelles, lions, zebras, water buffalos, impalas, giraffes and elephants. The Leader of the USSR delegation was the first to ask for the floor that Monday morning to thank the host government for their hospitality and the wonderful safari. It was the first time, he said, he had seen so many wild animals in their natural environment.

"Now," he concluded, "we must remember the giraffe this morning as we discuss the budget estimates and instead of spending so much time on detail, let us adopt the giraffe's overall view and see these figures in perspective."

Unfortunately my colleague had difficulties with his "r"s and said *giwaffe*. The Spanish, German, Chinese and Arabic booths were taking relay from the English booth for the Russian and by the time the sound got to them, it sounded like *dwarf*. So the Spanish, German, Chinese and Arabic-speaking delegates heard about the overall view of the dwarf. One by one the delegations took the floor to discuss the budget and referred to the magical dwarf with the overall view until he became quite famous - he probably went into their reports home too and to this day there may be people who believe there exists in darkest Africa a magical dwarf with an overall view... The Russian delegates from that conference must still wonder what they were all talking about.

If there is an Interpreters' Hell in the hereafter, I know just how it could be. In one of its chambers there would be rows of booths and you would have to work all day from relay. Into your headphones would pour words, strings of words without a connecting thread. No logic. Just words. And you would have to zing about inside your head trying to find a meaning, a link, trying to piece the words together to form a sequence. I know. It has happened to me.

To conclude this section on the use of relay interpreting, I am going to tell you a little story (taken from the AIIC *Bulletin*). I think it puts the whole subject of re-lay in a nutshell:

> *The captain's note to the chief officer: 'Early to-morrow morning there will be a total solar eclipse at 9 hours. This is something that cannot be seen every day, so let the crew line up in their best clothes on deck in order that they may see it. To mark this rare phenomenon I will myself ex-plain it to them. If it is raining, we will not be able to see it clearly. In that case, the crew should gather in the messroom.'*

> *The chief officer's note to the first officer: 'On captain's orders there will be a total solar eclipse early tomorrow at 9 hours. If it is raining, we will not be able to see it clearly from the deck in our best clothes. In that case the sun's disap-pearance will be fully observed in the messroom. This is something which does not happen every day.'*

> *The first officer's note to the second officer: 'On captain's orders we shall fully observe in our best clothes that the sun disappears in the messroom at 9 hours. The captain will tell us if it is going to rain. This is something which does not happen every day.'*

> *The second officer's note to the bosun: 'If it is raining in the messroom early tomorrow, which is something that does not happen every day, the captain in his best clothes will disappear at 9 hours.'*
> *The bosun's note to the crew: 'Early tomorrow at 9 hours the captain will disappear. It is a pity that this does not happen every day.'*

In conclusion, let me say that, as John Coleman-Holmes (1971) points out, conference interpreters are not the technicians they pretend to be. In fact they are part of "show biz". They are the cousins of actors, oddly enough not of translators. Even if they have to translate sometimes at high speed there is still no link between the two professions - their universes touch but do not intermingle. The translator never has to hand in an unfinished piece of work. He has his dictionaries, he can consult colleagues *viva voce* or by telephone. He has time to think, to make changes.

At the end of the day, he is not reduced to the exhausted state of an interpreter, whose brain feels like a lemon that has been squeezed dry, who is incapable of any intellectual effort or even any physical effort. Often he has to walk for twenty minutes until his brain is back into gear before he can drive his car safely. This is because for each conference (and for a free-lance there may be a different one each week) he has to learn a new vocabulary, a new subject; set forth in unfamiliar territory. This is why the first two days of a new conference are exhausting even if the subject is not technical. In spite of the new words, new concepts, new paradigms, the interpreter has to give of his best at every instant with no time for mental adjustment.

7

Modus vivendi
WORKING ARRANGEMENTS

What I am going to say on this subject is not a matter of rules and regulations, but rather of common sense.

As in all professions, working conditions have a bearing on the quality of your performance. You cannot do a good job unless you can hear clearly and see properly, have room to arrange your documents in front of you in the appropriate language versions and in good reading light, unless you are neither too hot nor too cold, unless you have fresh air to breathe so that you remain alert, your chair is comfortable and there is no noise to distract you. You should not hear the sound of your colleague's voices from the other booths, nor should you hear kitchen staff rattling trolleys of crockery along the corridor behind the booths.

You should not work unless these conditions are respected; to do so would be unfair to the delegates who have come to the meeting sometimes from a great distance and at great expense and have the right to hear and understand the proceedings clearly, but most of all because it is unfair to you and your reputation as a professional conference interpreter; your future career is at stake if you do not do well.

To work to the best of your ability, you must also have travelled in comfort if the conference is not taking place in your home town. You must be well rested and well prepared, having had a chance to study the documents beforehand, that is, having received documentation well in advance of the meeting.

You are, of course, free to interpret in bad working conditions if you wish and with sub-standard equipment but in that case you will be a sub-standard interpreter. That is your affair but do not be surprised if work offers cease to come your way.

Interpreters should therefore always endeavour to secure satisfactory conditions and study a contract (offer of work) carefully before signing it. Your contract should show the names of the colleagues on your team (there might be a colleague sharing your booth whose presence prevents you from doing a good job - in which case you might prefer to decline the offer) and which booth you will be working in. If you feel the subject to be discussed is too difficult for you because of your lack of experience it may be more ethical for you to decline rather than attempt something you feel you are unable to do well.

If you have doubts about any of the conditions consult a more experienced colleague. If you are still not satisfied, speak to the person who sent you the contract. It may be wiser to lose a few days' work but maintain a good reputation. That is the charm of working free-lance. You have the freedom to say "No, thank you" if you do not consider the working conditions satisfactory.

Your work is particularly dependent on the simultaneous interpretation equipment (see the section of Chapter 12 dealing with technical requirements) so you would be well advised to check that your contract specifies what type of equipment will be used, who the supplier is, and that the technician is satisfactory because his experience is important in ensuring the proper operation of the equipment.

In addition, you should ascertain that the teams of interpreters are formed in such a way as to avoid the systematic use of relay, that any texts to be read out will be given to you in advance insofar as possible, and that you will not be required to perform any duties other than those of conference interpreter.

There is, however, some need for flexibility. While the interpreter should not be required to perform any other duties, we must not forget that goodwill is also important. During my career I have been known to make a short translation during my lunch-hour or during the coffee-break when no translators were available - provided I was asked nicely.

As to manning strengths, normal practice is for there to be two interpreters per booth so that between them they cover all languages (with the exception of Chinese, Japanese and Arabic and any "rare" languages, where this may not be possible). In cases of unequal language distribution or in bilingual meetings teams of three interpreters are possible provided normal meeting hours are respected, i.e. two and a half to three hours per meeting. For very short meetings two interpreters might do.

In conferences where 90 per cent of the discussion is in English there may be only one interpreter in the English booth, provided he has all the necessary passive languages and that there is an English "B" in one of the other booths who is willing and able to take over if the English booth interpreter has to go out for any reason, has a coughing fit or needs help in finding documents or locating quotations. In two-way booths such as for the rarer languages mentioned above (Chinese, Arabic, Japanese, Korean and so on) three interpreters are the norm.

The work rota is established by the interpreters. Given the constraints related to quality and health, the normal working day for a conference interpreter is two sessions of two-and-a-half to three hours. If a meeting looks like going beyond the prescribed duration, there are tactful ways of indicating this to the Chairman. This is the responsibility of the team leader. We do not work for longer than the prescribed periods because the quality of our interpretation suffers if we are tired and we want to do a good job. This is why we do not charge overtime. It is not a matter of money. It is a matter of the number of hours the brain can cope with simultaneous interpretation and do it well. What we want most of all is to do a good job. If the Chairman wants to continue the meeting beyond the prescribed duration, another team of interpreters will need to be brought in to relieve the first team.

We owe the fact that we have reasonable working hours today to the negotiations in the past between our professional association and the United Nations Secretariat, resulting in our Agreement. In the early days during a very difficult, technical radio conference in Geneva I can remember working from 9 a.m. through until 5 a.m. the following morning on a few historic occasions - though I doubt if the discussions any more than the interpretation were particularly clear or lively during the second half of the meeting, speeches grew longer and more involved, and coffee-breaks more frequent. In those days we relied on plentiful supplies of strong black coffee to keep going.

There was also a time, some years ago, when the Non-Aligned Movement decided that, because of their budgetary restrictions, they would meet twenty-four hours a day in order to make maximum use of the premises (rent) and "facilities" which included the interpreters and equipment. It is true that they had a very long agenda. Interpreters then worked two-and-a-half-hour shifts, day and night, in rotation. A limousine would pick you up from your hotel at, say 3 a.m. and deliver you back again at, say 6.30 a.m. but I am afraid the standard of interpretation was not the best in those conditions. Anyway, there were not many members of the audience awake to listen.

Nowadays when the agenda is long and the duration of the meeting short, delegates are often given a time-limit for their speech, which may be reduced by half as the meeting progresses and time starts running out, so that a speaker wishing to make full use of this opportunity to inform the world of his research may have to read his thirty pages in the time it would normally take to read ten. The exercise thus becomes a race against time with "machine-gun delivery" which is impossible to interpret satisfactorily. Your only hope in this case is to have been given the text of the speech which you have read beforehand so that you can recognize the salient points and at least express those clearly.

Roles of chief or coordinating interpreter and team leader

To be successful, conference interpretation services need to be organized and coordinated by an experienced conference interpreter. The chief or coordinating interpreter is your ultimate authority. He serves as a bridge between the organizers and interpreters. He therefore has a dual responsibility towards the conference organizer and participants on the one hand, and on the other towards his colleagues, who, individually and collectively, count on him to ensure that optimum working conditions are provided as well as fair payment of entitlements. The coordinating interpreter therefore loyally safeguards the best interests of all parties concerned, while ensuring that expenditure for the organisers is kept at a minimum consistent with the service required. When approached by a conference organiser, he fully acquaints himself with the nature and subject of the conference and advises on the type of interpretation most appropriate. He recommends optimum teams, ensuring that all requisite language combinations are properly covered and other conference requirements are met regarding composition of teams, sufficient number of pivots, documentation, equipment, advice to speakers, etc. He may also advise about the most suitable premises and equipment in the light of ISO and IEC standards (see Chapter 12 for an explanation of these acronyms). He prepares detailed cost estimates and conscientiously fulfills all planning, administrative, liaison and supervisory functions. He ensures that the organizer provides members of the team with all documentation and information required for preparation for the conference (glossary, bibliography, explanatory material, past reports, etc.) as soon as possible after signature of the contract.

During the conference he sees to it that the papers for a particular meeting are provided in advance to the members of the team, especially if they are to be read at the meeting (when the subject so permits, he systematically advises speakers to speak without following a prepared text). He may organize, if necessary, a briefing session with the organizers to deal with practical problems such as obtaining missing documents, solving any organisational matters and problems of terminology. This briefing session is followed by regular contacts during the meeting with speakers and chairmen as necessary.

The coordinating interpreter selects the interpreters according to language combinations, interpreting skill and proficiency in the specific subject, such as previous experience with that particular subject or earlier conferences; and which interpreters' professional addresses are nearest to the conference venue, if there is equal competence.

If the coordinating interpreter does not head the team himself, he appoints a suitable team leader, fully acquainted with the required arrangements (generally the most experienced interpreter on the team), who acts as spokesman. The coordinator keeps a record of how many meetings each interpreter has done to ensure the workload is equally shared. He also works out the interpreters' programme and decides who will work where and when during the conference. When there is a large team of interpreters, there is often a noticeboard in the Interpreters' Lounge with everyone's assignments for that day, which interpreters have to check first thing in the morning, and before leaving for lunch. At large international conferences and at United Nations, ILO , ITU, etc. (see Appendix A for list of international organizations and specialized agencies of the U.N.) interpreters are given a telephone number to ring at lunchtime to obtain a recorded message giving their afternoon assignments and in the evening for the following morning's assignments (a different number for each booth).

The normal workload of the interpreters in the UN family of organizations and at the European Union is a maximum of eight meetings of two-and-a-half to three hours' duration per week. However, non-governmental organizations and the private market may pay higher rates but expect longer working hours (ten meetings per week). In all cases, exceptionally long sessions are split into several "meetings" (insofar as the interpreters' work programme is concerned) which means that a second team relieves the first. Night sessions are not followed by work the next morning. The aim is to enforce normal workload criteria over the week and avoid taxing the health of the interpreters.

The U.N. system of interpreters working eight meetings a week out of a total of ten has given rise to an arrangement where, in addition to the normal number of interpreters, that is, two per booth for European languages, there are in addition two "rovers" (*interprètes volants* or *paracheveurs*) for what is called *parachèvement*: the two "rovers", each of whom work in two booths, may work in say the English booth for half of the week and the Spanish for the other half or the French booth for half of the week and the Russian for the other half. The basic team recruited for the five-day week would thus have two half-days free at the discretion of the chief interpreter who organizes the timetable.

You may find that, although your contract specifies that you will be working for one committee, when you consult the assignments table in the Interpreters' room you are working on quite a different subject. Sometimes the day is split into four so you may find yourself interpreting in four different committees on four different subjects in the course of the day.

Working arrangements with colleagues should be based on a clear understanding of who does what when. Arrangements must take account of the needs of all booths, overall language cover, working conditions and the difficulty of the subject. Slavish adherence to the clock or to dividing work rigidly on the basis of the number of papers to be presented may serve neither your interests nor those of the delegates. In other words, flexibility is essential. It is, for example, rarely advisable to change interpreters in the middle of a speech unless it is a very long one and the first interpreter indicates to the second that he is getting tired and wishes to be relieved. In such a case, the change-over from one interpreter to the other must be seamless.

The team leader informs the Chief Interpreter if any changes to the programme are announced or any additional working groups are set up requiring interpretation.

I have explained in the section on Relay in Chapter 6 how the various language combinations are organized in a team. The team leader is responsible for ensuring all working documents are brought to the booths and for all contacts with delegates or the Chairman during meetings. For example, if the Chairman asks whether the interpreters are willing to continue beyond the normal time, say for fifteen minutes or an extra half-hour to enable a decision to be reached by the meeting, it is the coordinating or chief interpreter, or in his absence, the team leader who, after consulting with the rest of the team (generally a questioning glance through the glass window of the booth) will respond. It may be necessary to remind the Chairman if he forgets the time and the meeting lasts beyond closing time. After a leeway of some fifteen minutes, the chief interpreter or team leader may write a polite note to this effect and deliver it by hand to the Secretary. I generally prefer to allow some flexibility and say: "You have already exceeded the normal meeting duration by fifteen minutes. The interpreters are willing to continue for fifteen minutes more if you wish, but after that time interpretation will cease because interpreters have other meetings after lunch" (if it is lunchtime) or "because the interpreters have been working since 2 o'clock this afternoon" (if it is the evening). The note is then signed by the team leader (or chief interpreter). These are only examples - there are many ways of dealing with this problem which are acceptable provided they are dignified and courteous. For example, the team leader may prefer to go down into the meeting room and explain in a whisper to the Secretary of the meeting.

I am indebted to the AIIC *Bulletin* for the following extract from an article by Lord O'Hagan, the MEP for Devon, writing in "Europe 81" on the European Parliament:

"Some things have not changed at all. The excellent interpreters continue to go on strike when they have worked too long - thank goodness."

8

BOOTH BEHAVIOUR

Punctuality

The only people who must always be on time for meetings are the interpreters. Sometimes at WTO your 9 a.m. meeting did not start until 11 o'clock but the interpreters had to be there, ready, because the moment the private negotiations taking place all round the room were over, the official meeting would start and there was no knowing when that would be. The official meeting might last ten minutes and then adjourn. In UNCTAD the meeting scheduled for 10 o'clock might not start until twelve-thirty but similarly the interpreters had to be there and ready at 10. It is not a good idea to arrive at the last minute, hair awry and out of breath. From the delegate's point of view, it is most unpleasant to listen to a breathless voice, obviously unprepared for the meeting, panting into the microphone and switching off to ask in a loud, desperate voice: "Which Committee is this? What are they talking about?"

Your group of delegates might habitually arrive late but the day you do, you may find they were on time. Interpreters need to be in the booth fifteen minutes before the scheduled starting time to check whether there are any changes in the programme, any new documents have been circulated or any *ad hoc* working groups convened, and so on. You may find when you arrive at the scheduled meeting room that the venue has been changed and that your group is meeting in a different wing of the building that will take you ten minutes to find. Or that there has been a last-minute team switch because of a change in the languages required. Better be early so you have plenty of time to sort out the documents that will be needed, and find out where they are on the Agenda.

Team spirit and solidarity

Team spirit and solidarity are the order of the day. Your team will be judged as a whole. Try to help one another by sharing vocabulary, proposed translations for new words, new technologies and new scientific concepts that have come up. You may have a mental block about one word and it keeps coming up - that is when your colleague can respond to a signal of distress and give invaluable help. If you are experienced, do not keep your know-how to yourself. Do not forget that not only are interpreters judged as a team but also that we were all beginners once. Similarly, if a colleague doesn't know something, don't spread it around thereby creating a source of tension but rather try to help discreetly. Remember, though, that there is nothing more irritating than a colleague determined to help when you don't need it, who keeps pushing notes in front of you or, even worse, whispering suggested wording when you prefer to do it your own way ! If you want help from your booth mate, ask for it - scribble a few words on the notepad. If you do not, also say so. If you are a beginner and by chance know an expression or technical word which your more experienced colleague may not know, don't antagonise him by gloating over it - you may need his help on another occasion. The best way to help your colleague is to write your suggestion on your own pad in front of you, without any fuss, so that he can read it if he wants to.

While your colleague is "on the air" you may notice he hasn't realized the delegate is reading from a text and is struggling with something that in fact already exists in an official text. See if you can find it in the appropriate language quietly and place it in front of him discreetly, without disturbing him.

Sound levels

If there is a considerable difference in volume between your voice and that of your colleagues, the sound engineer will adjust the output volume whenever there is a switch from one to the other. Try to speak always from the same distance from the microphone and do not turn away while interpreting. Do not rustle papers, pour out water, drum your fingers on the work surface, etc. in front of an open microphone. Avoid noisy bangles in the booth.

Posture

Posture is important in voice production and the work is far less tiring if your posture is correct. A slouching interpreter will not sound bright and alert, nor even reliable. Think of all you have heard about body language. All of this also applies to your posture as you sit in the booth (See Chapter 12 regarding the Alexander Technique).

When not actually interpreting, do not leave the meeting room for longer than absolutely necessary and in your own interests avoid returning at the last minute before taking over the microphone. When not working you should relax but continue to listen to what is being said and be firm but courteous with people who drop by for a chat. If your colleague has to leave the booth for a short while, do not abruptly hand over the microphone the moment he returns - give him time to pick up the thread of the discussion again. Brief your colleague on how far the discussion has progressed and on anecdotes or unusual terms used by speakers. Likewise, if a new team is taking over after you, leave them a note in the booth telling them how far the discussion has progressed on which item and which document will be taken next, as well as any other useful information.

As a general rule, respect your colleagues' wishes (even unspoken) regarding socialising in the booth. Not every interpreter is able to deal with a speech from the floor and your life story in all the gaps. Do all you can to establish good working relationships with your colleagues - you all need to be able to depend on one another.

Even if you think you are one of the best known interpreters in the profession, introduce yourself to colleagues you have not met before. Experienced interpreters should make every effort to put newcomers at ease and beginners should concentrate on doing a good job rather than impressing their booth mate. It is good to include a beginner in a team because they are the next generation of interpreters. However, it is also a good idea to obtain the agreement of the more experienced colleagues first and be sure to put the beginner in a booth with an experienced, helpful colleague who will be kind and cooperative. Beginners should be used in meetings where they can prepare beforehand. It is unfair to offer them meetings which are difficult and require experience because they may jeopardize their future career.

Documents

Try to keep documents in logical order and by language - respecting whatever system is agreed between colleagues sharing your booth. When the meeting is over, it is well worth taking ten minutes to put all the documents back in order ready for the next day. When your colleague takes over from you, pass over the pile of documents in the right order if possible. If the organisers have asked that the documents be returned to them at the end of the meeting, be sure to do so.

Beware of handing over copies of speeches or documents to enquiring journalists or visitors. You have a duty of confidentiality. Always refer such requests to the team leader or chief interpreter.

Booth manners

Smoking is not prohibited in public buildings in all countries. However, never smoke in the booth even if there are no non-smoking signs - it is generally forbidden in conference rooms and booths anyway. Similarly, use perfume or aftershave sparingly. Too heady a scent can be as intrusive as tobacco smoke and becomes overpowering in a small enclosed booth. It is not advisable for the same reason to varnish your nails in the booth when you are not working or even during the coffee-break. Nor is it advisable to knit, sew, manicure your nails, or be seen to be reading a newspaper or snatching a late breakfast in full view of the delegates. Not only is such behaviour likely to disturb your colleagues but it is also unlikely to impress the organizers and delegates with your professionalism. Do not take your mobile telephone with you into the booth unless you have checked that it is turned off. Beware of blowing your nose or coughing with the microphone on. Pity the ears of the delegates listening to the interpretation.

Use the cough button

Do not switch the microphone off when coughing, pouring water, rustling paper, because an intruder has burst into the booth to bring documents, to ask your colleague a word you have not understood or to make a brief sarcastic comment about what the speaker has just said. When you do this, the delegates' listening to you will suddenly have their ears blasted with the floor channel which is probably gibberish to them and louder than the interpretation: there is invariably a difference in sound level. Use the cough button. Do not switch off your microphone until the speaker has finished. If your booth mate is working, go outside to cough or blow your nose.

Only interpreters may speak over the interpretation channels. Sometimes a visiting interpreter, who may be part of a delegation speaking a rare language such as Korean or Farsi, may come into the booth to interpret into English a speech to be delivered by his delegation. This is then interpreted into the other conference languages by relay.

Microphone manners

Before the first session of the conference it is advisable to check that you know how the equipment works, how to switch to the required channel if there is relay and that in general the equipment is working to your satisfaction, the headphones are comfortable and the sound is right for you. When you come into the booth for subsequent meetings, make sure the microphones have not been left on by mistake by the technician, or earlier colleagues. It would be embarrassing for your private conversation with your colleagues to be broadcast all over the room. Beware of forgetting to turn the microphone off when you finish a speech. By leaving your microphone switched on after you have finished interpreting you may be preventing delegates from hearing something the Chairman has said.

A professional interpreter turns the microphone on the moment he begins to speak and not before, and turns it off the moment he has finished. Failing to turn the microphone off immediately is courting disaster. Delegates do not want to year your comments, or the rustling of papers, coughing, nor do they want to hear the comments of your highly-strung colleague who erupts into your booth to let off steam about the stupidity of the delegate she has just interpreted. Beware of making comments - a microphone light may be hidden by a sheaf of papers. Do not laugh too loudly - this may be picked up by a microphone left on in the booth next door.

A survey carried out by Jennifer Mackintosh shows that delegates attach greatest importance to accuracy, clarity, correct terminology and completeness, and do not like too much lagging behind the speaker and pauses. (See Appendix B entitled "How to irritate your delegates without really trying"). They want interpreters

109

to concentrate on the essentials and to have an understanding of the subject under discussion. They want clear enunciation. I remember an embarrassing incident some years ago when the English booth, interpreting from Russian, gave the meeting the impression the Soviet Union was placing 45 vessels at the disposal of the World Weather Watch when in fact they were offering four to five.

Correct terminology is very important as is broad general knowledge and a wide cultural background. According to the survey Jennifer Mackintosh carried out, English, French and German are the most common languages, with English being used at 98 per cent of the meetings, French at 88 per cent, German at 61 per cent, Spanish at 41 per cent and Italian at 16 per cent. Lower down the list come Dutch, Russian, Portuguese, Arabic, Japanese, Chinese, Danish and Finnish, in that order. The survey indicated a direct correlation between pre-conference distribution of documents to the interpreters and high delegate satisfaction, particularly in the area of correct terminology and general understanding of the subject matter.

Remember, life is not always easy for delegates. Some have to wear headphones most of the time and they are less well protected from extraneous noise than we are. It is tiring enough to have to follow several days' discussions and when this has to be done via simultaneous interpretation equipment it becomes very demanding. So try to make your voice pleasant to listen to. Avoid a monotonous tone. Always seek to be clear and lively. It is advisable to keep your animation level similar to that of the speaker you are interpreting. Sometimes the speaker may be droning on in a peaceable manner, but if you switch to the various booths you might be forgiven for thinking that he was declaring war judging by the high-pitched tone coming from some of them.

If a speaker is having to use a language other than his normal working language, try to convey the message with clarity. Never alter the emphasis of what is being said, never let your own views on the subject show through your tone of voice. Your job is to communicate the speaker's intended meaning. It is only too easy for an unscrupulous interpreter to sabotage an argument especially if the delegates listening are monolingual. You have a responsibility and a duty to be accurate. It is dangerous, too, to try to improve on what you hear because sarcasm or vagueness may be deliberate.

The golden rule is: as literally as possible, as freely as necessary. Be fluent in your delivery and as close to the patterns of spontaneous speech as possible. Do not speak in sharp bursts followed by long pauses, nor in a sing-song voice. Do not speak in a soporific manner, especially after lunch ... Match your register to that of the speaker and the audience. If the speaker is using simple, plain words do not distort the original by using abstruse terms or arcane expressions. Conversely, do not lapse into a familiar, jocular tone or slang expressions on formal occasions.

Numbers

Always quote document numbers clearly, if possible twice. If your delegates still look lost, say the number again.

Try to form a partnership with your listeners

Ask for their help when documents are being distributed or if floor microphones are not working properly. Acknowledge their responsiveness. Enlist their help in slowing down fast speakers by saying something like: "We regret it is not possible to interpret accurately when a speaker is going at this speed. Please help us to help you understand by asking the Chairman to slow the speaker down." If you still don't get any response you may add: "We are doing our best under the circumstances but unless the speaker slows down the interpretation will not be complete." Do not shout this into the microphone or bang on the booth window. Quiet appeals for help through the microphone are much more effective. If the speaker's microphone goes off, it is better to say so quietly into your microphone so that your audience knows what is happening and that it isn't you who have dried up. If the speaker moves away from the microphone so that you can only hear faintly, do not try to interpret. You must only interpret when you can hear properly. If you make a mistake you are responsible for it and once you have imparted inaccurate information the deed is done and no-one will be interested in your explaining during the coffee-break that you couldn't hear properly. It is your duty to provide an accurate interpretation come what may.

Microphone feedback

A sudden high-pitched screaming noise may come through your headphones due to a speaker leaning too close to his microphone with his headphones on. Take your headphones off immediately before your ear-drums are damaged, preferably silently, and signal to the technician what has happened.

Introduce yourself to the technicians before the meeting. If you must make comments about volume or the equipment, do so through the team leader and politely. Remember how much you depend on the goodwill of the technician. When the meeting is over, do not leave without saying goodbye and thank you.

As Valerie Andersen has said: "Quality, like beauty, is in the eye of the beholder" - or rather "listener", in this case the delegate. When interpreting, try to convey an interest in your listeners' subject. See if you can communicate humour if the original does; show you take an interest in what you are doing. In a number of respects, interpreting is like acting, as I have explained in Chapter

6. Do not let your audience slip from your grasp. Watch the delegates listening to you for their reactions and hold their attention by being convincing and accurate. Make them forget they are hearing the speaker through an interpreter. Be helpful: repeat important figures or dates.

Accent

Try to adopt a "middle of the road" accent. For example, in the English booth, a strong Scottish, Welsh, Irish, Lancashire, Indian or Australian accent might be difficult for some of your listeners to follow, especially if English is not their mother tongue: think of the Norwegian, Thai, Swedish and African delegations who will be listening to the English channel. (Whatever you do, please avoid the ubiquitous twenty-seventh letter of the Australian alphabet: *haitch*.)

"Les microphages"

Some interpreters are "*microphage*" (they hog the microphone) and are reluctant to hand over to their colleague. If this happens to you, be tolerant and if they are doing a good job, listen and learn.

Boothmates and Team mates

Someone once said "An interpreter who is a bad colleague is a bad interpreter." It is true that the work of the team will be much better if everyone gets on well with everyone else. However, beware of the colleague who has a plane to catch in the middle of the last afternoon and leaves you alone to finish "the last half-hour". That half-hour may stretch to two hours. Beware too of the delegate who says "I have an important statement after the coffee-break and I want you to do it." You will feel flattered but upsetting the working arrangements (or boasting) will not improve your relationship with your team-mates. If it is possible to comply with the request diplomatically without it being noticed or causing any changes, so much the better.

Your team becomes your family for the duration of the conference. A warm relationship develops where you know one another's strong points and weaknesses and can help one another. This is even more so when you are away from home on a conference, perhaps all staying at the same hotel: a wonderful spirit of comradeship develops. If one team member has a headache someone will replace him while he goes to get an aspirin, if someone's wallet or handbag has been stolen on the city streets at night, the whole team will rally and pass the hat around. If someone has a personal problem, everyone will provide support. A good feeling of solidarity prevails and like Josephine Baker and her "*deux amours*" I have always felt I had two families: my own in private life and my professional colleagues and friends.

9

THOU SHALT, THOU SHALT NOT
DEONTOLOGY
ETHICS AND HONOUR
DUTIES AND RESPONSIBILITIES

The challenge of the third millennium will be ethics (Malick Sy, President of AIIC 1994-1999).

> *As new technologies open up a borderless world, authority is eroded and governments' ability to implement regulations fades. To ensure orderly business and harmonious relations between citizens, between business and consumers, we will have to rely increasingly on ethics, on our own ethical behaviour.* (Jean-Pierre Allain, President of AIIC, 2,000)

Each profession has its own Code of Ethics. It is just as important that a conference interpreter behave ethically as a doctor, surgeon or lawyer. The International Association of Conference Interpreters (AIIC) and The American Association of Language Specialists (TAALS) have Codes of Ethics which are binding upon all their members; NAATI and AUSIT have also published codes of ethics.

In short, a professional conference interpreter always behaves responsibly and in keeping with the dignity of his profession, respecting international standards of integrity, professionalism and confidentiality.

Observing the strictest secrecy is of the utmost importance. You may be called upon to interpret at sensitive negotiations; you will need to be very careful when you come out of the meeting-room. One tends to let off steam with colleagues over coffee. Beware of making comments about the discussion or the delegates' attitudes where others may hear you. Anyone overhearing your comments might be able to put two and two together. There could be serious repercussions, particularly with regard to financial aspects, changes in currency, the imminent floating of a company for example, imminent political decisions. One needs to be particularly careful of the media - reporters frequently gather in places such as the coffee bar to pick up information because they are in need of a story. I was even shut in a lift once by (and with) a newspaper reporter, anxious to find out what was happening in a secret meeting on the top floor of the United Nations building. He said he was willing to pay "my price".

(You want to know the end of the story? Well after a while I began to feel quite desperate because I was going to be late back into the booth but an innocent secretary saved me *in extremis*. She somehow succeeded in getting the lift to stop at her floor in spite of the fact that the reporter had his finger on the button all the time - I managed to rush out just as the doors were closing and race up the stairs.)

Professional conference interpreters also should not derive any personal gain from confidential information acquired in the exercise of their duties.

Another point to be made on the subject of ethics is that it would be unethical for an interpreter to accept an assignment for which he is not qualified - acceptance of an assignment implies a moral undertaking on the interpreter's part to work with all due professionalism and to a proper professional standard. So do not hesitate to turn down an offer if you think you are not sufficiently experienced to handle it or if it is too difficult technically for you to do it well.

An interpreter does not accept more than one assignment for a given period of time. There have been cases of "moonlighting" where interpreters worked for one conference during normal working hours (some U.N. meetings start at 10 or even 11 o'clock) and another from 8 - 10 a.m. or in the evenings. Working such long hours would surely prevent the interpreter from doing a good job throughout the day quite apart from the dishonesty.

Interpreters do not accept any job or situation which might detract from the dignity of their profession and refrain from any act which might bring their profession into disrepute.

Professional conference interpreters afford their colleagues moral assistance and collegiality, and refrain from any utterance or action prejudicial to the interests of their profession. They do everything possible to ensure the best quality interpretation and with this in mind they always endeavour to secure satisfactory conditions of sound, visibility and comfort. They do not work alone in a booth unless a colleague is available to relieve them should the need arise. They do everything they can to ensure that teams are set up in such a way as to avoid the systematic use of relay. They ensure that they and their colleagues have a direct view of the speaker and the conference room and refuse to work by means of television monitors (except in the case of videoconferences). They require that working documents and texts to be read out at the conference be given them in advance and prepare them diligently beforehand. They do not perform any duties other than those of conference interpreter at meetings for which they have been recruited as interpreters.

Conference interpreters do not accept a contract without knowing its precise conditions and ensuring that their identity and remuneration are known to the organizer of the conference.

They always remain neutral and refrain from trying to influence listeners by tone of voice or to let their own views on the subject being discussed shine through their words. This may be difficult if the subject is one you know a lot about (having done previous conferences) while some delegates are new and ask questions that you could answer. Be patient.   You are there to interpret, not to show off your knowledge.

At some large international conferences you may be working on four different Committees or groups each day - sometimes the working day is split up from 9 - 10.30 (coffee break) then from 11 until 12.30 (lunch), from 2 to 3.30 (tea break) and then from 4 until 5.30. The four meetings to which you are assigned may be groups of the whole, discussing strategy for the forthcoming Plenary meeting. The European group may meet to decide what they will do if the African group says so-and-so, but if the U.S. makes a certain statement they will do something else. Then you may work with the group of LDC's (Lesser Developed Countries) or the G7 (group of seven major industrialized nations) who discuss what they will say if the European group says this or that, or if the African group says so-and-so.   In the afternoon you may be with the Latin-American Group who also discuss how they will react to the other group's strategies. When the Plenary comes up, you may be the only person present who has all this information, but you must be wary of giving anything away even by your intonation or by your silences! Neutrality is part of the job.

Loyalty is sometimes a difficult matter. Generally speaking your loyalty must be to whoever is paying you even if another party has your sympathy. If you are working for United Nations, your loyalty is to U.N. and you are not answerable to anyone else, you may not receive instructions from anyone else - not even, for example, from the delegation of the country of your own nationality. So long as you are contracted to the United Nations you are a "custodian of international (rather than national) public trust."

Except in the case of public meetings, professional interpreters do not bring visitors into the conference room, family members or friends. Whatever the type of meeting, public or not, they do not bring visitors into the interpretation booths. Only interpreters and technicians have access to the interpreting booths. It goes without saying that only interpreters may speak over the interpretation channels.

It is not considered ethical to distribute your visiting cards or give your telephone number to conference participants (unless asked) or to engage in oneupmanship *vis-à-vis* your colleagues.

It is also considered unethical to try to get yourself replaced because you regret having accepted a three-day contract when, a few days later, you are offered a much more exciting two week conference in a country you would like to visit.

Improving your performance

It is the duty of all interpreters to keep improving their work. There are many ways of tackling this. In Australia, as I mentioned on page 71, we are lucky to have SBS television providing original news broadcasts every day in French, German, Chinese, Russian, Greek, Italian and Polish, enabling you to keep up to date with current affairs as well as keep your languages up to date as they evolve with time.

Self-monitoring is an excellent way of improving your performance. Buy yourself a twin track cassette recorder so that you can compare your interpretation with the original a few hours later while you still remember well enough what was said but are better able to judge your performance. Sometimes the technician may be able to help you by doing the recording for you. When you listen to your interpretation you will be able to evaluate its coherence, clarity and accuracy, and your errors of vocabulary and syntax, as well as repetitions and uncorrected slips of the tongue, will be glaringly obvious. It is useful to do this at regular intervals throughout your career to enable you to pinpoint irritating speech mannerisms, poor diction, choppy delivery and any other defects. When analysing your performance, pay attention to accuracy and faithfulness to the original and also to fluency, delivery, style and clarity of the message. (Before making any recording, however, it is wise to clear it first with the conference organizer for reasons of professional secrecy).

If you do not like what you hear, you may find you need to spend some time in a country where your languages are spoken - every two years is a good idea to keep your languages up to date. If the problem is one of content, you will need to fill in your knowledge of the areas in which you are weak. Pay particular attention to your voice. Voice is probably the feature in an interpreter to which delegates attach the greatest importance. So often excellent interpreters are poorly ranked by delegates because of an unpleasant voice or tiresome vocal mannerisms. Less able, less accurate colleagues are often preferred because of a pleasant voice and a reassuring delivery. It may even be necessary to invest in sessions with a voice coach. You can always ask a colleague with the right language combination or specialist knowledge of a particular subject to listen to you during a meeting and comment on content and delivery. This may be a constructive two-way process. As Karla Dejean Le Féal (1989) says:

> *What our listeners receive through their earphones should produce the same effect on them as the original speech does on the speaker's audience. It should have the same cognitive content and be presented with equal clarity and precision in the same type of language. Its language and oratory quality should be at least on the same level as that of the original speech, if not better,*

given that we are professional communicators, while many speakers are not, and sometimes even have to express themselves in languages other than their own.

Moreover, we know from surveys, round table discussions and private conversations with delegates that they are equally concerned about certain aspects of our output that we sometimes tend to neglect. They attach great importance to a pleasant voice as well as a steady volume, and are extremely sensitive to any background noise. Furthermore, they want interpretation to be truly simultaneous, i.e. without interruptions in the interpreter's speech, and without delays in the onset of interpretation whenever someone takes the floor. Rightly or wrongly, they assume that any such silence reflects a loss of information.

Conferences consisting mainly of discussions provide us with enough immediate feedback to judge whether the interpretation is effective and whether we use the relevant jargon correctly. Successful communication among the participants of the conference, however, does not necessarily mean that our performance actually lives up to the standards mentioned above. Other conferences consist mainly of the presentation of papers and feedback is almost entirely missing. In either case, alternative means of evaluating the effectiveness and the quality of our work have to be used.

With regard to improvement of performance, refresher courses for professional conference interpreters in most European languages are frequently held in London, Trieste, and at many European and American Interpretation Schools.

Working into your B language

Whether or not you are capable of working into your B language or languages depends on whether you fulfill all of the prerequisites for performing up to professional standards.

> *The two prerequisites most likely to remain unfulfilled concern the target language and the interpreter's background knowledge. Indeed it often happens at least in some countries and for certain languages that the interpreter does not work into his native language, but into a foreign language. Thus, the standard of language and oratory quality can hardly be met. Perhaps even more frequently, we do not have enough background knowledge - even though we may have prepared carefully for the conference - to live up to the standards of clear and precise re-expression of the original cognitive content in its entirety using the same type of language* (Dejean Le Féal 1982).

> *One of the main differences between our native language and a foreign language is that, however well we may master it, it is less developed. That is why we are not capable of using it as adroitly as we do our native language and that is also why, ultimately, we are not competent to judge whether it was actually used properly* (Seleskovitch).

Consequently, self-evaluation alone does not suffice for an interpreter working into a B language. The quality of the target language has to be assessed by a native speaker. The standard to be applied is the same as for interpretation into the native language. Regular evaluation by a native speaker of simultaneous interpretation into a B language would probably sharpen the profession's awareness of the highly erosive effect of simultaneous interpretation on performance in the B language (Dejean le Féal l985). Thus it could contribute to a healthy drive toward a more responsible use of this practice, to which, in my view, one should only resort in the exceptional cases where interpreters with the required language combination do not exist.

As for interpretation into English, such a drive would have the additional advantage of counteracting the present trend of reducing the number of working languages at international conferences. Indeed, if delegates received basic English (that is, linguistically substandard interpretation performed by English B interpreters) through their earphones less often, those who are not native speakers of this language would be less convinced that they understand English and less ready to forgo interpretation into their native language. The profession would benefit from this in terms of quality of service and in terms of a more even distribution of job opportunities for its members. Moreover, we as a profession should ask ourselves whether we should contribute to the mishandling of English and to the elimination of other languages from the international scene, or whether it is rather our duty, as well as in our interest, to help maintain the integrity of each language and to ensure its survival in international communication (Herbulot).

Emergencies happen to us all at some time - a colleague in another booth has an accident, is taken ill, or is unavoidably detained and arrives late for a meeting so that you are asked to step in and "cover" the booth for a while until a solution can be found - which means you have to work into your B language. In such a case, beware of colloquialisms. In my experience, it is particularly difficult to measure colloquialisms and slang in an acquired language. One is less sensitive to shades of meaning and degree so that one uses expressions in an acquired language that one would not use in one's own tongue. I have noticed this frequently in this country where immigrants often seem to think that the more they use colloqualisms, slang or swearwords, the better they are demonstrating their knowledge of English.

The advantages of foreign travel

Make the most of all the chances you get to practise your languages and update them if you can by spending an extra few days in a country before or after a conference. It is a mistake to arrive there just before the meeting and to leave the moment it finishes. If you can spend an extra few days there, visiting the country and getting to know the people, it will help you enormously in the future. A few days before the conference starts will help you to get acclimatized to the country, the people, and their mode of speech which will be invaluable in the booth when the meeting begins. A few days in Cuba will make the Cuban accent music to your ears when the Cuban delegate takes the floor and you will understand him so much better, however fast he speaks. The same goes for the Chilean or Argentine accent, not to mention the various French accents in Quebec, African countries and so on.

The interpreter as scapegoat

It has happened to us all at some time or another and it will happen to you. A delegate whose speech you know you have accurately interpreted takes the floor to say that his words have been misrepresented. It is natural to feel indignant. You are bursting with righteous indignation. But you cannot, as Anne Kerr pointed out (1988), start an argument with a delegate in the middle of a conference, even if you had the right to speak your own words. Jean Herbert once said:

> *In any international meeting there will be a number of people who understand both languages well enough to know you have not made a mistake. So you can forget your pride, for a start. My own method is to say, without expression:*

"Correction to the interpretation," and then give the new version.

He considered that this was a further means available to the interpreter of "carrying out his essential task of bringing individuals and groups together." Teddy Pilley said he would even bow slightly and say "I thank the honourable delegate for proposing a correction to the interpretation" and give the new version.

Altman (1989) tells of

a Spanish chairman who accused his interpreter of rustling papers in the booth and therefore rendering her interpretation incomprehensible (an accusation for which he later apologised publicly and profusely). The chances are that a moment of inattention had caused him to miss a point and that he had chosen this method of concealing his embarrassment. Sometimes "blaming the interpreter is a form of courtesy among delegates." It seems that to bear the brunt of such criticism is one aspect of the interpreter's role which s/he must, unwillingly, accept.

During discussions at a telecommunications conference where I was interpreting some years ago there was a long drawn out disagreement between the U.K. and the U.S.S.R. The U.K. delegate allowed himself to get quite carried away and was unpardonably rude. Either he suddenly realized he had overstepped the mark himself, or someone else pointed it out to him, because he took the floor again to apologize, saying the whole argument had been caused by a misinterpretation from the English booth. It was difficult for me to accept this because I knew I had made no mistake. I swallowed my pride, however, and carried on. At the end of the meeting, the U.K. delegate was waiting for me outside the conference building. He explained that he had gone too far and that when he realized this, accusing me was the only way he could think of saving the situation. I said I sympathized but my career was at stake and his complaint had been made in front of over a thousand people. The next morning a bunch of flowers was waiting for me in the booth.

10
TIPS FOR BEGINNERS

First and foremost: nerves. It is, to say the least, extremely daunting for an inexperienced interpreter to find himself in a glass booth overlooking an enormous hall with five thousand people listening to his every word. My advice is : forget yourself, forget it is you. Act the part of a conference interpreter.

A lot of famous actors and actresses have confessed that they are very shy people in real life, but once they are up on the stage being someone else, they are fine. Think of Italian waiters - they don't just wait at table, they act the part of the perfect waiter with the white cloth over one arm and all the gestures, posture, facial expressions and flourishes that the part requires. There are cases of stammerers in the interpreting profession - people who, in private life, cannot speak without stammering yet once up there behind the microphone, the stammer disappears. This is because they are not just John or Mary speaking, they are The Interpreter. Take a deep breath before you start and act the part of The Perfect Simultaneous Interpreter and you will be fine.

Another thought that helped me to overcome nerves in the beginning, especially in consecutive, was the fact that all I was doing was trying to help people understand one another. That thought has always made my role clearer in my own mind and somehow helped me cope with stage-fright.

Working on medical conferences is a problem if you have, like me, a vivid imagination. I have suffered the imaginary symptoms of every disease I have ever talked about, felt creatures crawling up inside the veins in my feet and legs during meetings of expert committees on bilharziasis (schistosomiasis), suffered diarrhoea, aches and pains in cholera control meetings, fever during expert committees on malaria, and felt sores about to appear on my arms during discussions on the leishmaniases. I could not help scratching arms and legs while talking about smallpox or malaria. Rabies symptoms were unpleasant too. I had to interpret conferences on orthopaedic surgery with my eyes closed while slides or films were being shown especially if there was blood. I almost fainted the first time I saw a surgeon making the first incision. Until I discovered my Secret Method: not to be me but rather The Perfect Imperturbable Professional Interpreter.

If you are feeling nervous, confide in your colleagues; often the entire team will rally to your support once they know there is a problem. Control your voice and delivery so that the nervousness is not perceptible to your audience. Keep your voice down, especially when interpreting a fast or difficult speaker. This will help you to remain calm.

If a particular speaker makes you nervous, try to imagine him looking ridiculous, in his underpants, or when he first wakes up in the morning with his hair untidy. He is only a human being like the rest of us, after all. If you find his accent difficult to understand, seek him out during the coffee break and ask him if he can hear the interpretation satisfactorily. By talking to him on a social level you may find him easier to understand later when he takes the floor during the meeting.

Stress and stagefright

You are working at super-high tension in closely confined quarters with a critical audience listening to your every word, which is at best extremely stressful. But being nervous is no excuse for doing a bad job. No-one is interested in whether you had a good night's sleep. Like the other performing arts, stage fright is normal and may improve the quality of your work but you must learn to master your nerves so that you *sound* calm, reliable and utterly sure of yourself.

An interpreter is entirely given up to his profession while the conference lasts. In the middle of the night you may wake up with a word burning in your brain: You should have said X and not Y. It will worry you, haunt you, but there is nothing you can do about it. What is said is said. This is just one of the agonies interpreters have to put up with.

Not only must interpreters be familiar with the culture and literature of each of their active and passive languages (delegates have been known to quote from Molière, the Bible, the Koran, Racine, Martin Fierro, Shakespeare, Cervantes, Tchekov, and to use proverbs that are untranslatable unless you are familiar with the culture associated with the language concerned), but they must also be up-to-date with current affairs and the international political situation so that they have an idea what a speaker is likely to say on a given topic before he starts to speak.

Imagine you are interpreting a vital speech on economics and the man next to the speaker coughs so you miss one key word. In simultaneous, you have no way of stopping the meeting to ask whether he said "above" or "below[3]" the figure he mentioned, and there may be six thousand delegates listening to you (especially if you are working in the English booth). If you have prepared well, studied the subject thoroughly and read about it in the press, you can make an "educated guess" which can be

---

[3] At a telecommunications conference dealing with the radio frequency spectrum, there were interminable discussions on the apportionment of frequencies above and below 27.5 MHz. An Italian delegate attending all of this series of conferences, who had to speak in French as Italian is not a United Nations working language, pronounced *en-dessus* and *en-dessous* in exactly the same way because of his Italian accent. It was vital for the audience to know whether he meant "above" or "below" as this separation of frequency bands was the crux of the debate.

adjusted if necessary later, probably in the next sentence. This is better than hesitating, losing control, giving in to panic and missing the next part of the speech. Conference interpreting is living dangerously: verbal acrobatics without a safety net.

Adjusting the Volume

A mistake beginners often make is to turn the volume up too high in their earphones for fear of missing something. They forget that it is important also for them to hear their own voice because if they do not, they will not finish their sentences properly or polish their delivery. The balance between the volume of the sound in your earphones and the sound of your voice is a very personal matter. Practise with the volume as low as possible. The louder the volume in your earphones, the louder you will speak and there is nothing worse than a booming interpreter who can be heard in the background on all channels, deafening all around and putting the technician in a flat spin. "Boomers" tend to be unpopular so if your colleagues in neighbouring booths close their doors rather pointedly you will know why. Beginners should make a conscious effort to lower their voices both in volume and in pitch (when nervous, one tends to raise one's pitch.) You will find that by adjusting the tone contol, that is, the balance between treble and bass, you can lower the volume, thus protecting your hearing.

Before you start work the first morning, check the equipment in case there is something you haven 't seen before. First, make sure you know how to switch the microphone on and off - in some convention centres I have worked in, the green light is on when you are free to talk to your cabin-mate, that is, the microphone is switched off - and the red light comes on when the microphone is switched on whereas in others on the contrary the green light comes on when the microphone is switched on. This is extremely confusing for the first hour or two. It is rather like driving in a country where traffic is on the other side of the road. Beware ! Check the cough-button, and the relay system and unless you work from Chinese or Arabic, check with the colleagues in the Chinese or Arabic booth to find out whether they will be working into English or into French.

Before you start, too, have a look at the list of participants if there is one (if not, look at the report of the last meeting where there will probably be one) to see if there are any difficult-to-pronounce names, or any English names you may not recognize in the mouth of a French, Spanish or Russian speaker. Make sure too you are up to date with the country names which may have changed following certain political events (the former USSR, for example, "Burma" or "Myanmar" - you must of course say the same as the speaker) and know when to say "People's Republic of" and when to say "Popular Republic of".

Delivery

A word about your level of animation. Try to adopt the same level of animation as the speaker you are interpreting. When you are off the air, it is interesting to switch to the various channels: the original may be a dull British voice, but sometimes the Spanish and Italian booths sound so animated you would almost think the speaker was belligerent while the French booth makes him sound alert and agitated. Do not go to the other extreme, however: a dead-pan monotonous voice, however accurate the interpretation, is not pleasant to listen to and tends to send the delegates to sleep, especially after lunch.

A pleasant tone of voice is important; however desperate you may feel, do not sound desperate. Try to sit back in your chair and feel detached enough to improve your style as you go, finish the sentences properly, and perhaps use different words from the speaker in order to get closer to his meaning. As you become more experienced and more confident you will learn not to follow the speaker too closely, but to sit back and put odd words in the little "pockets" of your brain to retrieve later when the speaker slows down.

Another problem arises when a delegate refers to the title of a well-known book, play or film - frequently the title is quite different in other languages and either you know it or you don't. The English title of Malraux's *La condition humaine* has nothing to do with "human" or "condition".

Accuracy

According to B. Grote (AIIC), reporting on an information meeting between five interpretation "users" and thirty-five conference interpreters in 1980:

> *delegates felt that interpreters should consider themselves part of a complicated "thinking machine", that, painful as this may be to us, the best interpreters were those one could simply forget, that interpreters should take their vocation literally and "interpret" the original speaker as faithfully as a piano soloist interprets a sonata.*

In case of doubt: accuracy comes before style.

Fast Speakers and Economising your Voice

It makes all the difference in the world if you have been able to read and prepare the text beforehand. However, whether or not you have been able to do this, the strategy applied by experienced interpreters is to condense. This can be done without any loss of information. This is called *macroprocessing* and is necessary when the source text information is so dense that there is not enough time to convey everything into the target message, whatever the speed of the speaker. According to Marianna Sunnari of the University of Turku in Finland:

> *when working with structurally different languages such as Finnish and Indoeuropean languages, macroprocessing is needed even in an*

132

"ideal" situation, where the speaker is speaking without a script and the interpreters are familiar with the speaker and the topic. Novices, who do not master this strategy, fail to produce a coherent output message.

In any case, you must learn to economise your voice. You may be using it the whole, long day. You can learn to economise the effort required so that you won't be too tired as the afternoon wears on and if the speaker is going hell-for-leather you will find it less tiring if you speak softly.

Difficult speakers

Some people do not have the knack of public speaking: they mumble or gabble their words. Everybody has heard and had difficulty understanding speakers like these in their own language too. The more practice you can get listening to speakers like this the better. Working in booths other than the English, you will need practice too to understand the different types of accent and imperfect English you will have to interpret - delegates from Brazil, the Middle East, Japan, Norway, often Germany, Czeckoslovakia as well as India, Pakistan and some African countries often have to use English instead of their own language. Practice makes perfect.

Remember that you must not try to improve on what the speaker says, even if it seems to you that he is talking nonsense. You cannot know what tactics, what strategies are at play. All you are asked to do is to interpret accurately and to respect the register of the speaker.

Keep up your languages

There is a saying I have heard, generally applied to "grey power" (that is, those rather long in the tooth) : "Use it or Lose it!" This saying applies to interpreters' languages at any age. You must use your languages, read in them, speak in them, listen to them spoken or you will forget them.

Those of us interpreting from or into French are fortunate in having New Caledonia so close (only a couple of hours' flight from Sydney and closer than Perth) where we can brush up our French and keep it up to date. We can also listen to their radio broadcasts in French and, by means of a dish on our rooftop, even receive television programmes from Nouméa.

Languages evolve all the time. If you left Guatemala or Argentina ten or more years ago, you can be sure the language you speak is not the same as is spoken there today and you will need to make a conscious effort to keep in touch. Quite apart from that, your Spanish will now be contaminated with the language being spoken around you. You may not even realize you are saying "el reporte" instead of "el informe". English short cuts also have an insidious way of insinuating themselves into other languages. So you must be constantly on the look-out for anglicisms in your speech. It is essential to read newspapers and literature from the countries whose languages you work into and from in order to keep them up to date. It is no good just glancing at the headlines and reading only the subjects of personal interest. Thorough reading is required with an open mind as to type of language used, shades of meaning, paying particular attention to current affairs.

As W. Keiser (1975) explains, beginners must also *acquire total mastery of the jargon typical of international negotiations and meetings i.e. terms and expressions directly related to conference procedure, the organization of meetings, voting, the amendment of texts such as resolutions, the preambular as opposed to the operative sections of resolutions, etc. Useful words: The Chair - to chair - the Chairman - Madame Chairman - The President - To call the meeting to order - to close the meeting - to adjourn the meeting - vote - ballot - casting vote - roll-call - secret ballot - to give the floor - to call on - filibuster - delegate - substi-*

tute or deputy - representative - credentials - proxy - delegation of powers - plenipotentiary - Standing orders - agenda - draft agenda - approval of agenda, resolution, statement, declaration, decision - preamble - items on the agenda - to delete an item - agreement - undertaking - provision - entry into force - ratification - signatories, etc.

In simultaneous interpretation, the interpreter is at the mercy of the speaker and must learn to construct his sentences with flexibility, especially when interpreting from and into languages with different syntax. He must also be prepared to handle heavy, verbose or flowery speech, to change the order in cases where logical progression differs according to different cultures, to cut lengthy sentences into several short ones, and even find vague expressions and padding to overcome temporary difficulties, that is, while you are waiting for the speaker to clarify something incomprehensible he has just said.

The interpreter is a professional speaker. He must therefore be able to adapt his style to his audience and carry the original message in the way it would have been delivered by the speaker had he addressed the audience in the language into which the interpreter works.

If you are a beginner, you can also learn a lot from listening to experienced colleagues working in your languages to see how they tackle a particular difficulty or subject. When you are not actually on the air yourself, switch over to the other booths to hear the words being used - this may be of great help because the delegates speaking those languages will no doubt use similar wording later. This is also an excellent way to improve your vocabulary in your passive languages.

Your Conference diary

Keep careful note of all your conference commitments to avoid any overlapping or duplication. Reply promptly to telephone or email offers of work. If you are not available, the recruiter will need to contact someone else and cannot afford to waste precious time. Be sure to check your messages daily, wherever you are, and respond to them, otherwise you may find you don't get a second offer.

Open your documents early

Be sure to open e-mails and download conference documents immediately, even if you do not need to study them until later. Contracts, programmes or details of change of venue may be hidden among them and organisers are justifiably irritated when you ask for information that has already been sent to you. Do not leave it until the last minute because you also need to see, well ahead of time, how difficult the subject matter is. Some conferences require more preparation than others - you may need to Google a number of reference papers on a difficult subject before you start work on the conference documents themselves. On the other hand, if the subject-matter is easy, or one that you have done frequently in the past, three or four days may be enough. But - better safe than sorry.

Preparing for a meeting

It is a good idea to work out your own system to keep track of documents, past and current, on a particular subject or for a particular organisation. You will need to work out your own method for indexing key words, including titles of officials and committees with their translation into each of your working languages. The better your mastery of the organisation's structure and jargon, the better your chances of being recruited again. It is also important that freelance interpreters identify with the "corporate image" of the organisation.

At least two weeks before the conference you should be able to download a complete set of documents in each of the working languages containing, for example, a full programme, agenda, list of participants, minutes or previous meetings, reports, invitations and all the documents which will be available to the other participants or which might be helpful in the preparation for the conference. Minutes of past meetings and proceedings of earlier congresses are very useful too.

However, unfortunately you will not always receive documentation in advance: it may happen that, upon arrival at the conference venue, you are given a USB key containing the documents in which case a lot of last-minute preparation will be required. There may also be a laptop awaiting you in your booth so that you can plug in the USB key and retrieve the documents, having them on the screen while they are being discussed.

Make sure you keep time free before the meeting to study all of these papers in depth. If this is the first time you have worked on the particular subject, you should also research it as much as you can to give you some background understanding that will help you cope with fast or difficult speakers and give you the feeling you are on top of the subject. Some people think interpreters simply transliterate words without understanding the idea conveyed by the message, but interpreters know that it is quite impossible to reproduce messages without a full comprehension of what the speaker wants to say and this, in turn, is impossible without some knowledge of the subject matter. The various search engines on the internet are of course invaluable for this purpose. The first time you work for an International Organization it is advisable to ask them for a set of the Basic Texts governing that organization: Charter or Constitution, Statutes, Standing Orders and so on, which you will keep with the glossary you have prepared during the meeting for future reference.

When sorting out the conference documents you are about to study, you will need a system to index them so you can find any document you need in the booth in a hurry (for example, Committee documents, Plenary documents, working documents, conference room documents). Pay particular attention to key words and also the titles of officials (which vary according to the organization, for example in some there may be a Deputy Secretary-General, in another a similar post may be called Assistant Secretary-General or Vice-Secretary-General). Prepare your own multi-lingual glossary, noting carefully the "in-jargon" of the technical or professional organization concerned. You will find that "Commissions" are generally bigger than "Committees" and "Committees" more permanent than "Working Groups."

You will also need to list the official names of the various Committees (Standing Committees, and so on) in your languages for each Organization to keep on file. It would seem that "Executive Committee" is obviously *Comité ejecutivo*" and "*Comité exécutif*" but it may not be in some organizations. In the International Telecommunications Union where telephony is concerned a "Recommendation" is not "*une recommandation*" but rather "*un Avis*" and an "Opinion" is "*un Voeu*" in French . "Steering Committee" or "Management Committee" has various translations depending on the organization, as well as "Council", "Board", "Governing Body", "Junta", "working group","*ad hoc* group" and "task force". Sometimes there seems to be no rhyme or reason, but that's how it is and you just have to memorize these idiosyncracies. (Also, "*le Comité exécutif a renvoyé la question pour examen au Comité X*" , "referred" in English and "*remitió este asunto a la consideración del Comité*").

"*Trimestriel*" is nothing to do with "three" in English ("Quarterly") and in budgetary matters "*imprévus*" is mostly "contingency" or "unforeseen".

Preparation was much easier in the old days of "parallel pagination" in all languages even though the

English pages were much shorter than the French and Spanish. To save paper, parallel pagination has long been done away with so it will take longer to find the same place in all texts. When you do, highlight the words you want to remember. The next step is to write your glossary. If I am working in the English booth, on one page I write down recurring English expressions, names of people with their titles, etc. If you have one active and two passive languages, the rest of your glossary will be in three languages so you would divide each page into three columns with the active language in the last. I generally organize mine into groups such as names of committees and official groupings on one page, acronyms and abbreviations on another, technical words on another, general vocabulary on another, etc. to make them as easy as possible to find in a hurry. Some colleagues prefer to organize their glossaries alphabetically. In any case, it is worth while taking the time to write very clearly and print difficult words because you will not have time to puzzle out what you have scribbled. If some kind colleagues lets you share his handwritten vocabulary, I would copy it out in my own writing first to help me remember it and secondly to be sure I can read it in an emergency. Once you have finished this task and learnt it all, I suggest you get up early on the first morning of the meeting and go through your vocabulary again in a concentrated fashion to set it in your mind for the day. I have always found it useful, too, on a difficult technical conference, to get together with colleagues from the other booths just before the meeting starts to compare the translations of unusual words and expressions - sometimes they have found different equivalents, based on one of the other languages. You will find Day 1 of most conferences very tiring - it is better not to have organized any strenuous social events for that evening - but as from Day 2 the vocabulary seems to come naturally. I prefer to devote all my time to the conference while it lasts, and not make any private social commitments. You do not know in advance whether you will be required to work late, or at a night meeting and trying to change plans at the last minute is an unnecessary hassle when you are in the booth trying to concentrate perhaps on a new subject.

Dictionaries

It is worthwhile to invest in the latest versions of specialized dictionaries to help you study at home and to enable you to prepare your own glossary to take with you into the booth. Do not clutter up the booth with a pile of dictionaries, however, you won't have time to consult them while working and the glossary you have prepared will be much more useful. It is not "done" to stagger about with bags of heavy dictionaries or to moan to all and sundry that the meeting is difficult. You will notice that the top professionals always give the impression that everything is easy (they do their preparation in private), that they know it all (they arrive in the booth empty-handed or carrying a newspaper in case they are bored). That is fine when, to top it all, they then proceed to give a brilliant performance.

Nowadays, excellent dictionaries are available on the internet and preparing glossaries is greatly facilitated by using a silent laptop or "Palm" that you can take with you into the booth.

Taking notes in simultaneous

While your colleague is working, it is a good idea to listen and take notes of any expressions that might recur. This is also an excellent opportunity to switch to the other booths to hear the terms being used. Note-taking in simultaneous is particularly important in the English booth because you may not be working for some time, and then suddenly be plunged into a high-speed statement without a "warm-up" period. In any case, be sure to note down all figures and dates as you hear them, for accuracy's sake.

Texts of speeches given to you beforehand

Scientific, medical and technical meetings make much use of written material which, as W.Keiser (1975) says, runs against the very essence of conference interpreting, which is oral. Speakers at such meetings generally read, and read exceptionally fast.

Do not rely, however, on the speaker reading the whole text word for word so that all you have to do is sight translation. It often happens that, as the meeting progresses it gets behind schedule and the Chairman cuts down the time allotted to each speaker. In the worst case, the speaker may then read his paper (which may represent his life's research work of which he is particularly proud) word for word but at top speed in order to fit into the time slot, making it impossible to keep up with sight translation - sometimes you will lose your place, panic and miss a few sentences until you find it again and the result will be an incoherent approximation of what is said and there is also a good chance you have missed out the main points. An experienced speaker will summarize his paper, which is preferable and easier to interpret provided you have read the full text beforehand carefully, paying particular attention to difficult expressions and technical words and highlighted figures, dates, names and acronyms, for which you will have found the equivalent. Acronyms and abbreviations are the tools of our profession: they can save precious speaking time so write a list of them clearly and have it in front of you in the booth. If you are pressed for time when preparing the text of a speech about to be made, skip to the end and be sure you have the last few sentences prepared and polished, so that you can at least end on a confident note.

Briefing sessions

Briefings can be extremely useful and also help to establish an intelligent professional image. Experts usually appreciate intelligent questions and are prepared to answer them, to explain a term or a process, a piece of machinery or an operation and this also helps them to understand the needs of interpreters and increases their confidence in our professional ability. Briefing sessions with experts from different language groups are most useful after the interpreters have had an opportunity to study the documents and immediately before a session.

Preparation of personal Glossaries

A self-compiled glossary is like a trusted friend through the years. I base mine on personal mental association and subject. As Francisca Melero (AIIC) says, glossaries outline and identify a given subject matter, and give you a prior indication as to what terms of art are likely to come up in the context of the meeting concerned. Dictionaries do not do this, they are cumbersome and their use is slow. In any case, they would have to be multilingual and subject-related to be any real use in the booth. When you compile your glossary make sure you have a logical system for sorting by subject, organisation, committee, etc. in alphabetical order for each language, enabling you to identify terms with the organisation that uses them in that particular way.

Melero goes on to say that "home-grown" glossaries are "Brain Energy Saving Devices":

> *No matter whether you are a relative newcomer to the subject matter of the meeting and therefore expect having to cast around for every other technical term that comes your way, or whether you are an old hand at it and just need that extra amount of security resulting from a list of terms of art in front of you - in either case you will find that the brain energy you would have to branch off your energy output mainstream to pinpoint the right word at the right moment can be channelled towards more productive aims : improving on your linguistic quality, style and conciseness, paying attention to your voice (pitch and modulation) and other ancillary requirements. Whenever I am working I can feel physically that*

my energy output represents a two-prong flow, and I am always relieved whenever I can shut off one prong.

Last but by no means least, when the chips are down and you have no documents and the subject is highly technical, you can do a very decent job just relying on the glossaries provided you have studied them beforehand.

Here, for example, are the subjects I worked on during a three-month period in Geneva:

- The standardization of synthetic fibre (when I thought the Italian delegate said "fibrocitis" he was really talking about fibre sizes).

- Sexual abnormalities of the newborn child (where I learnt about some weird practices in remote parts of the world and contraptions placed upon new-born boy babies to ensure their procreation facility didn't disappear).

- Radiocommunications (peak-rain conditions, the effects of canting raindrops on propagation, line-of-sight, nominal boresight, DBS systems, feeder link transmitters, earth station receivers, rain fade constraints, power flux density, antenna characteristics, beamfit and synthesis calculation, orbital separation, time division multiplex, elevation angles, gain patterns, up links and downlinks, sidelobes, aggregate weighted carrier to interference ratio, spurious emissions, refractivity, vestigial sideband, double sideband, single sideband, effective versus apparent radiated power, effective isotropically radiated power, MUF and LUF).

- Metallurgy (not my cup of tea).

- Tick-borne encephalitis (mainly about the sterilisation of the tick - no, not with a minute scalpel but rather by irradiation), haematoprotozoal diseases of livestock: piroplasms, anaplasms, theilerias, rickettsias, transmissible pathogens, hybridisation of tick species).

- Forestry (rehabilitation of degraded land, windbreaks and firebreaks, soil and water conservation, forests and woodlands, watershed management, agro-silvi-pastoral development, depletion of ground water, sclerophytic bushes, scrubs, shelter belts).

- Orthopaedic surgery and Anaesthesiology (complete muscular relaxation, blood flow, induction time, quinine derivatives, pupillary reflexes, cardiac arrest, nerve blocks, caudral, sacral, brachial, plexus and spinal blocks, distal retrograde flow stump pressures).

- The calibration of eggs (egg marketing).

- Telephony - automatic switching systems (start-stop systems, asynchronous network - automatic digital data error recorders, companders, clear-back signals, dipoles, directional couplers).

- Cancer research (too much vocabulary to include here).

- Cardiology (bacterial endocarditis, valvular prostheses, congestive heart failure, arrhythmia, salmonella septice-mia, mitral stenosis, hydrostatic pulmonary edema, ve-nous return, hemodynamic management, post-streptococcal valvulopathies, wedge pressure, balloon valvuloplasty, angina, chronic hypoxia, commissuratomy, thrombo-embolic, pulmonary shunts, glomerulonephretic immune-complex type, capillaroscopic anomalies, mitral leaks,fungal endocarditis, Osler's nodes, Roth's spots, immunoglobulins,Aschoff nodules, mechanical asystole, epithelioid cells).

- Telephony and the creosoting of telegraph poles (and how they put carburundum in p.v.c. telephone cable sheaths in India to wear away the teeth of the hungry chewing termites)(commonly known among interpreters as the Toothless Termite Committee).

- Communicable diseases (oncocerkiasis, relapsing fever, trachoma, yaws, plague, measles, cholera, tinia, smallpox, kidney-flukes, trematodes).

- Breastfeeding and the reason why in some African countries women could not give both breasts to the infant (because one was reserved for the husband).

There was also a meeting about the cloning of rabbits but I have forgotten the title of the conference and two days on The Peaceful Uses of Outer Space (which the Interpreters called The Useful Pieces of Outer Space).

As you can imagine, each meeting required specialized vocabulary. Moral: keep your glossaries in good order so that you can find what you need when you need it, and keep adding to them as research develops on the different topics and the vocabulary evolves. Conference interpreting is very difficult and tiring for the first few years, until you have become accustomed to the terminology of the organizations you work for. After a while, however, as you develop your own glossaries and become used to the jargon used by each client, it will be far less tiring and you will become more confident. For each meeting there `will be less vocabulary to learn; all you will have to do is update your glossaries.

To cheer you up: most of the larger international organizations such as UN, ITU, WMO, and so on which have permanent translation sections have had Lexicons or Glossaries of technical terms prepared by their translators. These are generally available free of charge to freelance interpreters and translators working for them.

I am afraid you will just have to learn beforehand the acronyms specific to each conference you do. And keep your list of them to be added to in the future.

Some useful vocabulary

Most professions have their own jargon which, some say, is intended to "keep outsiders out". Conference interpreters need to learn the jargon of each profession so that, when they speak, they sound like a physician, meteorologist, brain surgeon, geologist, and so on. They must also be familiar with colloquialisms, quotes, proverbs,

145

and common slang expressions in all of their working languages. They must also be on guard against language contamination i.e. contamination by the language spoken in the country in which they live, "faux amis"(false friends), anglicisms in French, gallicisms in English, and so on, and should have at their fingertips a plentiful supply of synonyms, clichés and language patterns. You will find some suggested useful books to read at the end of this book under "Further Reading."

Quick, off the top of your head, what is "nozzle" in your other language(s)[4]? And what about "Foot and Mouth Disease"[5] ? (nothing to do with feet or mouths.)"*Tirer la jambe*" is a false friend if you compare its meaning to that of "pull your leg" in English. Another false friend frequently encountered: "*Ce n'est pas un hasard* ..." which is not the same as the English word "hazard". "Sustainable" development ? ("*durable*" according to official UN terminology but sometimes (Program Action 21) "*soutenable*" or even "*écologiquement soutenable*". "Straddling" stock ? (*stock trans-zone*). An interesting snippet I found somewhere: "Mitterand remains the aristocrat of French politics while Balladur is labelled BCBG (*bon chic, bon genre*)."[6]

Beware of public-servantese. *Dickson's Word Treasury* (Dickson 1992) calls this "the D.C. Dialect" (DCD; c.f. the book of that name by Paul Morgan and Sue Scott, exploring the new language in terms of ten easy lessons (be impersonal, be obscure, be pompous, be evasive, be repetitious, be awkward, be incorrect, be faddish, be serious, be unintelligible). Examples:

English	*DCD*

---

[4] *col de tuyère* in French. Other possibilities: *bec (tuyau), canule (séringue), suceur (aspirateur), pistolet (pompe à essence), buse (soufflet)*

[5] *fièvre aphteuse* in French (zoonosis)

[6] Sloane Ranger?

begin	implement
break-in	entry operation
cover-up	contain the situation
criminal conspiracy	game plan
fired	selected out
kidnap	segregate out
won't work	counterproductive
workable	viable

Some of the examples of bureaucratic gobbledy-gook quoted in *Dickson's Word Treasury* are:

Anticipatory retaliation: Attacking your enemy on the assumption that he would do the same if given the chance.

Information processing center: A typing pool.

Intermodal interface: A term that was translated by former Transportation Secretary William Coleman as, "When you get off the train, a bus is waiting."

Recreational eco-unit: A garden."

He also refers to "Medicant: the jargon of people in medicine who say "deglutition" when they mean swallowing, or call a headache "cephalalgia."

Australianisms

One of the things I love about Australia is the creativity that goes into the evolution of the English language with such words as "milko", "garbo", "cuppa", "rort", "stouch" "spruker","larrikin", "smoko" (I cannot vouch for the spelling of any of these, they do not appear in any of my dictionaries). However, none of these words should, of course, be used in the booth. Nor should baby-talk such as "coffee and bikkies" or "tummy". (One cannot help a smile at the thought of a medical conference where the interpreter talked of "tummy pains!" or "chemist" instead of "pharmacist".)

Australianisms do however present a real problem. Australian delegates, probably because they are mostly monolingual, use local colloquialisms which are difficult to transpose into other languages and seem quite unaware of the fact that everything they say is being painstakingly translated into French, Spanish, Russian, Arabic, Chinese, Japanese and so on. Sometimes they use these expressions deliberately believing them to be amusing. Surely the top priority of a conference speaker is to be understood ....

Living in Australia, we hear expressions like "things are crook", "headless chook", "scumbag" and "fair dinkum" so often on the radio and television we might be forgiven for thinking they were English. They are however Australianisms and probably will not be understood at an international conference by many of those listening to the floor channel i.e. listening to the original English, such as delegations from India, Pakistan, Sri Lanka, Thailand, Myanmar, Kenya, Norway, Sweden, Denmark, Finland, etc. as well as the United States of America and Canada. The non-English-speaking delegates are more fortunate because you will be able to interpret them in a way they can understand.

Before interpreting at your first international conference, therefore, it might be a good idea for beginners working in booths other than the English to give some thought to how you would interpret the following, all of which I have jotted down at recent international ministerial meetings at Parliament House in Canberra:

- "Bottom of the harbour scheme" (explain what it means, for example: a scheme whereby a company is purchased, stripped of its assets and consigned to oblivion);
- "for defo reasons" (defamation - heard at a publishers' conference);
- "I am happy to see flax still gets a guernsey" (at a wool producers' conference);
- "whether we all get our snouts in the trough or whether we all back off a bit";
- "a motherhood statement";

- "It's a two bob each way situation";
- "You can have your cake and eat it";
- "It's a rat-race out there" (that's a hard one to translate);
- "ballpark figures", "double-dipping", "sunset provision";
- "if we're fair dinkum about these rates";
- "non-performing loans", "get on the gravy-train", "the countries who copped a hiding during the war", "Cash Flow Enhancement Programme", "snags" (Australia) and "bangers and mash" (U.K.) (at a conference on food and the retail industry);
- "to cut off our noses";
- "dag";
- "rubbery figures"; and
- "razor gang" (which is not as bloodthirsty as you might think - it means a committee involved in reviewing expenditure).

A former Prime Minister used all the following expressions in one session when I was interpreting for him: "The two concepts are pegged", "We were investing our dollar while everyone else was having a barney in the Middle East," "The Americans are mucking around with their currency", "We are running twin deficits", "there's plenty of money sloshing about", "The Australian dollar is a commodity-driven currency", "and that is when we started sucking in all the producer goods", "investment shot through the roof", "the interest rate literally took the stuffing out of the place" and "the little countries keep getting ripped-off".

When I was a beginner, I decided how I would translate "*couper les cheveux en quatre*" but am still waiting for a French delegate to say it so that I can talk about "capillary quadrisection", much more satisfying than mere "hair-splitting", though I doubt if I would have dared.

Millions, billions, trillions or milliards and billiards

First of all, let me confuse you. In the United States of America and France a trillion is a thousand billions (that is, 1 followed by 12 zeros), equivalent to an English billion. However in Great Britain and Germany, a trillion is 1 followed by 18 zeros. What the British and Germans call a trillion is what the Americans would call a quintillion. What the Americans call a billion, the British call a milliard.

In the United Kingdom, a billion is a million squared, a trillion is a million to the power of 3, a quadrillion is a million to the power of 4, a quintillion is a million to the power of 5, etc. The *Oxford Dictionary* gives the word "milliard" in English meaning "a thousand million", which is the same meaning as that of the "milliard" in French, Russian, Spanish, Italian and German. So you cannot be criticised in Australia for saying "milliard" in English when you hear "milliard" in French, Russian, Spanish, Italian or German. This is certainly the easiest solution and saves mental acrobatics.

Just count your blessings that you are unlikely to come across firkins, rods, poles and perches, a barleycorn (one-third of an inch), a mease (500 herrings), a pig (British measure of ballast equal to 301 pounds), half-crowns, florins, shillings or farthings.

Use of lap-tops

Nowadays many interpreters bring their personal laptop to the booth containing the conference documents as well as their glossary which also enables them to keep up-dating it as they go along throughout the day while their colleague is working. It also has the advantage of enabling reference to past conference vocabulary for that organization or on the same topic. It is, however, important to be as discreet and quiet as possible to avoid distracting your colleague and a soft-touch key system is preferable to prevent the clicking sound which might be picked up by the microphone.

The laptop should be able to be connected to the internet in the booth and have a reasonable amount of memory. It is sometimes a great help if your colleague working beside you can search, in a flash, for the key word that persists in eluding you.

Binoculars

A pair of binoculars might be useful in the booth if you are working in a large hall such as Brisbane, Canberra, Melbourne, Adelaide or Sydney Convention Centre, or anywhere where there are 1000 delegates or more.

Accreditation and language claims

When the time comes to seek accreditation as a professional conference interpreter, be modest. You may be able to get by in local conditions, working with colleagues who are friends and will help you out if necessary, but not when working on an expert international team with colleagues you have never met before. So do not claim too many languages when you first begin, and do not claim any languages of which you are unsure. Due to unforeseen circumstances you may suddenly find yourself acting as pivot in an important meeting on a difficult subject, working from one of your "shaky" languages. Well may you regret having been so rash - you could ruin your reputation and career for good. Imagine how you would feel if your colleague has to leave the booth for a moment and the Chairman announces an unexpected speaker on the subject of "The Kinetics of the Reaction Inactivation of Tyroserose During its Catalyzing of the Aerobic Oxidation of Catechol". (*La kinétique de l'inactivation par réaction de la tyrosérose durant sa catalysation de l'oxydation aérobique du catéchol.*)(Coleman-Holmes 1971)

151

John Coleman-Holmes, in his book *Mâcher du Coton* (1971), describes "Corinne Mauffetard" who has not spent enough time preparing for the conference because the documents she received were so boring, difficult and off-putting. She tells herself she'll get by when the time comes. When it does, she speaks too close to the microphone, in a panic-stricken high-pitched voice, constantly correcting herself to improve on what she has just said. She cannot keep up so leaves out one sentence in three. When she gets too involved in one sentence and cannot find a way out, she jumps ahead to what the speaker is now saying leaving a trail of *non sequitur*. The only words that are always clear are the "Thank you, Mr. Chairman" and the beginning and the end.

It is true that delegates rarely complain. Colleagues are another matter however - while they say nothing and grimly pretend to read a document with headphones firmly clamped in place, they do not miss a single syllable. They know that no-one will say the bad interpretation was the work of Corinne Mauffetard, but rather that it was "a woman's voice", or that "the interpretation was bad". Colleagues react by trying to limit the harm done and get her away from the microphone but this is as difficult a task as trying to remove a lion cub from its mother. However, Corinne Mauffetard will not be offered any more conference contracts ....

This was before the days of "*Les juifs et les gentils*" (during the Pope's visit to Geneva) and the "*marineros congelados*" at the WHO Sperm Bank Conference.

A little later in his book, Coleman-Holmes describes "Bertha Frühlingsweihe" who never talks nonsense. She has even been known to say into the microphone in a dignified voice: "The interpreter apologizes but has not understood the speaker", which made her famous among colleagues. The audience listening to him in the original had not understood either. Before reaching this point, she let the speaker go ahead to avoid the hypnotic effect of following word for word, giving her time to find out what he meant and produce a clear sentence. She only used his words (or their equivalent in her language) if she judged them to be best. She knew how to re-think his words and express them in her language, leaving out what was unnecessary. She spent many long days before the conference studying the documents and noting down terminology and ideas. She copied them all down in a glossary, one glossary for each subject and each employer and recited them to herself. If the documents were late in reaching her, she telephoned and pestered those concerned until they arrived. Some clients dropped her preferring more easy-going interpreters until an important, difficult, technical conference came along. Then they knew they needed Bertha who could be relied upon for accuracy, rather than someone who would merely get by.

Would you rather be Corinne or Bertha ? I am sure that Corinne does not feel fulfilled ("*bien dans sa peau*") and happy in her job whereas Bertha no doubt does. Perhaps it would be best to be somewhere between the two.

Give as good as you get

You must give your listeners exactly the same as you are getting in your earphones. You cannot take it upon yourself to change, improve or correct what the delegate says. So if the Chairman says "It is now four o'clock" and you know it is five o'clock, all you can do is say: "The Chairman says it is four o'clock".

Proverbs and Jokes

Generally speaking, proverbs cannot be translated. You hear "*Les absents ont toujours tort*" but in English the only proverb about absence that springs to mind is "Absence makes the heart grow fonder", which is completely different. "An apple a day keeps the doctor away" in French would probably be: "*Après la soupe un verre de vin remplace une visite chez le médecin.*"

So you see you will need to keep a few useful proverbs up your sleeve "*por si acaso*". The eminent Eric Simha of WHO fame used "*il ne faut pas essayer de tondre un oeuf*" if working into French and he couldn't think of anything else and Pierre Lambert frequently referred to "*la plus belle fille du monde*" (a French saying about the most beautiful girl in the world being able to give no more than she has). Another of his passe-partout proverbs in English was "You can't boil an egg twice!" and "You can't make an omelette with breaking the eggs" ("*Pour faire une omelette il faut bien casser les oeufs*").

What is a good joke in one language may not be at all funny in a different culture and what we find correct may be offensive to others. So be careful. You might also like to keep a joke up your sleeve, in case someone tells a joke you don't understand. It would be a pity for the delegate concerned to lose face because no-one laughs. Better by far for you to tell your own joke so that the delegates listening to you laugh at the right time, thus keeping everyone happy. I have my own little story that I can drag out or keep short and snappy, depending on the time it has to fill, about the man painting the ceiling, perched at the top of a ladder, in a lunatic asylum. Another man comes along and says:"Hold on tight to the paintbrush, I need to borrow the ladder a minute!" Some interpreters have been known to say coldbloodedly into the microphone: "Would you please laugh: the speaker has just told a joke I did not understand." But I find that rather lacking in imagination.

Cocktail Parties and Receptions

If you are invited to social occasions, do not stand in a huddle with your colleagues, do not grab a plateful of food and stand next to the buffet to be in the best position to grab more. Circulate. Introduce yourself to the delegates listening to your booth, ask them if they can hear you satisfactorily. You may even ask them about an expression you have had difficulty with. They will be happy to make your acquaintance and to help you if they can. Seize the opportunity to do a little for Public Relations. Consider yourself an ambassador for the profession and for the colleague who recruited you. With luck, what happened to me once may never happen to you: On the occasion of the election of an Australian delegate to a high-ranking position at an international conference overseas, I was asked to interpret his "thank you" remarks at a celebratory reception. When I took my position on the stage next to the elected official, he announced: "The interpreter will now sing 'Waltzing Matilda' in French and Spanish".

Apart from such situations, coffee breaks, receptions, luncheons and dinners do afford opportunities for improving the image of the profession. However, if you have a question for a delegate, introduce yourself and put your question succinctly. Do not monopolise the delegate's attention as meetings give participants a chance to make useful contacts and deal with business and professional matters; if the interpreters take up too much of their time, they may resent it.

Sometimes speeches are made at conference receptions or dinners. There is no obligation upon the interpreters to interpret these if they have already worked six or seven hours that day. However it is an elegant gesture if they do and works wonders for our public relations. Personally I enjoy rendering speeches of this kind and have rarely refused. (It goes without saying that no extra charge is made.)

Overtime

Free-lance interpreters are hired by the day and are not paid overtime. You cannot provide high quality simultaneous interpretation for more than seven hours in one day. Once you have worked six to seven hours no matter how much extra you might be paid, your work will be sub-standard. If conference organizers require more than seven hours' interpretation on any one day, they need to recruit a second team of interpreters. The problem generally arises towards the end of a conference, when the Chairman realizes how much of the agenda still remains to be dealt with and how little time is left. As the deadline approaches, people start to panic and this is when night meetings are convened.

With a second team of interpreters this can be organized, and the team covering the night meeting is generally free the following morning to recuperate. International conferences do not respect office hours. At some of the larger United Nations conferences, you may be working from 8 a.m. until 9 a.m. and then be free until 3 o'clock in the afternoon, and work until 7 p.m.. It is very difficult to make private arrangements and one's social life has to be left in abeyance until the conference is over because you never know in advance when you will be free and there is no guarantee you will be free in the evenings. So be warned: conference interpreting is not a nine to five job.

Copyright[7]

The interpreter's contract should specify that the interpretation is intended solely for immediate audition in the conference room. Without the prior consent of the interpreters involved, no-one, including conference participants, is entitled to make any tape recording of the interpretation for any other than internal purposes, such as the writing of minutes and reports within the organization.

If recordings are made nevertheless, the interpreters involved may request appropriate remuneration

---

[7] Based on the provisions of international copyright agreements administered by the World Intellectual Property Organisation (WIPO) and UNESCO, containing practical information on the conditions governing the use of recordings made of interpretation at conferences.

for it in accordance with the provisions of international copyright agreements.

It must be remembered that conference interpretation is an oral intellectual exercice, quite distinct from drafting a written text. Any attempt to put the content of recording of conference interpretation into written form, without considerable preliminary editing, can only yield questionable results. Spoken language is never completely transferable into acceptable written form. The interpreter concerned is entitled therefore to listen to the recording of his interpretation and edit it as he thinks fit, with the help of the technician, before the tape is released.

The Universal Declaration of Human Rights (10 December 1948) recognizes in principle the protection of the moral and material rights of authors in relation to their works.

The protection of intellectual and creative works and their use by third parties are subject to national legislation, bilateral agreements and international agreements, in particular the International Copyright Convention and the Berne Convention for the Protection of Artistic and Literary Works. The performance of conference interpreters is thus protected under international law. The Berne Convention provides protection for the interests of authors; translations are protected as original works and translators are protected as authors. When fixed in material form of any nature whatsoever (printed, sound or audiovisual recording, records, discs, magnetic tapes, videograms, slides, films, wire, cable, transparencies, photocopies, microcards or any similar method) the performance of the conference interpreter becomes a translation within the meaning of the Berne Convention; the exclusive rights foreseen in the Convention therefore apply to the author, that is, to the interpreter.

The assignment of copyright must be made in writing. The organizer must therefore apply for permission beforehand, and *no interpreter may be recorded without his knowledge and consent.*

Model contracts to cover the assignment of copyright in connection with recording of conference interpretation have been prepared by the interpreters' professional association specifying the type of use to be made of these recordings; any use not specifically provided for remains the property of the author. An individual contract must be established for each interpreter, i.e. for all interpreters working in the language or languages being recorded including any interpreters acting as relay or pivot. Each contract must be signed by both parties.

Interpretation at press conferences is, however, specifically excluded from these provisions and cannot be charged extra under copyright. Re-broadcasts of interpreted versions of a press conference may - details must be negotiated. Clients often refuse to grant copyright for press conferences because of the ensuing difficulties in the event of resales. Colleagues might therefore prefer to waive their rights but ask for greater remuneration because of the stress involved. The same procedure could be adopted for news bulletins where the World Intellectual Property Organization has stated that "*droits patrimoniaux*"(economic rights) cannot apply.

When approached with the request that another microphone be placed in front of me by radio or television news reporters at conferences in Australia, I have generally considered this a useful publicity exercise and have agreed on condition no more than five minutes' recording was used. This sort of publicity is very precious to us in this country where the public is largely unaware of our profession. It may be possible, also, to obtain that in exchange a reference to the interpreters be given and to their professional accreditation, status, and so on.

However, if you discover at the end of a session as I did once, coming down the main stairs of the Convention Centre in Manila, that copies of the tapes of the session are on sale in all conference languages, and order forms are being handed out - then you must take immediate action to inform those responsible:

- that they should have obtained the interpreters' prior consent;
- that an agreement has to be drawn up and signed immediately; and
- that a percentage of the sales figure from the tapes is due to the interpreters under copyright law.

As mentioned earlier, I have also always insisted on my right to vet any recordings made of my interpretation and to edit them later, as I felt necessary.

Copyright when working for Television

The World Intellectual Property Organization (WIPO) has stated clearly that although it is possible to waive one's "economic rights"(that is, rights to remuneration), one never loses the "moral rights" (that is, the rights to edit, to prohibit publication or to prohibit any changes being made subsequently). This means that colleagues could waive their right to copyright for television whilst using the above ruling to help them obtain, for example, the screening of the name of the interpreter and/or the fact that he is member of a professional association. Newscasts however are not covered by the Berne Convention so are not copyright protected except for repeat broadcasts.

Lunchtime

Go for a walk outside, preferably alone, to give your voice a rest and oxygenate your brain rather than staying in the convention centre in the electric light and air-conditioning.

Dress

Dress to fit in with the meeting, not for effect. You may find yourself having to provide consecutive interpretation at a luncheon or because the equipment breaks down, so do not count on the anonymity and seclusion of the booth.

Compliments

If a delegate compliments you, be loyal to your colleagues and include them in the tribute. Try to cover up for any shortcomings in the team and never criticise colleagues to others.

If someone mentions recruiting you for another meeting there are two ways of handling the situation. If you have been recruited by a colleague (whether a member of the team or not) note down the person's name and address and pass it on to the recruiting colleague. In return, that colleague will almost certainly include you in the team if your language combination and domicile fit. If you were recruited directly by the organization, there is nothing to prevent you organizing a team for a future meeting if asked. When doing so, always refer to the rules regarding team strengths, fees and per diems and ask for advice from a more experienced colleague if necessary. Acquaint yourself with the Guidelines for consultant interpreters published by AIIC and the interpreters' code of ethics. Remember that your team should convey as favourable an image of the profession as that held by the person who asked you to recruit. Do not use mediocre interpreters or make up a team of beginners just because these are easier to get hold of. There should never be more than one beginner in a team, and a beginner should never be pivot.

If you remember all these tips you will soon be The Perfect Imperturbable Simultaneous Interpreter you were pretending to be when you were nervous at the beginning of this Chapter.

11

A WORD IN THE EAR OF THE CONFERENCE ORGANIZER: IS INTERPRETATION REALLY NECESSARY ?

No meeting can truly be called "international" or a "World Congress" unless interpretation is provided. If 50 or 5,000 delegates have paid or been paid to attend a conference they are entitled to understand the proceedings, especially if they have had to travel half way round the world to get here. I wonder how many speakers have addressed symposia and wondered why there were no questions asked afterwards during the question-and-answer time ? Did it cross their minds that it may have been because there was no interpretation and the audience had not understood enough to ask questions ? Lack of interpretation may offend in some cases. De Gaulle said he did not need an interpreter when he went to England, he knew English well enough. Then he upset everyone by "demanding" things he only meant to "ask for".

One conference organizer told me he was thinking of sending out a letter to all countries asking them to send only English-speaking delegates to a forthcoming medical research conference. What he failed to understand is that experts in the highly specialized fields covered by international conferences cannot be expected to speak any language other than their own to do justice to themselves and to their research. The conference organizer concerned attended a medical conference in Madrid shortly afterwards. Not only the welcoming speeches but the whole of the inaugural day of the conference was in Spanish and even the technical part of the session that followed had more Spanish spoken than any other language. The last straw was the closing Press Conference which was almost entirely in Spanish. The delegate concerned reluctantly had to turn to me for consecutive interpretation of the questions into English.

No sensible world leader professes to be a linguist. It would be too embarrassing to be caught out by a word he didn't understand. Quite apart from providing understanding, interpretation also gives status and prestige to the speaker and - a precious advantage in delicate negotiations - consecutive interpretation gives him time to think between statements, time to reconsider what has just been said and to prepare his next statement. At a press conference, for example, even if you understand the other language, you hear the question twice if you use an interpreter. In the old days at United Nations both the Soviet and French delegates always insisted on full interpretation even though we all knew they spoke perfect English at cocktail parties and receptions. It was part of their prestige always to speak through an interpreter as though the interpreter were a shield, enabling them to take a step back from the action.

The provision of interpretation considerably increases attendance at international conferences which means greater receipts, i.e. the cost-benefit analysis is more favourable. In large congresses the cost of interpretation as a percentage of total expenditure is comparatively low. When delegates are free to express themselves in their own language - even people who seem quite fluent in their second language - the full significance of what they say is much more apparent, and their enthusiasm can communicate itself much more effectively. There is no doubt that participants are much happier when they can use their own language and the conference is a greater success.

Interpretation also puts order into a discussion, preventing several people from trying to speak at once or cutting in. It generally means that speakers are clearer, more succinct and prepare beforehand what they are going to say rather than "thinking aloud." It therefore has the effect of shortening meetings and making them more constructive, less impulsive. In fact, interpretation seems to be to everyone's advantage.

It is a good idea first to decide which are the countries most likely to contribute to the scientific or political input of the meeting - in other words, which languages are they likely to speak ? Secondly, which are the countries who have the most to learn from the conference? (That is, which languages do they understand ?) The answer to these two questions should determine the interpretation requirements of the meeting.

If the meeting is to be held in an area which is attractive for reasons of economy, but which has very few meetings in the course of a year, it is possible that there will not be enough professional conference interpreters available locally for the simple reason that they would not be able to earn a living. This would, therefore, mean flying in interpreters for the meeting. The cost involved is absorbed by extra registration fees. It is essential to ensure that in all the preliminary publicity mention is made of the languages in which speakers will present their papers and those into which interpretation will be available. Naturally, the preliminary brochures will have to appear in all the languages foreseen for the conference. Once a budget has been established, it will be obvious that the amount involved, although high, is low in proportion to the total budget figure on which the registration fee is based.

If you think free-lance conference interpreters and translators are highly paid, you should remember that they do not work 365 days a year or even 250. The average number of days worked per year in Australia is about

50 whereas in Europe the norm is closer to 150, which is quite a strain when you are starting out on a different subject every few days. Also, the time spent on preparing for a conference is unpaid (except for briefing sessions which are the exception rather than the rule.)

It often happens that interpreters spend more time studying for a conference beforehand than they do actually working under contract. I have spent more than three weeks preparing for a difficult technical or medical five-day meeting and that is no exception. Furthermore, free-lance interpreters have no superannuation unless they make their own arrangements and pay for it out of their earnings, nor are they entitled to sick leave. They are also expected to travel frequently at their own expense to the countries where their languages are spoken in order to keep their languages up to date. The unpredictable free-lance lifestyle while pleasant does give rise to extra expenditure due to the constant travel and absence from home such as upkeep of home and garden, child-care, and so on.

Moreover, it is to everyone's advantage that world standards prevail both regarding quality of performance and hence fee structure to enable the free circulation of interpreters referred to in Chapter 3.

Using the other party's interpreter

There are many pitfalls when Australian government officials, ministers and businessmen travelling overseas use interpreters and translators in the service of another government. The question of loyalty arises - the interpreter's loyalty is bound to be to those employing him. The fact that most Australian delegates are mono-lingual means that they have no idea whether they are being given the full picture; they are at the mercy of the other side, which can hardly strengthen their position, especially in the case of sharp business deals. In political situations, they may even be given a biased version of an event or situation. Everyone, even interpreters, have their own agenda - some rise above it if they are professionals, others do not.

A case in point was raised on the Australian broadcast news at the time of writing. The Dalai Lama requested the Australian Deputy Prime Minister to return to Tibet but not to use an official Chinese interpreter, that is to say provided by the Chinese Government, this time as he did on his previous visit. What the Dalai Lama is saying is that the Australian Deputy Prime Minister, in order to get an impartial picture or both sides of the story, should take his own Australian Chinese interpreter with him.

Some years ago at a high-level Ministerial meeting in Canberra, a pale nervous lady sitting next to the Prime Minister kept fidgeting with the papers in front of her and dropping her pencil on the floor. I had been recruited by the Quai d'Orsay to work for the visiting French Prime Minister. During the coffee-break she came over to express her admiration for what we were doing and ask if we would continue. When I asked what her role was, she confessed she was the interpreter for the Australian Prime Minister, but she had been told only at 4 o'clock the previous afternoon so had had little time to prepare. "In any case", she said,"I couldn't do what you do. I was told to come here because I have just come home from a two-year posting in Paris. I can ask my way in the street or order in a restaurant but I could never hope to understand the finer shades of meaning in a diplomatic discussion or trade negotiations when the speakers are eloquent, educated people." In other words, in Parliament House in Canberra both sides were dependent on the interpretation provided by the visiting statesman. Let us hope things have changed since those days. Interpretation is a highly specialized skill quite apart from knowledge of languages. We must not forget, too, that there are different levels of understanding of a foreign language.

Loyalty, Allegiance and Trust

A conference interpreter recruited by the United Nations or one of its Specialized Agencies is in fact recruited (and paid) by all the members of United Nations, and thus owes loyalty and allegiance to all the countries (delegates) participating in the conference. He must not favour any party or speaker, must keep his counsel, remaining impartial and neutral. Like all employees of the United Nations, he must not accept instructions from any one country or act in the interests of any one country in the carrying out of his duties because he is custodian of an international public trust.

During bilateral trade or diplomatic negotiations the situation is rather different. You are hiring the interpreter and therefore he, while respecting the international interpreters' code of ethics and professional behaviour, owes allegiance to you and will ensure complete communication, thus putting all chances on your side. If the interpreters you have hired are competent professionals, you will be given a full understanding not only of the words spoken, but also of the asides and any behaviour which might otherwise perplex you due to cultural differences. A competent interpreter will also convey to you any underlying meanings that may not be apparent at first sight. Body language and gestures are important too and vary in different cultures. For example, if you are negotiating with a Spanish delegate and he points with one finger to his eye, do you know what that means? If the delegate you are with is French, and he does the same thing, it means something completely different - do you know what that gesture means in France ? Your own interpreter will explain these things to you but you can hardly expect the other side's interpreter to do that. Why should they? Their loyalty is not to you. (In France this gesture means 'I don't believe what you are saying' or 'My eye and Betty Martin!' whereas in Spain it stands for '¡Hay que ver! i.e. 'this needs looking into!'

Another thing to remember is that a professional interpreter is bound by a strict Code of Ethics which guarantees confidentiality.

Hiring interpreters in good time

The most experienced professionals are engaged way ahead of time - in some cases three, four or even five years ahead. If you want the best professional interpreters available it is a good idea to contract them well in advance. According to statistics, the busiest times of the year are February, March and April and September, October and November.

Bad use of interpreters

Sometimes interpretation is provided and not used. I have worked at meetings where the French booth worked hard all day but no-one was listening to them because the French delegation preferred to listen to the original in English. The interpretation was used only when they spoke in French. It is a good idea to find out before the conference what the actual needs of the various delegations are, and discuss these with the consultant- or chief-interpreter.

Sometimes interpretation is provided and not used properly. Recently a group of wealthy French businessmen came to this country to study investment possibilities. Interpreters were recruited once again by the French side but not by the Australian and told to provide consecutive interpretation. The Australian delegates told us not to bother, they all "understood French" (their self-esteem would not allow them to own up to not understanding French). The French, who felt it more courteous to use the language of their hosts, said they did not need us because they all "spoke English". They did, with heavy French accents (businessmen are not linguists) that made them largely incomprehensible to the Australians, although their English was no doubt far superior to the Australians' knowledge of French. The interpreters sat in silence, everyone was very polite. The Frenchmen had no idea what the questions were about because the Australian accent is almost impossible for them to understand. During the coffee-break following each useless session various delegates would sidle up to the interpreters and ask what had been said. It was not easy to remember. Large sums of money were being spent on fares, hotel accommodation, meals and so on and time spent away from work, but most of this expenditure was wasted because no message was getting through.

So you have decided to hire interpreters?

We, the interpreters, share a common interest with you, the conference organizers, in wanting to provide our customers with a high level interpretation service. The interpreters you recruit may well be your client's main point of contact with your company. Remember that interpreters are business travellers too, working for one conference after another, and that they should be provided with the same standards as you would wish for yourself regarding seats on aircraft, hotel accommodation, restaurants, etc. While you have breaks in between asking questions and receiving answers, or during interventions that do not concern you, the interpreter must concentrate intensely all the time, and keep this up for a number of hours. Whereas your tension ends with the end of the meeting, the interpreter is probably going on to another assignment with similar stress and strain.

The best procedure is to enlist the assistance of an experienced professional to act as your consultant interpreter, who will need information about the conference subject, languages, number of meeting rooms and concurrent sessions, draft programme and schedule of sessions, interpretation facilities available and conference venue before being able to give an estimate of the cost. The consultant interpreter will then :

- sign a master contract with the organizer, stipulating the rights and duties of both parties;
- select the team of interpreters best suited to the conference requirements and avoiding the use of relay insofar as possible, starting with local conference interpreters available and only if none is available with the required language combination bringing in interpreters from the Region. If there are still certain language combinations required which are not available locally or in the Region, then interpreters may have to be brought from overseas;
- prepare a letter of appointment or contract for each interpreter to be signed by the conference organizer;
- ensure proper working arrangements for the interpreters
  during the conference; and
- serve as a link between the interpreters and the organizer.

The functions of interpreters do not include the written translation of texts.

The languages used at United Nations conferences are English, French, Spanish, Russian, Chinese and Arabic. The languages used at most international conferences held in Australia are English, French, Spanish and Japanese; on rare occasions, Russian, Chinese, German and Italian.

Choice of mode of interpretation

Because a number of critical choices have to be made (Keiser 1975) regarding the type of interpretation and the interaction of the languages it is important that the providers of the interpretation service be given adequate information regarding the meeting. The consultant recruiting the interpreters needs not only factual information, that is, details regarding the timetable, subject matter, conference languages, conference style (free discussion or formal programme with speakers), recording requirements but also less tangible information about the aims and objectives of the parties involved, the purpose and status of the meeting, the general background as well as the language distribution of the participants. The consultant recruiting the team of interpreters will work closely with you to ensure that the interpretation makes a positive contribution to the success of your conference.

As to the mode of interpretation chosen, each corresponds to a specific set of requirements(Keiser 1975). For example:

Consecutive interpretation

- Suitable for meetings conducted in not more than two languages.
- Delegates have more time to collect their thoughts and prepare their reply.
- Speakers tend to be more concise.
- The Chairman has better control over the discussions.
- May not require any special technical facilities if the venue is not noisy.

Contrary to what is generally thought, this method does not double the length of the meeting because speakers are more concise and interpreters generally give their rendering in less time than that used by the speaker. It also enables delegates to ask for something to be repeated if they have not understood, whereas in simultaneous mode a misunderstanding may go round in circles and take much longer to clarify.

Consecutive interpretation is therefore particularly suitable for work in small committees, discussion groups, detailed negotiations, drafting/editorial committees and question-and-answer sessions of the press conference type.

A combination of "whispering" and consecutive is often used where there are only one or two delegates speaking a different language from the rest. In this case one of the two interpreters sits between the two delegates and whispers simultaneously, while the other sits on a chair behind. Every half-hour they change over. When the delegate speaks, his intervention is interpreted into the language of the meeting in consecutive mode.

Interpreters should be seated as close as possible to the chairman, have a full view of the participants and be able to hear them clearly. They should be provided with facilities for taking notes. If the room is darkened for slide projection, small table lamps should be provided for the interpreters.

It should not be forgotten that the interpreter works as a mediator between human beings and not as an anonymous cogwheel in an inhuman clockwork which is how it tends to be in the case of simultaneous interpretation. Thus, the most rewarding activity for the interpreter - and it is quite rare today - is consecutive interpretation because he is then physically present with the speakers and can gauge directly how successfully he has performed his highly skilled work. The physical isolation, the banishment into gloomy oblivion behind smoked glass, imposed by modern interpreting facilities, robs him of human contact and joy in his achievements. Not surprisingly, those interpreters who work on satellite conferences from the "other" end have particularly commented on their alienation and the lack of incentive in this type of conference. It is probably that the delegates feel the same way. The ultimate appeal of any convention or meeting has always been the human contact, the group experience, the opportunity to talk to other people face to face and to learn from them. This is a simple human need.

Simultaneous interpretation

Best for meetings with more than two languages, or meetings where lengthy papers or speeches are being given. However, delegates are prone to speak more often, forgetting they are being interpreted. Simultaneous is not efficient for the drafting of texts. It requires a larger number of interpreters and special soundproof booths and sound equipment, as well as the presence of a sound technician. With simultaneous interpretation, stricter enforcement of rules of procedure by the Chairman is necessary.

Let us assume that all this has been done and that you have recruited the best team of interpreters available. In order to make the best possible use of them and ensure that everyone is satisfied and the conference a success, here are a few points to bear in mind.

Qualifications and experience of interpreters

Some people believe that if you are bilingual you can interpret, which is about as true as saying that if you have two hands you can automatically be a concert pianist. The most expensive meetings are those ruined by bad interpretation. It is unwise to try to economise by using "cheap" interpretation, i.e. non-professionals - it is probably better to have no interpretation at all rather than mediocre interpretation because delegates trust what the interpreter says even if it is wrong and the discussion may be led astray; misunderstandings may persist long after the meeting is over. In some cases such misunderstandings have been known to result in the cooling of diplomatic relations between countries. In others, they have proved extremely costly in terms of money and the effectiveness of the conference as well as goodwill towards the country concerned. As Confucius said: "If language is not in accordance with the truth of things, affairs cannot be carried on to success".

If you use professional, qualified interpreters you can expect accuracy, reliability and quality of performance. The interpretation service is always "made to measure" to suit the requirements of each meeting. As with all aspects of the conference business, success on the day depends on careful preparation and good coordination. It is therefore important to hire experienced interpreters with appropriate qualifications such as full membership of their international professional association and/or NAATI accreditation as a Senior Conference Interpreter (former Level 5). Conference Interpreters accredited at Level 4 are beginners and do not have sufficient experience; to achieve the best results, therefore, there should not be more than one Level 4 interpreter in the team, the remainder all being accredited at Level 5.

Some interpreters have extra responsibilities. The English booth is generally in direct contact with both Chairman and Secretary of a meeting and must be mindful of any problems their colleagues in other booths may encounter. Also it frequently happens that 90% of the audience is listening to the English booth, as well as minute-writers and in an English-speaking country like Australia also press reporters. Pivots also have a special responsibility *vis-à-vis* their colleagues who are in fact most vulnerable "users". As Sergio Viaggio, Chief Interpreter at the United Nations Office in Vienna, stressed at the Melbourne FIT[8] Congress, " a pivot who does not interpret with those who must relay from him primarily in mind is wanting both as an interpreter and as a colleague."

Delegates who understand more than one language may say that the interpretation is better than the original; in fact, this should be so because a professional interpretation should have no repetitions, no hesitations, no mistakes and no self-corrections.

As explained in Chapter 10, no recording or broadcasting of the interpretation may be done without prior authorization of the interpreters involved; royalties in respect of copyright will need to be negotiated.

Scientific, Technical and Medical Meetings

To interpret at scientific meetings is a difficult task because of the constraints and stresses which are added to those of normal conference work. Impromptu

---

8 Fédération Internationale des Traducteurs, XIVth Congres held in Melbourne, February 1996

speech is easy to understand and to interpret. A speech written in advance and read aloud, designed to be understood not by laymen such as interpreters but by the experts to whom it is directed, is quite different (Déjean Le Féal 1982). The speaker is not thinking aloud when he reads, his delivery is faster than normal speech, the tone produced by reading is monotonous and more difficult to empathize with and there are no repetitions or redundancies.

Speakers tend to read exceptionally fast under the stress of addressing a public gathering and also because of constraints imposed by the limited time at their disposal due to the large number of communications or papers on the programme (see Chapter 10, section entitled "Texts of speeches given to you beforehand") so that frequently they are not even understood by the delegates speaking the same language. And all this often in a new field of scientific research where terminology barely exists in some of the languages. In meetings of this type, two interpreters per booth are indispensable because of the team work required. They help each other find documents, look for passages quoted from the text, and may even go out to look for missing texts. If a speaker is racing along at high speed reading an esoteric technical paper, the interpreter may need to draw breath at the end and take a few minutes to recover: in this case his colleague will take over even if it is not time for him to do so according to the half-hour schedule. There is only one way that simultaneous interpreters can cope with high-speed technical, scientific or medical papers and that is by having read the texts beforehand and prepared them. Even then, it is important that all participants in the communication chain be made aware of the interpretation problem, from the chairman of the meeting to the secretary, the delegate and the operator of the simultaneous interpretation equipment. It may be necessary for the Chairman to make an announcement to the effect that speakers should preferably summarize their papers rather than reading them out at high speed.

It is also helpful if the programme of a meeting is scheduled in such a way as to avoid overloading it with papers. The speaking time allotted to each speaker should be defined beforehand by the number of pages that can be read at normal speed within this time slot. The reading speed should not exceed 100 words per minute, that is, three minutes per double-spaced typewritten page. Speakers should be given the assurance that the parts of their paper they do not have time to read together with supporting documentation will be published and available to all delegates or form part of the Proceedings of the meeting. The Chairman should be prepared to intervene to ask speakers to slow down if necessary (when requested to do so by the interpreters' teamleader). However, speakers who speak too slowly are as difficult to interpret as those who speak too fast because the output is disjointed and, depending on the language, the interpreter may have to wait for the second segment before he can interpret the first.

If films, slides or transparencies are to be shown and require interpretation, the screen must be clearly visible from the booths and the interpreters need to be given a script or copy of the texts to be projected in advance. The narration is generally faster and more compacted than normal speech delivery.

If your conference deals with highly technical matters, it is advisable to ask your consultant interpreter to recruit professional interpreters specializing in that subject.

Documentation

Interpreters have a wide range of knowledge but cannot be experts in all subjects. In order to familiarize themselves with the topic of your conference, they need the conference papers in all languages well in advance.

They will study these documents and prepare their own glossaries. This will help them gain a better idea of the subject under discussion and understand your speakers better, especially those who have difficult accents or speak very fast.

Many international organizations, specialized agencies of United Nations, now send their documents to delegates, translators and interpreters overseas by means of the Internet, saving themselves the trouble of photo-copying and going to the post office as well as saving a lot of time since this may take a matter of seconds rather than the time it would otherwise take for documents to be posted from Europe to Australia or New Zealand, for example. With this method, the interpreters can download the texts themselves and print out only the parts they need. The minimal cost of sending documents via the Internet is also a consideration.

As well as the agenda and written speeches, interpreters need minutes of previous meetings on the same subject, background information on the organization or association, some information about key speakers and their titles, and the names of the officers of the organization.

Conference secretaries must ensure that interpreters have a complete set of documents in all languages and rush to them any working documents distributed in the course of the meeting. There is nothing more frustrating for the qualified professional interpreter than to see his efforts thwarted and the delegates dissatisfied because he was not able to do his job properly through lack of preparation of texts (Keiser 1975).

Tips for speakers

If you have a written text or notes for your speech, whether or not you intend following them closely, please hand them to the conference secretariat for distribution to the interpreters to enable them to familiarize themselves with the subject and terminology. You are free to depart from your text or add to it as you go along. Professional interpreters are bound by secrecy and the content of your document will remain confidential at all times. Your text will be returned to you upon request.

Before starting to speak, to ensure that your microphone is switched on, say a few words such as "Good morning" or "Thank you Mr. Chairman" rather than blowing on to it or knocking it, which will be amplified in the interpreters' headphones and cause a loud unpleasant noise. Please do not speak too close to the microphone (this creates interference) and avoid leaving your receiver set close to the microphone when speaking to prevent feed-back whistling.

If you need to move away from your seat to point at a slide or transparency projection, make sure you have a neck or lapel microphone because otherwise the interpreters will not hear you, however loudly you speak, and you will not be interpreted. Similarly, if you are speaking from the rostrum or a lectern and want to reply to questions from the floor, make sure you have a receiver set with you to follow the questions as they are interpreted.

When presenting your paper please speak into the microphone and do not just read but rather deliver it in an oral style at normal speaking speed. Speak very clearly especially when quoting figures, dates, names of places and people and formulae.

What not to do

I have heard conference organizers say simultaneous interpretation was useless. Discreet enquiries among professional interpreters present at the congress concerned revealed that 2000 doctors had come to listen to a few experts working in a fast-developing and highly specialized branch of medicine. Thirty scheduled speakers had been fitted into three four-hour meetings. They had been told in advance that they would be given thirty minutes each. However, the first two speakers on the first morning took the time of four so the following speakers were asked to cut their presentations down to 15 minutes. At the following meeting, the time allotted per speaker was further cut to ten minutes. The result was that speakers tried to read fast enough to present the whole thirty-minute paper in ten minutes. They were not even understood by delegates who spoke the same language! Others skipped paragraphs so that, even if the interpreters had a copy of the speech, it was impossible to follow. And all this in a new field of research where terminology barely existed in some of the languages. The interpretation may have been poor but the miracle is that there was any interpretation at all.

Booths and equipment

The success of a multilingual conference largely depends on good interpretation, and this is only possible provided the technical facilities are satisfactory and the technicians competent. No simultaneous interpreter can provide a professional standard of interpretation unless he is receiving good sound and the equipment and working conditions respect minimum professional standards. The equipment is provided separately from the recruitment of the interpreters because two distinct specialist activities are involved. However, the equipment supplier and the coordinating interpreter or consultant recruiting the interpreters will usually be in contact at all stages of the conference.

Each delegate should have a headset with channel selector and volume control. The conference secretary, sound engineer and chief interpreter should decide on the best microphone layout for the meeting. Provision should also be made to ensure that not more than one microphone is on at a time, as dual transmission interferes with reception.

Your equipment supplier should provide the whole system including microphones, amplifiers and headsets, in order to avoid technical hitches. (The hotel microphone and amplifier or PA system may not be compatible with the simultaneous equipment.) To enable speakers to move away from the rostrum, a roving lapel or neck microphone should also be provided, as mentioned on page 178.

Australia is a member of the International Standards Organization (ISO)[9] so the international standards approved by them apply in this country and all interpretation booths, whether built-in or portable, should be in conformity with ISO[10] standard No. 2603 for built-in booths and ISO 4043 for portable booths standards (1998-11-15, available on the AIIC website, from AIIC Secretariat or from the headquarters of ISO in Geneva. They should have a height of 230 cms., a depth of 240 cms., and a width of 250 cms.(measured at table level), with a window over the full width. The working surface should have sufficient legroom and a minimum width of 50 cms., providing enough space for equipment and documents. Generally speaking the booths should be roomy and comfortable, sound-proof and adequately ventilated with a fresh air inlet and an exhaust fan, both of which should be silenced. The resulting carbon dioxide concentration in the booth, when in use, should not be more than 0.10% as sustained mental effort is hampered at higher concentrations. From the booths, the interpreters must have a full view of the chairman, speakers and screens or blackboards. In addition to volume control, tone control is also necessary to enable the interpreter to strike the right balance between treble and bass and set the volume lower, thereby protecting his hearing. Each interpreter should have a separate headset, incoming channel selector and volume and tone control. A light should indicate when the booth's microphone is on. If

---

[9]International Standards Organization, Varembé, Geneva, Switzerland (also offices in Sydney, from which copies of standards may be obtained)

more than one language is to be spoken from a single booth , an output channel selector is necessary. Adequate lighting without glare in the form of small reading lamps should also be provided.

It should always be technically possible to work both ways from one booth, whatever arrangements may have been made, to cover unforeseen problems.

The booths should have appropriate lighting and ventilation (fan) but these should not be heard in interpreters' earphones or feed back into microphones. There should be enough space for interpreters to spread their documents out in front of them (often in the case of drafting three language-versions are required), and if possible a shelf above the window for the Basic Texts of the organization which may occasionally need to be consulted, such as Constitution, Voting procedures, Rules of procedure and any other reference books.

There should be a door (easy to open and noiseless) or heavy curtain at the entrance of each booth to ensure that they are soundproof. A carpeted floor is preferable. A large window at the front and sides of each booth is necessary to ensure maximum visibility of the room, and to ensure that interpreters can see their colleagues in other booths.

Details of wired, wireless, infra-red etc. systems, as well as humidity and temperature measurements in booths ("comfort index"), may be obtained by writing to the Technical Committee of AIIC.

Each interpreter should be provided with a comfortable chair with a good backrest (preferably on wheels), a notepad and pencil, and a glass or bottle of fresh water at the beginning of each meeting.

Except for the technicians, the interpreters' booths should not be accessible to the public or anyone else.

Sound

There is no doubt that the quality of the sound transmission is the most vital factor for the interpreter; he needs a far higher than usual sound level since he must listen and speak simultaneously.

Earphones must be light-weight and provide sound in both ears, that is, not stereo. They must be mono headphones and never have thick padding on them. *Under no circumstances should interpreters ever hear their own voice in their earphones.*

Each interpreter must have his own volume control switch. It is impossible to work correctly without this. Interpreters should also be able to control tone settings for their own headsets. There should be a cough button so that the interpreters do not need to switch off their mikes which causes a break in the sound heard by the audience, especially as there is generally a difference in volume when the floor is heard as compared to the interpretation.

Electrical equipment must be in conformity with IEC[11] Standard No. 914 entitled: "Conference systems: Electrical and Audio Requirements" or IEC 764 (FM transmission) for infrared interpretation systems. (These numbers may change when the standards are revised from time to time).

International simultaneous interpreting contracts specify that the interpreters on the spot are the sole judges as to whether the equipment is functioning adequately to permit interpreting to a proper standard. If in their judgement it is not, they are not bound to provide simultaneous interpretation during the entire period of malfunction.

In the case of videos being shown with a sound track (that is, commentary), a separate channel must be

---

[11] International Electrotechnical Committee, Varembé, Geneva, Switzerland (also offices in Sydney from which copies of standards may be obtained).

provided for the sound from the projector to the interpreters' earphones. It is impossible for them to understand and interpret using the public address system in the hall. As Dr. H. Kolmer says:

> *If the commentary is spoken faster than normal speech and especially if it is on a specialized subject, the interpreters need to be given a copy of the text beforehand to prepare, or to be given at least one showing of the video beforehand so that they know what to expect.*

> *In the case of complex audiovisual performances requiring a rehearsal in order to coordinate the performers, the technical equipment and the interpretation, the interpreters must be included in the rehearsal (and, unless the rehearsals are held on the same day as the performance, also paid for that extra day). In such shows, everything must run like clockwork, with strict synchronism, which means that the interpreters should be consulted to ensure that their various translations produce texts of roughly equal length.*

Visibility from the booths

It is generally accepted that communication is based 7% on the meaning of words, 38% on intonation, and 55% on visual cues.

It is therefore essential that the interpreters have a clear view of the meeting room and can see the speakers, especially the Chairman. Simultaneous interpretation cannot be performed well unless the interpreter can see the speakers, their facial expressions, body language, when they are about to speak and any gestures they may make. All this helps them to enter the speaker's train of thought. The use of television screens as a substitute for a direct view of the speaker and the conference room is not acceptable in a conference environment. In very large halls, however, tv sets as an additional aide may be useful, especially with a camera giving close-ups of speakers, and of graphs or figures projected on a screen (which must also be directly visible from the booths).

There must also be visibility between booths so that interpreters can communicate with each other (by sign language!), and also be aware of any difficult situation or problem taking place in the colleagues' booth.

The technician

Close coordination is necessary between the operators of the simultaneous interpretation equipment (as they will be connecting and disconnecting speakers' microphones) and the interpreters and chairman - strict enforcement of rules of procedure, for example, regarding priorities as to who has the right to speak first, is of paramount importance. Before the first meeting begins, the consultant interpreter or chief interpreter (team-leader) and the chief technician generally check that the equipment is working properly.

The interpreters also rely on the intervention of the operator of the equipment when the audiosystem becomes destabilized by acoustic feedback causing loud screeches in the earphones and damage to the interpreters' hearing if they have the volume turned up high. Also, within the auditorium, the placement and mounting of microphones should be such that they cannot be knocked over inadvertently, causing great distress to interpreters wearing earphones adjusted to picking up the sometimes faint voices of speakers. Similarly, the wiring should be covered and secured in such a way that normal access to and from the delegates' positions does not disturb it.

Within the auditorium, the use of a public-address system for a particular language (such as English, in Australia) is highly undesirable; it is unfair to those listening to other languages who find it most distracting. If any channel is to be broadcast over the P.A. system it should be the floor channel. In an ideal situation in a carpeted room with a well-arranged system the general noise level in the meeting room is very low - in fact since all delegates are wearing headphones anyone coming into the room would find silence. In Australia, delegates from this country tend not to wear earphones until someone speaks in a language other than English . Then there is general panic to grab earphones and put them on, frantically find the right channel etc. with the result that the first sentence or two of the intervention is not heard.

Conference venue

It is essential to choose a suitably designed conference venue equipped with properly maintained installations or to hire mobile equipment from a reliable supplier. You should also check that the required number of booths, as described in this Chapter, are available. Your consultant interpreter will help you ensure that the facilities are adequate. Professional conference interpreters generally carry check lists to enable them to ensure, in case of doubt, that the facilities comply with the international ISO standards.

Australia has modern convention centres in Adelaide, Sydney, Canberra, Melbourne, Brisbane and Cairns. The Sydney Olympics in 2000 boosted the fairly new conference industry in this country as Australia became "the flavour of the month". World-wide the conference industry is thought to be worth more than $US100 billion, and according to the Amsterdam-based International Congress & Convention Association, Australia's share of the international conference market now ranks it tenth in the world behind the U.S., U.K., France, Japan, Germany, The Netherlands, Canada, Italy and Austria. In 1994 the Association of Australian Convention Bureaux said the conference (domestic and international) industry's annual value in this country was somewhere between $1.8 and $2.2 billion although some believe this figure to be excessively conservative and the Melbourne Convention and Tourism Authority claimed the figure was closer to $3 billion while the Sydney Convention and Visitors Bureau said almost $1 for NSW alone. The new Brisbane Convention Centre hosted some 45,000 delegates in its first year of operation and having secured 51 international conventions up to the year 2003, injected about $375 million into the local economy. The centre's flexibility (it can be configured as one 24,000 square metre, pillarless space) as well as its communications system, enabling clients to interface computers, telephones and faxes directly with their own offices, make it a most attractive proposition. In 1999 it hosted the XIIIth World Congress of the Deaf with some 5000 delegates.

Architects continue to design conference centres with windowless meeting rooms for some reason best known to themselves. I think these architects should be condemned to work eight hours a day in a windowless room for a given period of time; this might change their minds. A boring technical meeting on a subject in which you have no interest whatsoever becomes torture in a windowless room. I could never understand what architects have against real daylight. My favourite meeting rooms are in the ILO building in Geneva. I look forward to working there because from the interpretation booths, through the large windows, we have a view of green grass and trees and a brown horse contemplating life with serenity.

"Classroom seating" is the preferred arrangement, i.e. delegates are seated at tables where they can consult their documents, take notes and place their laptops. This system also enables them to get up and walk along to consult with a colleague if necessary. Cinema-type seating is not generally acceptable. At large conferences, such as the one which took place in Sydney Town Hall in 1999, where there were 1,200 or more delegates, some delegations consisted of over two dozen people. In this case, the leader of each delegation and one or two other delegates were seated at the table, the remaining members of the delegation being seated on chairs behind them for easy consultation.

Photocopier

It is advisable to have a photocopying machine handy to enable texts of speeches from delegates to be photocopied rapidly - if possible close to the booths to avoid having to run upstairs and down corridors to reach the conference secretariat.

Interpreters' room

If possible, especially in the case of a large team of interpreters and conferences with written texts to be read out which the interpreters need to prepare beforehand, a room should be made available or an area where the interpreters may study the conference papers when they are not working in the booth, and where messages may be left for them. It is also useful for delegates to know where they can find the interpreters to hand in written speeches before meetings and sometimes explain their slides or papers to them beforehand. The interpreters' room should be as close as possible to the booths.

Using interpreters on TV

Interpreters should be provided with background information such as a press file, interviewees' latest books, records or whatever and a brief CV if possible a few days before the interview. If this is not possible, the interpreter should be given an opportunity to ask questions before the show either of the guest's impressario, manager or even from the guest himself while he is being made up. It is also useful for the interpreter to hear the guest's voice and accent beforehand. If the anchorman has a written set of questions, a copy should be given to the interpreter.

In addition to the provisions above under "Booths and equipment","Visibility from the booth" and "Sound", the following points need to be borne in mind.

During interviews only the microphones of the interview partners must be switched to the interpreter, for example, the talkmaster's and the interviewee's, but no additional microphones.

The reproduction volume over the P.A. system needs to be adjusted as low as possible in order to prevent the interpreter hearing himself too loudly so that he cannot concentrate on the conversation he has to translate. The interpreter needs a direct connection to the sound control room and the outside broadcast van so that he may speak directly with the sound control engineer and other participants at all times. In other words, interpreters must be able to contact technicians through an interphone system which does not interfere with the broadcast.

Interpreters should be able to see the set and all the people on it. If this is not possible for technical reasons, interpreters must be provided with 2 large colour TV monitors, one showing what the viewers are seeing at home and one showing the rest of the set (this is necessary if only to know when the foreign guest is on the set and when he or she has left).

The interpreters' booth or booths must be soundproof and must not be "live", that is, it should be possible to switch off all mikes so that interpreters may communicate with each other, if necessary, without being heard by the people on the set or even worse by the TV audience. Should several interpreters be used, several booths may be necessary depending on the languages and interview partners (for example, male/female voices). A fast and spontaneous dialogue between persons who may even continuously interrupt each other (interview situation) can only be translated in the best possible way if there are two interpreters, each with his own microphone. Interpreters must all be able to see one another to coordinate their work in a dialogue situation. A relay button is also useful to enable the interpreters to hear one another if they wish to ensure they are using the same terminology as their colleagues, for example. A "cough button" is essential - nothing is more unpleasant for the listener than to hear the interpreter blowing his noise or clearing his throat into the microphone (it happens to us all) . While interpretation into one language by one interpreter should not last longer than thirty minutes if it is to be well done, a lot depends on the individual situation and even a one-hour speech, for which hopefully the text is available beforehand, is better translated by only one interpreter on television because a sudden change of speaker's voice is disconcerting to the listener.

Earphones and microphones as well as those of guests and anchor persons must always be tested before the programme by the interpreters themselves and, if the guests have not arrived, by technicians seated in guests' future positions and using their earphones. It is preferable to have a trial run with the actual guests, if only to ascertain that they understand the language they will be hearing and know how to use the equipment (it is often the first time they encounter simultaneous interpretation).

New Technologies

Tele-conference : any form of communication between two or several participants in two or several different places and relying on the transmission of one or several audio signals between those places.

Video-conference: a tele-conference comprising one or several video signals which convey the images of some or all the participants.

Multi-lingual video-conference: a video-conference in two or several languages with interpretation (consecutive or simultaneous).

Tele-interpreting: interpretation of a multilingual video-conference by interpreters who have a direct view of neither the speaker nor their audience.

When doing a "spacebridge" or duplex transmission, testing is of paramount importance. The people at the other end will usually be hooked up by a satellite connection and this must be checked. It is also of paramount importance that the PA systems at the other end do not cover the sound or do not send back the interpreters' own voice, as is often the case in these situations. This makes interpretation technically impossible. The "other end" may be a third world country with poor installations and untrained technicians : all this must be checked by the network well in advance.

In the case of pseudo-live or pre-recorded programmes, it is advisable before the programme to check that questions and answers have been synchronized properly. If there are inserted visual sequences such as film-clips, etc. the technicians must ensure that the interpretation has finished before it is covered over by the sound track of the insert. A continuity script or log of the programme is important; in cases of pre-recorded programmes with inserts this is even more important.

Under the terms of the Universal Convention on Copyright and the Berne Convention for the Protection of literary or artistic works, interpreters' names and professional affiliation must be mentioned in the credits, either flashed on the screen during the actual interpretation or at the end with the other credits.

In the case of television, as in that of international conferences, booths whether built-in or portable should always be in conformity with ISO standards, that is, ISO 2603 for built-in booths and ISO 4043 for portable booths. Electrical equipment should conform to IEC standard No. 914 on electrical and audio requirements for conference systems.

Videoconferences[12]

---

[12] "Visioconférence" in French. "Teleconferencing" is used for conferences taking place by telephone.

The first remote conference interpreting tests carried out by the United Nations via satellite between New York and Vienna took place at 10 a.m. (Vienna time) on 9 August 1982 and although everything went relatively well technically, the main problem for the interpreters in New York was that it was 4 o'clock in the morning. Since then, UN has carried out experiments with links between New York and Buenos Aires and others, and will continue in the hope of improving present-day techniques.

At the present time, the Council of Ministers and the Council of the European Commission are working on videoconferencing networks between all European capitals and have a programme (INSIS) to study the development of long-distance computer networking in Europe.

According to the IEC Standard for conference audio systems the frequency response must range from 124 Hz to 12.5 kHz. The ISDN (Integrated Services Digital Network) Videoconference Teleservice network provides a bandwidth between 4 kHz and 7 kHz at the very best, which means technically it is unsuitable for simultaneous interpretation(Bros-Brann 1996). This conclusion was also drawn by the European Telecommunications Standards Institute (ETSI) after an experiment carried out with the cooperation of the Technical Committee of AIIC in 1992. The experimental conditions included sound of 7 kHz with a bit rate of 384 and 3.1 kHz with a bit rate of 128, representing the upper and lower end of ISDN sound quality. Even the better ISDN sound quality is therefore much lower than the 12.5 kHz stipulated for interpretation equipment in the ISO and IEC Standards. ETSI concluded:

> ... we now know that the lower levels of video and audio bandwidth do not support simultaneous interpretation, leaving open for further study the possibilities for the higher level, especially with further improvements in codec (i.e. coder-

decoder) design leading to improved picture and above all, sound.

For now, sound quality with ISDN can only be improved to the detriment of picture quality and vice-versa. Sound and image are both, however, vital for high-quality simultaneous interpretation.

As far as audio quality is concerned, there are two choices on the ISDN: l) good quality sound with a 7,000 Hz passband (corresponding to the hearing of an elderly person) and lower quality with a 3,000 Hz passband.

In January 1997 a videoconferencing demonstration was held in Montreal with three professional speakers, one speaking from the main conference room and the other two from a studio in the adjoining room. The interpreting booths were outside the main conference room. The interpreters were able to compare satellite broadband sound with improved telephone copper cable, that is, ISDN sound. This demonstration confirmed the earlier conclusions of ETSI that with the present ISDN videoconferencing system, accurate interpretation cannot be guaranteed.

A dedicated end-to-end high-quality television (satellite) link provides a satisfactory pass-band which gives the interpreter excellent sound conditions. But the cost is far greater. For example, communication by ISDN costs roughly the same as a telephone call whereas the use of a satellite link costs some US$60,000 per half-hour. A businessman would probably find the ISDN system perfectly satisfactory for a business conversation and would not understand that this sound quality is not sufficient for a professional interpreter to give of his best. Efficient communication is best served by all interpreters being at the same place as the speakers.

Even more than in conventional conferencing, the presence of an experienced coordinating interpreter is essential. He should participate fully in the preparation of the conference, with the video and sound technicians as well as with the conference officers. Remote conferencing will often justify the coordinating interpreter's playing a purely managerial role during the conference and the appointment of similar coordinators at each location. In remote conferencing, interpreters normally work no more than three hours a day (especially in the case of different time zones when they may be working unusual hours). If more working hours are required, manning strengths are increased correspondingly. Standard booths and equipment are used. Sound quality must be at least equal to that required in ISO Standard No. 2603. Interpreters are provided with high quality uninterruptedly displayed colour images with visual display units of at least 40 cm diagonal or video projection of the speaker in close-up, the audience and the chairman and conference officers. Any speeches being read that have not been copied for the interpreters are also displayed to them, as well as any other visual material shown to the audience such as slides, graphs, and so on. Any other material that can help the interpreter overcome the handicap of not being in direct contact with the conference may also be displayed, such as : the agenda, voting results, list of participants, session timetable, and so on. A communication channel should be permanently available between the coordinating interpreter and his counterpart at the other location or locations, and there should be permanently available call lines with the Chair, sound and video control. There should also be a facsimile, telecopying or teletransmission facility continuously available to transmit speeches, lists of speakers or participants and as back up to the coordination channel mentioned above.

Voice-recognition computers are sometimes used for translation but the computer first has to be "trained" to recognize the voice and pronunciation of the speaker. My experience of voice-activated switching for simultaneous interpretation has not been positive because the first word or two are generally lost; in animated discussions those first few words may be of vital importance in order to understand what follows.

The European Union has an internal computer network called "Intranet" (as opposed to Internet); it may soon be possible to contact the Chairman via the computer screen in front of him to tell him when the interpreters do not have a document or when a speaker is talking too fast. When using laptops or notebooks keyboards should not be placed too close to the microphone because the sound of keying may be disturbing to the delegates; thought is being given to rubber or soft plastic keys that would be noiseless for use in interpretation booths.

Lunch

One important aspect of trade talks if they are to be successful is respect of the other party's customs. In France, Switzerland and most European countries, people eat a hot meal at lunchtime with meat and vegetables, salad, cheese and perhaps fruit, accompanied by wine and followed by strong black coffee. Everything stops for two hours for this purpose. Business is done over a leisurely meal. Often this is where the real negotiations take place (later ratified officially in the conference). It seems uncivilized to Europeans to have a short lunch break and offer sandwiches and bottled orange juice. If Australia wants to do business with France they should sit down unhurriedly at a table dressed with a starched white tablecloth. Why not include a wine-tasting to introduce them to the excellent Australian wines and get them in a receptive mood ? On one occasion when I was interpreting at diplomatic talks in Canberra, the Australians stood up at 12.30, declared the meeting would resume half an hour later, and disappeared into their offices to eat their sandwiches from the top drawer of their desk. I saw them and so did the visitors because they even left their office doors open! The French group waited hesitantly and finally asked where they could get lunch. They were directed to the staff cafeteria in the basement where sandwiches, Mars bars and instant coffee were available but nothing the French would call lunch: no steak, no vegetables or salad, no bread rolls, no glass of red wine.

At a meeting held in a prestigious Canberra hotel on another occasion the announcement was made: "You are all invited to lunch in the Griffin room at 12 noon." We waited politely until a few minutes after twelve before wandering into the Griffin room. A crowd of European delegates were waiting outside to be called in to lunch - they could see no set tables inside. After a while, waitresses came round with trays of sandwiches, glasses of so-called fruit juice and mineral water. Most delegates declined politely. Hoping to set an example, the interpreters signalled to the delegates standing nearby to help themselves. "No thank you," they replied. "We prefer to wait for lunch."

Coffee Bar

The importance of the conference coffee bar must be stressed. The object of a conference is after all to bring people together formally and informally to promote better understanding of one another and a better understanding of other people's problems. On many occasions, compromise solutions to international problems are found during informal discussions over coffee, and later ratified formally in the conference room.

And if, after all I have said, you are bringing 2000 delegates to a medical conference in Melbourne or Sydney next year and you go for a cheap sewn-up package deal needing no more than your signature, without qualified professional interpreters of international standing and with sandwiches and synthetic orange juice for lunch, then all I can do is wish you the best of luck.

12

HEALTH, DEALING WITH STRESS AND HEARING PROBLEMS

Simultaneous interpretation, like being an opera singer or an actor, is an adrenalin-based profession. We are subjected to constant stress and shut up without fresh air in air-conditioned often over-heated booths inside conference rooms, working in artificial light all day, frustrated by having to repeat other people's opinions which may be different from ours, unable to express our own feelings and thoughts. We are dependent on electronic technology we often do not understand. It is a sedentary existence which over-values the world of the mind and of ideas. In between conferences we travel frequently, spend hours waiting in airports or queueing up at immigration desks after sleepless nights in planes. After years of this lifestyle we are particularly sensitive to bright lights and noise and many of us, after working with headphones (monophonic sound) for so long, develop a selectivity problem with our hearing. We become irritated and cannot hear dinnertable conversation if there is background noise. We over-react to loud noises and panic, for example, if there is a loud crash nearby.

The best way to survive this lifestyle is to compensate for it by what we do outside the booth.

I believe some sort of manual or physical outdoor hobby is important. When I get home from a stressful conference and exhausting air travel I feel an urgent need to walk and also to do some gardening. When I have soil all over my hands and I am kneeling, planting and weeding I feel at peace with the world again. Gardening is a good way of resting the brain and giving it time to work through all it has absorbed . It is also an optimistic activity because when you are planting you are working for the future.

Some colleagues take up manual activities such as woodwork or other handicrafts, others are artists, dancers, singers or play an instrument. Some are keen on hiking, swimming, jogging, yoga, skiing, sailing or keep-fit classes. The most balanced interpreters I know share their time between two careers, the other being manual or physical. Irène Testot-Ferry (who lives in Paris and was one of the founders of AIIC) was also a racing car driver and has in her home in Paris shelves full of cups and trophies from the great European car rallies. Many AIIC interpreters are also architects, professional singers, lawyers, psychiatrists, athletes and seem to gain in stability from juggling two careers.

In the golden days of interpreting in the 1960s and 1970's in Europe when there were fewer interpreters and as much work as one could want, some of the better-balanced interpreters in Geneva and Paris would wisely limit themselves to 200 days' work a year. It is a good idea to avoid going straight from one conference to another without a break in between. Interpreters who accept all offers however much travel is involved, and even if one conference follows another, burn themselves out and often suffer nervous disorders later in life.

It is a good idea to go for a walk when you come out of a conference session to unwind rather than jumping straight into your car and driving off into the traffic. While interpreting your brain is working on a different level and at a different rhythm, you are concentrating so hard that your environment is only of secondary importance. If you continued in that way walking along the street you could walk in front of a bus. A ten-minute "decompression period" is a good idea.

Stress and the Alexander Technique

All interpreters have to cope with stress which is unfortunately unavoidable. Fortunately, however, there are ways of minimising it. Over the years various suggestions on ways to combat stress have been discussed at professional interpreters' meetings. An effective method is the Alexander Technique which was originally designed to help singers but has been shown to be of great help to a number of colleagues, especially when sitting in the booth towards the end of the day. I refer in particular to the invisible piece of string attached to the crown of your head, gently pulling upwards...

In the late 19th century, F.M. Alexander, an Australian by birth, discovered that, through habits acquired in early childhood, whenever we prepare for movement or sometimes merely think of it, we tense, shorten and narrow the torso and disturb the balance of the skull at the atlanto-occipital joint. We may also stiffen the muscles of the neck before speaking, tense the vocal muscles and produce an altered voice sound.

Anna Cooper (1983), a qualified teacher of the Alexander technique, describes how she first encountered it when nerves affected her interpreting voice:

A voice specialist said that voice exercises would help but that he thought a course of lessons in the Alexander Technique would be more far-reaching. Since the voice exercises lacked appeal (e.g. punching myself in the stomach while producing a "lowing" sound - preferably alone in a car at a red traffic light to avoid embarrassment) and the Alexander Technique seemed to amount to a pleasant sensory experience whilst sitting or lying down, I was readily persuaded. The first series of lessons showed me how I "used" my body, how this affected my whole being and what I could do about it. The work, manual though non-manipulative, is also therapeutic and relaxing, and after the course I glowed with a feeling of wholeness, health and a newfound ability to abstract myself from trying situations and the realiza-

tion that the problem I had faced in my early days had nearly disappeared. The half-hour lessons involved nothing more strenuous on my part than thinking but the benefits seemed to be cumulative.

As she continued to take lessons whenever possible over the years her

> *curiosity was awakened by the fact that the subtle adjustments the work teaches enabled me to make major changes in my attitudes and reactions if I wanted to. As an interpreter I found it easier to relax on the job and also to switch off completely afterwards.*
>
> *The Technique is a way of learning to use the body in an efficient and non-harmful way. Central to it is a new balance of the head on top of the spine and resisting the forces which tend to shorten and narrow the torso.*
>
> *Most people do not think consciously about how to use their bodies unless things go wrong. They pursue their activities in whichever way is most familiar, and see fatigue, strain and stress as the unavoidable consequence of sustained activity. A good example is a difficult session in interpreting, when we will be stiffening the muscles of the neck and shortening and narrowing the torso, not to mention other stress habits such as fiddling with the pencil, paper or microphone, swinging backwards and forwards on the chair or tensing the vocal muscles and producing an altered voice sound - the writer's own experience. Then things ease and we relax. However, relax we may but we do not return to neutral and in this, as in any other stressful activity, the effects on the functioning of the body and the personality build up not only during the day, but over the months and years.*

According to Anna Cooper, neuro-muscular reactions and tension patterns occur in response to every kind of stimulus, physical, emotional or other. When the conscious control learned from the Alexander Technique is applied, the student can learn to recognize the tension patterns causing "mis-use" of the body and right himself by going back to neutral.

Alexander called this neutrality the "primary control." It is a special balance of the skull on the spine which has been found to promote release of tension throughout the body and to allow optimal psycho-physical functioning. Brain and body are intimately connected in cause and effect and in the Alexander Technique we tend to think of a person as an indivisible psycho-physical unit, termed by Alexander the "self". Primary control is not a contrived balance of the head, but a dynamic relationship between head, neck and back in which the vital organs have been found to be in an optimal functional relationship with one another. It is also a state in which the Alexander student feels most effectively in control of his emotions and his mental concentration. By dint of constant training in "good use of the self", therefore, people become able to cope with many physically, intellectually or emotionally demanding situations and also may find that chronic conditions stemming from harmful use or the body are relieved or disappear.

According to Michael McCallion in "The Voice Book" (1988), F. Matthias Alexander was born in 1869 in Tasmania. He was an actor, a singer, but mainly a reciter. He was a successful performer first in Melbourne and then all over Australia and New Zealand but was constantly plagued by vocal strain and sore throats, his voice failing completely at times, although medical examination showed no cause for this. Since his voice functioned well normally, i.e. when he was not performing, he felt there must be something he was doing during performance that caused the trouble and after a lengthy process of self-observation, studying breathing methods, etc. he realized that when he spoke he tilted his head back, thus slightly shortening his neck which led to a poor use of the breathing mechanism. In producing the necessary volume of sound for performing, this was exaggerated.

As a result of these studies, others noticed an improvement in his voice and many actors, singers and reciters wished to study his method. He soon had a large practice and a number of members of the Melbourne University Medical Faculty were among his pupils. In 1904 he moved to London where he set up his practice, working with many of the great actors of his day, including Sir Henry Irving, Beerbohm-Tree and Lewis Waller. He wrote and published three books entitled "Man's Supreme Inheritance", "Constructive Conscious Control of the Individual" and "The use of self", and died in 1955 in his 87th year.

Booth temperature

Studies have been carried out by Ingrid Kurz and Herbert Kolmer concerning temperature and CO_2 and O_2 level increases in the booth by the end of the working day, showing the importance of air renewal and the negative effect inadequate air-conditioning can have on individual performance.

Air Travel

During long air travel it is worthwhile "switching off" and resting. Taking a lot of reading material with you and counting on the travel time to study documents is not a good idea. One should also avoid alcohol because of its dehydrating effect, and over-eating. I find the best way to travel is to put myself in "alpha-state", that is, complete relaxation, so that when I arrive, whatever the time and time-zone, I do not suffer from jet-lag and am fit, wide-awake but well rested and ready to tackle the new situation. It is certainly advisable for beginner interpreters to learn relaxation techniques to help them cope with the unstable lifestyle which incidentally is also often the cause of difficulties in social relationships.

In the case of frequent long distance travel it is advisable to dress carefully to avoid anything too tight, wear comfortable shoes and loose clothing with "support-hose" of the type worn by air hostesses to prevent swelling of the ankles.

Hearing problems

After some years of working with earphones you may find your ear has become accustomed to having the sound very close so that you do not have to distinguish between what you want to hear and background noise. Later in life, when you retire, you may have to re-train your ear gradually to pick up normal sounds the non-earphone-wearing way.

When working in consecutive, you should not be embarrassed to ask a speaker to speak up - after all, it is in his interest to be heard. If a small group is meeting in a large room, suggest they move to one corner rather than sitting in the middle. If you sit in the corner, facing out-wards, you will find you hear (and see) everyone better and the speaker may not need to raise his voice. You could say: "I don't have a hearing problem, but would you mind speaking up?"

After a day working with earphones, choose a corner table when you enter a restaurant. If you are at a party at a friend's house, try to stand in a quiet corner. In a concert hall, if you can choose where to sit, start by wandering around until you find the acoustically quiet spots - there are always dead spots due to the construction of the building - pillars, doorways and windows all play a part. The best place to sit, acoustically, is about four or five rows from the front and in a fairly central position.

Most of the acoustic energy in normal speech occurs within the frequency band 500 - 4,000 Hz. The most common hearing risk to interpreters is the feedback both within and above this band above when the speaker approaches the microphone with his ear-phones on and a high pitched screech comes through. Rip off your ear-phones as fast as you can when that happens (this is the natural reaction anyway) and turn the volume right down. Make sure the speaker concerned realizes what he has done and doesn't do it again. Speak to the technician and ask him to explain to the delegate concerned. There is a certain lasting danger to the very sensitive hair cells in the cochlea when this happens. As Herbert Kolmer points out:

these hair cells are sensitive to sound levels and unnaturally high decibels cause them to wilt and die. These cells do not grow again once dead.

Hearing ability is also subject to aging - the ability to hear high frequency sound gradually disappears in about half of all men in their sixties and five to ten years later in women. This is called presbycusis.

Acoustic shock occurs when a microphone is banged and results in a transient reduction in hearing ability which may last a few minutes. If a microphone is knocked over the transient effects will last longer - if the volume was turned up high because the interpreter was straining to hear the speaker's first words, sickness and a form of concussion may result, lasting a few days or more depending on the severity of the trauma.

Audiometry has undergone much the same technological change as all other sound equipment over the years, but is still mainly a matter of human interpretation of human response to a set of sound signals. After investigations by the AIIC Health Committee in 1989, Ingrid Kurz stated that preliminary findings did not indicate a professionally induced hearing impairment among conference interpreters. However colleagues are recommended to undergo audiometric tests early in their career in order to be able to prove unequivocally a hearing impairment in case of a work-related accident.

13

HOW TO BECOME A CONFERENCE INTERPRETER

René Pinhas, AIIC, Paris, said that a would-be interpreter needs an "innate talent", without which interpreter school training is useless. Schools can only develop such innate talents. Let us assume that all readers of this book have that innate talent.

Before signing up for a course, anyone contemplating training as a conference interpreter would do well to consult a practising interpreter able to provide guidance as to the languages in demand; there is no point in training in languages where there is already a glut of interpreters.

If in addition to your mother tongue, you have two or three languages which are of a sufficiently high level to enable you fully to understand a statement made in those languages, if you also have a good understanding of the culture and are well-read in the literature of the countries where your languages are spoken, then you may consider embarking upon a two-year post-graduate course in interpretation and translation techniques.

At the time of writing, the only internationally acknowledged conference interpreter training course in Australia is at the University of Queensland (Department of Asian Languages and Studies), Japanese-English and English-Japanese. This Master of Arts course is NAATI-approved; those who pass the final examinations obtain NAATI accreditation as a conference interpreter (former NAATI Level 4) as well as a Master of Literary Studies degree in Japanese Conference interpretaton/translation. It is a two-year full-time course for students with a degree from a recognized university and evidence of appropriate linguistic skills in English and Japanese. There are two AIIC members on the teaching staff.

Contact: The Director, MAJIT, Department of Japanese and Chinese Studies, University of Queensland, St.Lucia Q.4067 Australia

Interpreter training courses in the Asia-Pacific region

We have heard of the following interpreter training courses available in the Asia-Pacific Region but this list is for guidance only, incomplete and without guarantee. Some of the names of those concerned may have changed since the time of writing. The following however may be able to provide information:

Cambodia
The Australian Centre for Education,
#4-6 St. 75, Sangket District,
Phnom Penh,
Cambodia
Tel/fax (855) 23 426608

Cambodia Development Resource Institute,
CDRI, P.O.Box 622,
Phnom Penh,
Cambodia
Tel/fax (855) 66094/25103

The following two institutions trained interpreters during the UNTAC period but since then insufficient information is available.

China
Prof. Zhuang Yichuan, School of Interpretation and Translation (former UN Training Programme).
Beijing Foreign Studies University, P.O.Box 16, BFSU
2 North Xisanhuan Avenue, Beijing 81, P.R.C.
Tel (86-10) 842 2277 Ext.386 Fax 8423144

Hong Kong

Dr. Cecile Sun, Course Leader (former United Nations, New York, interpreter), Interpreters' Training, Department of Translation, Chinese University of Hong Kong, Shatin, New Territories,
Hong Kong.
Tel. (852) 2603 5173 Fax 2603 5270

Mr. Y.P. Cheng, Course Leader(AIIC, former Government Chief Interpreter), Interpretation, Department of Chinese, Interpretation, Translation & Linguistics,
City University of Hong Kong,
Tat Chee Avenue, Kowloon Tong,
Hong Kong.
Tel. (852) 2788 9577 fax 2788 8706

Dr. Jane Lai, Course Leader, Translation,
Department of English Language and Literature,
Hong Kong Baptist University,
Kowloon Tong, Hong Kong.
Tel. (852)2339 7191 Fax 2338 0874

Dr. John Minford, Course Leader, Interpretation,Department of Chinese, Translation & Interpretation,Hong Kong Polytechnic University,Hung Hom, Kowloon. Tel. (852) 2766 7445 Fax 2334 0185

Ms Agnes Au (Tel. (852)2867 2937 Fax 2537 1520), Chief Interpreter, Simultaneous Interpretation, and Ms Anita Chan, Chief Conference Interpreter, are in charge of the Hong Kong Government Training Course. 23/F Queensway Government Offices, 88 Queensway, Hong Kong

Indonesia
At the moment Indonesian-English translation only is taught. An interpreter training course is however planned.
Pusat Penerjemahan,
Mr. Benny Hoed, Director,
Universita Indonesia,
Jl. Salemba Raya,

Jakarta 10430.
Fax (62-21) 315 5941

Japan
Prof. Masaomi Kondo (AIIC), Course Leader,Interpreter Training Course,Department of Economics, Daito Bunka University,1-9-1 Takashimadaira,Itabashi-ku, Tokyo, Japan.Tel. 81-3 3935 1111   Home Tel./fax 81-493 34-5587

Mr. Hara, ISS Interpreter Training Centre,Okina-cho 1-4-1 Naka-ku,Yokohama-shi, chome 231,Yokohama, Japan.Fax 81-45 663-1963

Mr. Tatsuya Komatsu, President,The Simul Academy, Kowa Building No.9, 1-8-10 Akasaka, Minato-ku, Tokyo 107, Japan. Tel. (81-3) 3586 3571 Fax 3583 8336

Korea

Hankuk University, which is sponsored by the government, trains translators and interpreters with Korean and one or two European languages:
Dr. Inn-Ung Lee, Dean of Language Department,
Ms. Choi SoheeJung-hwa (AIIC),Director, Graduate School of Interpretation & Interpretation (GSIT), Hankuk University of Foreign Studies,270 Imun-Dong, Dongdaemun-gu, Seoul 130-791,Korea. Tel. (82-2) 963 0550 Fax 963 8780

There are two courses: A two-year course for those who work in Korean plus one foreign language; and a three-year course for those who work in Korean plus two foreign languages. In the first year of both, the main focus is on developing basic interpreting and translating skills including note-taking, sight translation, language proficiency as well as international law, economics, domestic and international politics, social affairs and technology etc. Consecutive interpreting is also begun in the first year. Simultaneous is taught in the second year together with more consecutive interpretation. The courses are very intensive. Typically a student would spend five hours a day in class and simultaneous interpretation booths plus another five hours of private study in the library or language laboratory, six days a week for two or three years. Successful graduates are awarded an MA degree at the end of the course.

Macau
Ms Manuela Paiva e CostaActing Director, School of Languages and Translation, Macau Polytechnic Institute, P.O.Box 286,Macau. Tel. (853) 578 722 Fax 308 801

Taiwan
Ms Michelle Wu (AIIC candidate),Interpretation Section, Graduate Institute of Translation & Interpretation, College of Foreign Languages, Fu Jien University, Hsin Chuang 24205, Taipei, Taiwan ,M.A. Programme Tel.(886-2) 902 1292 Tel/fax 902 9623

Thailand
Asst. Prof. Nuangnoi Boonyanate, Director, Office of International Affairs, Chulalongkom University, Bangkok 10330, Thailand. Tel.(66-2) 218 3331-5 Fax 216 1299 E-mail Internet: ARTPNB4@chukn.car.chula.ac.th

Vietnam
Mr. Pham Sanh Chau, Head, Interpretation Division,Foreign Ministry of Vietnam,Hanoi, Vietnam. Tel. (84) 44 30173 (direct line) 44 58201 Ext. 309 Fax 44 59205

Whatever your languages, it is advisable to take a postgraduate diploma or master's degree in interpreting. Courses are available all over the world, for example in Europe and America (Paris at the Sorbonne (ESIT)[13] and

---

[13] ESIT (Ecole Supérieure d'Interprètes et de Traducteurs) is a component of the Sorbonne University. The course is postgraduate. Entrance requirements include a university degree in an appropriate faculty (for example, arts, law, economics, political science); a thorough command of English and French as well as proficiency in at least one other European language; and success in an oral examination that tests general knowledge, precision and speed of thought,

ISIT, Geneva University (ETI)[14], Georgetown University, The Monterey Institute of International Studies, California, Moscow (State Institute of Foreign Languages), Trieste, Vienna, Heidelberg, Cairo at the Al-Alsun Language School and in England at Bath, Bradford, Kent, Salford and Surrey universities and at the Polytechnic of Central London, which runs separate high-level courses in conference interpreting and technical and specialized translation).

A language degree is not an absolute prerequisite. A degree in economics, law or a scientific/technological discipline may be of greater value if the candidate can also offer the necessary advanced linguistic ability in three or more languages. A combined degree in a language with a commercial or technical subject can also be a useful background. Both interpreting and translating are suitable as second careers; previous experience in other fields can be a distinct advantage.

Schools offering courses for school-leavers may provide a four-year programme while training courses for

---

breadth of vocabulary, and capacity for a high level of concentration, combined with the ability to dissociate, so that the language one is listening to does not contaminate the language in which one is simultaneously expressing the same thought. Teaching is in twenty-five to twenty-seven language combinations, including Japanese-French. The staff of ESIT is composed entirely of professional translators and interpreters.

[14] ETI (Ecole de Traduction et d'Interprétation), Université de Genève, 102 bvd. Carl-Vogt, CH-1211 Geneva, Switzerland. For details of the next certificate course check website at:http://www.unige.ch/formcont/certininterpre2000.html, where you will find French and English versions, as well as on-line registration forms. The staff is also entirely composed of professional translators and interpreters (members of AIIC). ETI also runs courses in interpreter training for candidates with: a diploma in conference interpreting; a language combination including at least two of ETI's working languages which are English, French, German, Italian, Spanish, Arabic (seminars are held in English and French); and a letter of intent. The Certificate in Interpreter Training for conference interpreting aims at providing experienced conference interpreters with the necessary theoretical, methodological and practical background for training interpreters in an academic setting. The curriculum devotes sixty hours to seminars, twenty hours to course observation, fifteen hours to seminar paper and five hours to examinations. Information may also be obtained from: Barbara.Moser@eti.unige.ch.

post-graduates and mature students may be much shorter and more intensive, requiring a higher entry standard. Candidates for these courses are assessed on language skills and breadth of background culture - political, economic, technical, etc. The Geneva University course requires four languages and the syllabus provides for a course in parliamentary procedure and a year to be spent at a foreign university in a country speaking the candidate's study language.

Short courses claiming to train conference interpreters in a few weeks or months are totally unacceptable. Short courses to update practising interpreters (refresher courses) in subject matter and language are highly recommended. In-house training courses are provided by some international organizations such as United Nations, New York, and the Commission of the European Community in Brussels[15], especially in cases where there is a

---

[15] The Joint Interpretation-Conferences Service of the Commission of the European Communities in Brussels provides interpretation at the meetings held by the Commission, the Council of Ministers, the Economic and Social Committee and the European Investment Bank. With a total of well over 500 posts, it is by far the largest interpretation service in the world.

The Commission of the European Communities brochure entitled: "Short Courses for Student Interpreters" published by Joint Service Interpretation-Conferences: "The aim of the course is to provide accelerated training of conference interpreters who will meet the professional requirements of the Joint Service Interpretation-Conferences. It is open to young university graduates in any discipline (law, economics, sciences, etc.); no prior knowledge of interpreting is needed. Candidates must not be more than 30 years old, speak English, Danish, Dutch, French, German, Greek or Italian and express themselves freely, clearly and accurately in public, thoroughly comprehend at least two further languages from this list, irrespective of speaker or subject matter, and be well informed on current affairs, particularly economics and politics. Initially selected candidates must l) successfully undergo an aptitude test for interpreting at which they will have to demonstrate their command of languages and general knowledge as well as their powers of concentration, rapid analysis of arguments and oral expression and 2) undertake, provided they pass the relevant tests, to remain in the employment of the Commission in Brussels as interpreters (temporary staff) for a continuous period of at least two years reckoned from the end of the course.

The course lasts six months; the proposed starting date is indicated when candidates are invited to take the aptitude test. The initial training contract is for 2 months, which is extended by 2 months and then another 2 if the student interpreter is successful at the tests prior to each expiry date. The

shortage of interpreters for a given language. These courses are open only to university graduates (law, economics, science, and so on) or in some cases to student interpreters.

Once you have finished your training and succeeded in obtaining your diploma, and/or NAATI accreditation (at former Level 4), you will have become a beginner conference interpreter. You may well discover that you learn more then from working with professional colleagues than you did during your formal study. It is customary not to have more than one beginner per team at any conference.

You will need to read newspapers to keep up to date with current affairs and the literature of the countries speaking your languages (active and passive). The good interpreter is the one with the newspaper under his arm.

United Nations interpretation tests

From the interpretation point of view, Australia is a little pond containing some big fish. Once you start working out in the wide world, you will find you are a very small fish in a great big pond and there are many brilliant

---

course is based on work done individually. Student interpreters benefit from advice given by qualified interpreters as well as from a multi-lingual environment and access to the facilities offered by an international organization.

Trainees receive a grant and are covered by group insurance against accident and sickness. A household allowance is payable for 180 days in certain circumstances and an education allowance for children in full-time regular attendance at an educational establishment, depending on the age of the child and level of schooling, as well as the place of the establishment. Trainees have access to the Library and restaurants of the institutions and the Information office keeps a register of vacant accommodation which they may consult. At the end of the course, student interpreters sit a professional examination. If they are successful and have been declared physically fit, they are given a two-year contract as temporary staff which may be renewed once only for a maximum period of one year. The Commission organizes open competitions for the recruitment of interpreters in accordance with its needs, i.e. the working languages required.

interpreters working from and into a large number of languages. Should you decide to try for the United Nations interpretation test, prepare thoroughly beforehand. It is no good going along *en touriste*. You must be in fine fettle, having meticulously prepared vocabularies in the subjects most likely to be aired, with nerves of steel and the confidence of someone who works regularly. You are not given the subject of the speech beforehand. Before each segment, a voice tells you who is about to take the floor, and on what occasion (for example: "You are about to hear the delegate of Nicaragua, speaking at the Commission on Human Rights in October 1992"). The speech begins immediately, often at high speed and lasts from eight to ten minutes; there are four segments per language and a break of about 30 to 40 seconds between each segment. Anyone interested can obtain United Nations documents in their various languages as well as copies of past UN language exam papers and dates of forthcoming examinations by writing direct to United Nations Language Services in New York or Geneva.

The AIIC booklet entitled *Advice to Students wishing to become conference interpreters*[16] contains much useful information.

Training

According to research on emerging markets, demand is increased by quality supply. Clients who would otherwise "make do" would use good interpreters if they knew of their existence. Also, the existence of high-level courses presents a favourable image of the profession and enhances its status. The availability of qualified conference interpreters with more than two languages is a prerequisite for the emergence of true multilingual conferencing.

---

[16] This booklet is published by the AIIC Training Committee in English and French. It is updated every four years on the basis of a questionnaire sent to all institutions teaching interpretation.

Teaching staff should be practising interpreters but not necessarily holders of a PhD. It is important that teaching staff be able to continue interpreting at conferences; the authorities should not place obstacles in the way of this. Even if lessons have to take place at weekends or in the evenings (at ETI, Geneva, lessons are sometimes given for example between 7 and 9 a.m. or after 6 in the evening) this inconvenience is minor compared to the advantage of having a teacher with an up-to-date knowledge of current problems and requirements, who can provide conference documents hot from meetings thus making courses alive, current and exciting and inspiring students with enthusiasm for their future career.

The importance of screening

Training institutions should not, however, raise false hopes. It is no good training people who stand little chance of success in the profession. This is why stringent admission requirements and rigourous screening of students beforehand is so important. Accepting borderline students in order to increase the numbers is shortsighted; failures are not good for the reputation of the training course. Screening is also needed to eliminate candidates with an unsuitable personality, speech defects or mannerisms needing correction. Selection is advisable also after the first term of the course.

Schools

Teaching should be at a postgraduate level. The course leader should be a working conference interpreter. The target language should be the A language of the teacher. Both simultaneous and consecutive interpretation should be taught; teaching should start with consecutive and build up to simultaneous once the student has a firm grounding in the techniques of consecutive. *Retour* (working both ways, language-wise) should be taught in all consecutive, but only where possible in simultaneous (that is, a "retour" should not be forced into what is a genuine passive language). Relay techniques should also be taught, both at the providing and receiving ends. Sight translation is essential. Elocution and voice production training should also be available.

Courses should also cover international law, conference procedure, the conduct of meetings, for example, chairmanship and voting methods. Regular speakers might include a retired UN official, for example, or a specialist on international organizations from Foreign Affairs. Court interpretation, court procedures and terminology would also be useful. It is important to teach students where and how to find references, how to use reference libraries, etc. when preparing a subject for a conference. Each student should expect to spend three hours working by himself/herself for each hour of teaching received.

Choice of languages

The languages offered in any one year and the number of students in each language group should be strictly limited to foreseeable market requirements and may need to be rotated as the years go by to avoid flooding the market with a particular language combination. Students of the widest possible variety of mother tongues (compatible with market requirements) should be admitted and courses should not be limited solely to A- language speakers of one country.

Asian languages

It is the official philosophy of ESIT that simultaneous interpretation is the same whatever the languages. Students learn the principles and techniques in central methodological courses and then apply them to their languages.

Whereas one year in the country of the B language, in addition to the two-year course, seems sufficient in the case of Western languages, a longer stay may be necessary in the case of a speaker of a Western language wishing to interpret from or into Asian languages (such as Japanese, Chinese or Korean), and vice-versa.

Examinations

In all cases at least one prospective employer (chief interpreter or recruiter) should sit on the Jury in addition to internal examiners and working conference interpreters.

Failure in consecutive interpretation should be eliminatory as it is a tool for logical analysis of discourse and is fundamental to good simultaneous interpretation.

Simultaneous interpretation should cover both a general (political-economic) subject and a technical subject which the student has been able to prepare. The reason for the latter is not to prove the student's capacity to memorize twenty technical terms, but to judge his or her ability to prepare a technical meeting.

The ultimate criteria for assessment should be:

- Would I want to have this student working as a professional interpreter at my conference?

- Would I want to work with this person as a colleague? and/or

- Would I be happy to take relay from this interpreter?

Students should be able to re-sit the entire examination in all languages only once, and no partial re-sittings should be allowed.

The diploma awarded should show clearly the active and the passive languages in which the student has passed in simultaneous and in consecutive; that is, their A, B and C languages. Certificates for partial success should not be issued.

There is only one thing to add: Good Luck ! (or *Merde* !)

14

OTHER AREAS
WHERE SIMULTANEOUS
INTERPRETATION IS USED

Television and Radio

Precision and good diction are essential. The inter-preter's style and delivery need to be particularly smooth and clear, regardless of the original, because audiences are accustomed to the well-trained voices of newsreaders and commentators and do not understand or appreciate the very different demands made of interpreters. It is also important to start speaking right away because the usual delay while you wait for the speaker to get under way is unsettling to listeners. Also there must be as little overhang as possible once the speaker has finished.

In interviews, the interpreter must try to match the interviewer's timing in order not to lessen the effect or take the punch out of questions and answers. It is advisable to have as many interpreters as there are speakers to avoid problems of speaker identification for listeners or viewers and to ensure that each interpreter can cut in as soon as his speaker starts.

While the sound engineers are experts in their field, they may have little experience of interpreters' needs. When you arrive at the studio for the first time you may find you are expected to work from a little out-of-the-way cubbyhole with no direct view of the speakers but a tv monitor instead. You may be given heavy stereo headsets and no volume control. It is therefore important that you contact the broadcasting organization well in advance to give them a list of basic technical requirements, perhaps in the form of a memo for the chief sound engineer. If there is to be a scripted exchange, make sure you are given a copy of the script beforehand so that you are able to read and prepare it. There should be two tv monitors in the booth: one to follow what is going on in the studio and one showing what the viewer sees on his television set.

Conference interpreters are accustomed to audience feedback. The fact that there is none in this type of work makes it more difficult - you feel as if you are working in a vacuum. Sometimes the assignment is very short so there is no "warm up" time to enable you to get into your subject. Beware too of acoustic and visual distractions and disturbances from the newsroom and technicians. Media work is generally considered to be more stressful than conference interpretation, particularly as interpreters often have to work outside normal working hours.

Cool nerves are required as well as good technique and considerable skill. Occasionally, creativity is required in case of a break in sound for a few seconds or atmospheric noise on the line, in which case the interpreter has to reconstruct insofar as possible the missing fragment in order to avoid hesitation or silence. Interpreters need presence of mind in such cases and some acting ability.

There is no doubt that this type of work considerably enhances the professional image of conference interpreters.

Subtitling and dubbing

Successful motion picture translating is increasingly vital to the cinema industry as a large part of the income derived from a foreign film depends on the excellence of its translation. In the case of subtitles or surtitles (used for opera), this is not a case of translation or interpretation but rather of summarizing since they are run at a maximum speed of eight syllables per second reading time and have to be synchronized with the action insofar as possible. I am told that in Australia (where the SBS, Special Broadcasting Service, regularly televises news bulletins and foreign language films with subtitles) one second corresponds to one word, two seconds to one line of twenty-six characters, two-and-a-half seconds to thirty-three characters, three seconds to one and a half lines of forty characters and four seconds to two lines; that is fifty-two characters. Clearly this is very different from conference interpretation.

Subtitles are also used sometimes in the case of the various English dialects and other non-standard forms of English that may be difficult for the viewer to understand, or when the sound recordings are of poor quality.

Dubbing (the replacement of one language by another in live sound) is closer to simultaneous interpretation but more complicated. As Eugene Nida (1964) explains:

In this type of translating there are several important factors: (1) timing, both of syllables and breath groups; (2) synchronization of consonants and vowels with obvious lip movements by the actors ("lip sync"); (3) words appropriate to the gestures (some words just do not fit a shrug of the shoulders); (4) characteristic differences of dialect in the various actors; and (5) timing of humour or expressions which produce special responses from other actors. To make matters even more difficult, there is an increasing tendency to shoot close-ups of the actors.

Of course, it is possible to make a number of formal adaptations without destroying the meaningful content. For example, Caillé (1960a, p.118) cites the instance of a French film in which "l'Amérique du Sud" was translated into English as "in Mexico". The substitution of this phrase permitted a very close parallelism of lip movement, timing of stressed syllables, and overall similarity in total speed of utterance.

I must confess being rather shocked at the surtitles shown during *Carmen* and other operas in this country when the register was not respected with the result that dialogue such as "What are you up to ?" "What's going on?" and use of the word "Mum" instead of "Mother" was used, quite inappropriately for the time when the action was supposed to be taking place.

Court interpreting[17]

In the Middle Ages many interpreters came to be employed in an official capacity at the courts of the various kings and emperors as court interpreters. In modern times, the development of the institution of the law courts has led to an increased demand for foreign language services, particularly with a view to assuring full access to the protection of the law and justice to people who do not speak the local language.

What follows basically concentrates on the principles of court interpreting. Subject to legislation modifying the operation of Australian common law,[18] the judge who presides over a criminal or civil trial has a discretion to permit or to refuse to allow a witness to give evidence through an interpreter. (In other words, there is no common law right to an interpreter.)

More detailed information is available by reference to the "Further reading" section under "6. Court Interpreting" at the end of this book.

---

[17] The interpreter's oath in English courts is as follows: "I swear by Almighty God that I will well and faithfully interpret and true explanation make of all such matters and things as shall be required of me according to the best of my skill and understanding." Taken from: Archbold, op.cit., Section 349, p.125. 64. Archbold, Op.cit., Section 346, pp. 123-124.

[18] For an overview of South Australian and Victorian legislation concerning the use of interpreters in those States's Courts, see: Commonwealth Attorney-General's Department. *Access to Interpreters in the Australian legal system. Report.* Australian Government Publishing Service: Canberra, ACT, April 1991, Chapter 3.

This profession is very different from conference interpreting and extremely demanding. In addition to the human responsibilities concerning restriction of personal liberty, the owning of property or even more serious consequences which are at stake, there are many pitfalls. Not only do you have to operate in accordance with legal requirements and court practice but you are also subject to on-the-spot decisions by presiding judges as to what you should interpret. Sometimes a judge's direction to interpret or to refrain from interpreting a question or evidence is preceded by an application for interpreting or for the disqualification of an interpreter, during which the judge formally gives reasons for his/her decision to permit or refuse to allow the use of an interpreter. Sometimes a judge spontaneously directs an interpreter to interpret or to refrain from interpreting a question or evidence, without giving explicit reasons for the direction. None of these constraints exist in conference interpretation.

Interpretation versus Translation

There appears to be a problem regarding the definitions of interpretation and translation insofar as the Courts are concerned. Whereas for conference interpreters this is clear cut because "interpretation" refers to the spoken word and "translation" to the written, for lawyers "interpretation" also has a specialized, intra-lingual meaning. Interpretation is the process of determining, through the application of common law and statutory rules of construction, the meaning of enactments by legislatures. For example, "interpretation" describes a court's determination of the meaning of words in a statute which a party alleges are equivocal or unclear. The specialized, intra-lingual meaning which "interpretation" has for lawyers and the ordinary dictionary meanings of "interpretation" which give an impression of imprecision, of various possibilities and different understandings, seem to foster widespread misconceptions that interpreting is an inherently unreliable, impressionistic process, and that "translation" is a more accurate process[19].

Justice

Justice must not only be done; it must also be seen to be done. Unfortunately, with this in mind, it may be that some believe that "any interpreter is better than none." Justice may appear to be done if an interpreter is present, however unsatisfactory he may be. Using an unqualified or incompetent interpreter however is a serious matter and grossly unfair to non-English speaking parties, whose personal liberty may be at stake, as well as to their English speaking opponents or co-defendants. (In such cases, it might be better to have no interpreter at all because errors on the part of the "interpreter" may have dangerous consequences especially if monolingual English speaking or non-English speaking protagonists do not realize that the interpreter is incompetent.)

Choice of mode

There was a limited amount of rudimentary simultaneous interpretation in the 1930's but simultaneous interpretation can be said to have started on a large scale in court with the four-language post-war Nuremberg trials of war criminals. Since then court interpretation has mainly been consecutive (traditionally sentence-by-sentence or liaison mode) rather than simultaneous, which is not normally used in single-defendant trials although it is becoming standard practice for international events. (A noteworthy exception, however, is the mode of simultaneous and/or consecutive interpretation pre-

---

[19] For example, the Supreme Court of New South Wales unanimously concluded that "interpretation" necessarily alters the meaning and register of speech: *Filios v Moreland* (1963) 63 SR NSW 331 per Brereton J @ 333. The same Court and the Majority of the High Court of Australia expected "literal translation" to enable counsel and non-English speaking witnesses to "really hear" and be "heard" by each other as though they all spoke English: *Filios* per Brereton J @ 332-3; *Gaio v The Queen* (1960) 104 CLR 419 per Dixon CJ@ 421; Fullagar J@ 428-30; Kitto J@ 430-2; Menzies J@ 431-3.

scribed by the United States' Congress for use in civil and criminal trials and in *habeas corpus* , grand jury and pre-trial proceedings commenced by the United States Government in federal District Courts. At the direction of Congress, the Administrative Office of the United States Courts tests candidates for Certification as Federal Court Interpreters in "criterion-referenced performance" Oral Examinations of the modes of simultaneous and consecutive interpreting, prescribed by Congress, and in sight translation. Oral court interpreter certification tests, prescribed by a number of the States' judiciaries, including New Jersey's, are based to varying degrees on the simultaneous, consecutive and/or sight translation sections of the Oral Federal Court Interpreter Certification Examination.)

The Klaus Barbie trial in Lyon, France, in 1987 used consecutive interpretation from German into French and whispering from French into German. Perhaps simultaneous interpretation from booths might have afforded the interpreters some protection by separating them from the action and avoiding the impression that they were on the same side as the accused because they spoke their words. Being spontaneous, simultaneous interpretation also enables a more faithful delivery and greater accuracy with regard to tone, verbal mannerisms, manner of speech and impact in general.

The Demjanjuk trial held in Jerusalem in 1987-8 had thirteen interpreters working from and into six languages, three of which were used throughout:

1. Simultaneous was used to render the entire proceedings into English for the English-speaking defence counsels as well as the foreign press;

2. Consecutive was used to render the entire proceedings into Hebrew for the record and as a matter of official policy;
3. Whispering was used to render the entire proceedings into Ukrainian for the defendant, and the questions into

German, Russian and Yiddish for the witnesses speaking these languages; while

4. Liaison was used in rendering the defendant's testimony from Ukrainian into Hebrew (because no professionally trained interpreters were available for this combination, a non-professional was hired who found the liaison mode more manageable than full consecutive).

Ruth Morris[20], a conference interpreter of long standing who is also a student of sociolinguistics, language and the law, believes

> *that to some extent it is possible to use simultaneous, which obviously has considerable advantages over consecutive in preserving spontaneity and dynamism. However, given the difficulties of querying material, the interpreter may be put in a position of having to guess at unclear material, which can have unfortunate consequences for what should be an "utterly" accurate rendering. To some extent, therefore, I have come to the conclusion, albeit rather reluctantly, that it might be better to revert to a form of electronically-assisted chuchotage (whispering) simply to ensure that the interpreter is not as isolated and "invisible" as otherwise can happen. Monitoring can also be carried out somewhat more readily under those circumstances: obviously consecutive is best when it comes to chal-*

---

[20] Ruth Morris (AIIC), a former Brussels-based staff interpreter for the European Communities, now a freelance interpreter and translator in Israel, teaching at the Bar Ilan University, Israel. When studying for her MA in Communications (Hebrew University of Jerusalem), she came across the English case of Iqbal Begum, a Pakistani woman whose life sentence had been successfully appealed on the ground that she had not understood the interpreter provided at her trial, which led Ruth Morris to conduct research into the Impact of Court Interpretation on Legal Proceedings. PhD (Department of Law, Lancaster University, U.K.) on Images of the Interpreter: A Study of Language-Switching in the Legal Process. For a list of her publications, including one coauthored with Jean Colin, see the "Further reading" section ("6. Court Interpreting") at the end of this book.

lenges and corrections. This issue is one which should be looked at fairly and squarely by interpreters, court staff, judges, and lawyers in advance, and the various factors explained and taken into account. Non-interpreters generally have no idea whatsoever of these matters.

Margaret O'Toole[21] points out that in Australia's adversarial judicial system a breach of common law rules of procedural fairness or the inability of a party to exercise fundamental rights to natural justice can cause a criminal or civil trial to be unfair. The exigencies of a fair criminal trial and a fair civil trial differ and depend upon the circumstances of particular trials. Therefore, she argues, the modes of interpreting and/or translation which enable a deaf or non-English speaking party and an English-speaking opponent to exercise their respective rights and to discharge concomitant obligations depend upon the jurisdiction where proceedings are heard; upon the issues raised prior to and at trial; and upon the capacity of each party to hear, read, understand and speak English and the other language(s) in which evidence is signed, written and/or spoken.

The unavailability or inaccuracy of simultaneous interpreting, consecutive interpreting, sight translation or written translation could cause a criminal or civil trial to be unfair. For example, a government's ability to warn a monolingual non-English speaking suspect of his/her right to silence, to charge the suspect with a serious crime, or to understand the suspect's response, could depend upon the accuracy of consecutive interpreting dur-

---

[21]) Margaret O'Toole is a Judge of the Compensation Court of New South Wales. (The Compensation Court is a specialised Court of statutory jurisdiction which determines claims by workers for compensation for work-related personal injuries. As Justice Michael Kirby points out in *Gradidge v Grace Bros. Pty.Limited* (1988) 93 FLR 414 *per* Kirby P @ 419, the Compensation Court's proceedings frequently involve non-English and limited-English speakers.) I am grateful to her for referring me to Australian, English and American cases describing fundamental rights and obligations of parties to adversarial litigation, and duties of trial judges.

ing a police interview. The government's ability to confront the accused at trial with the allegations on which the charge is based could depend upon the accuracy of written or signt translation of documentary evidence and upon the accuracy of simultaneous interpreting to the accused of counsel's questions to witnesses, of oral evidence, of legal argument and of judicial rulings.

The exercise of the accused's rights to be present at trial, to hear and to challenge the government's case, to mount a proper defence to the charge and to address the court in legal argument could depend upon the accuracy of consecutive interpreting of the accused's intructions to and advice from counsel, prior to and during the trial. If the accused elects to give evidence, the extent to which s/he can defend the charge could depend upon the accuracy of consecutive interpreting: the trial "will be unfair if the interpreter lacks the skill and ability to translate accurately the questions asked by counsel and the answers given by the accused person."

The role of the court interpreter

The interpreter must at all times be seen to be, and be impartial. It must not be forgotten that, unlike the conference interpreter, the court interpreter does not have and should not appear to have, a "client".

Margaret O'Toole points out that in Australia, trial judges and jurors base and are entitled to base crucial findings of fact, based upon the demeanour of witnesses. Explanatory gestures or obtrusive behaviour by a court interpreter could distract a judge or jury from forming a reliable impression of a Deaf or non-English speaking protagonist. Therefore court interpreter's demeanour should be as neutral and as unobtrusive as possible.

The role of the court interpreter is indispensable and even crucial in society today and should not be underestimated. According to González, Vásquez and Mikkelson (1991):

As minority populations are assimilated into various world societies, these societies become increasingly aware of the barriers language differences present to the administration of justice and other government services. In point of fact, court interpretation is the newest and most vital form of interpretation in the United States.

Margaret O'Toole notices that in New South Wales the languages used by non-English speaking applicants for workers' compensation vary with the origins of Australia's recent refugees and migrants. She has the impression that over the past fifteen years interpreting has been requested most frequently by Arabic, Croatian, Greek, Italian, Macedonian, Portuguese, Serbian, Spanish, Turkish and Vietnamese speakers.

A third of the population of Australia is foreign-born, the community contains some eighty distinct ethnic groups speaking more than sixty different languages. Some individuals have not and may never attain fluency in English. For these people the communication barrier and cultural difference between Australia and their country of origin prevent them from fully exercising their legal rights, duties and entitlements. Many Aborigines, as well as others, share this problem as they do not speak English at a level enabling them to understand the formal register and legal terminology of the Australian system of law.

In Australia,"You shall truly and faithfully interpret the evidence." [22]A variety of other interpreters' oaths and affirmations is used in Australia's courts and tribunals. In 1995 uniform evidence legislation prescribed an oath or affirmation for interpreters used in the

---

[22] Laster and Taylor's *Interpreters and the Legal System* (1993) covers, in an Australian context, the legal 'right' to an interpreter; interpreters in criminal investigation, courts and tribunals; the role of interpreters and their strategic importance; and interpreter accountability and ethics.

courts and tribunals to which the Acts apply, to the following effect:

> *I swear... by Almighty God .... / I solemnly and sincerely declare and affirm that I will well and truly interpret the evidence that will be given and do all other matters and things that are required of me in this case to the best of my ability.*[23]

I must admit I am curious as to the "other matters and things" the interpreter might have to do and hope these words refer to sight translation and nothing else. The interpreter is there to interpret; that is all she should be asked to do, with the exception of sight translation if necessary.

The subjects being interpreted may be emotionally draining, sordid, or unpleasant. What you are saying may be contrary to your own beliefs. Discussing details of torture, sexual assault, etc. may not be an agreeable way to spend your day. Some of the Nuremberg interpreters found that while they managed not to think about it at the time, the horror came back to them in nightmares. Winning or losing the case may well rest on the interpretation which is a heavy burden for the interpreter and one that should not be taken lightly.

Like lawyers, interpreters are professionals and should be treated as such. Lack of understanding of the role of the interpreter and the problems of interpretation on the part of judges and counsel make the interpreter's task particularly difficult, especially as the interpreter often feels he is directly in the "firing line". Judges and cross-examiners sometimes indicate they have difficulty in understanding what the interpreter is saying, thus encouraging the interpreter to try saying the same thing again in other words. Then they pick up on the fact that different words have been used and ask : "Just now you

---

[23] Evidence Act 1995, Act No.2 of 1995 (Cth), section 22 and Schedule; Evidence Act 1995, Act No. 25 of 1995 (NSW), section 22 and Schedule.

said ....., now you say .... ! Did he say this or that?" which tends to unnerve the interpreter. The brief of the counsel for the defence may be to discredit the witness he is cross-examining which may mean also discrediting the interpreter, who is also probably unaware of where the particular line of questioning is leading.

Requirements

Accuracy is paramount; the interpreter must on no account attempt to clarify or improve when a speaker is being vague. Here lies the big difference between court and conference interpretation: in adversarial court proceedings, the judge or jury has the role and the responsibility of finding facts and is entitled to make crucial findings of fact based upon the assertiveness, clarity, hesitancy, inconsistency or imprecision with which documentary, oral and signed evidence is expressed. Roseann Dueñas Gonzalez, an American linguist who studies the registers of courtroom protagonists' speech, and Holly Mikkelson, a Spanish-English Court Interpreter, Federally certified by the United States Government who teaches at the Monterey Institute (González, Vásquez and Mikkelson 1991), point out:

> *The true message is often in how something is said rather than in what is said [in court proceedings]; therefore the style of the message is as important as its content...*

Clearly it is important that the interpreter make no attempt to polish, improve or even make sense.

González, Vásquez and Mikkelson (1991) argue :

> *The Court interpreter is required to interpret the original source material without editing, summarizing, deleting or adding while conserving the language level, style, tone and intent of the speaker or to render what may be termed the legal equivalence of the source message.*

Confident, clear, unwavering delivery is important, in a voice that is sure to be heard by all. The interpreter needs to be firm and even assertive to avoid having his confidence undermined and ensure his role is respected by the court. For this reason, it is a good idea to insist upon a glass of water, a notepad and a pen before starting work to draw attention to your needs, and important to inspect the court set-up beforehand to check that seating arrangements, visibility of documents (closed-circuit TV monitors), acoustics and so on are satisfactory.

Secrecy is once again absolutely essential and discretion outside the courtroom of the utmost importance. Interpreters must beware of chatting over coffee or lunch to the person sitting next to them.

Court interpreters should be fully familiar with the legal system, court procedures, customs, culture and regional linguistic variations both in the place where the interpreting is performed and in the place of origin of each person whose speech the interpreter interprets.

Constraints

Instructions from the bench to the court interpreter to caution the witness, instead of addressing the witness directly, are inappropriate because the interpreter's only task is to interpret.

In her review (Rich 1994) of the *Handbook for Legal Interpreters* by Ludmilla Robinson (1994), Minako Rich (AIIC, Australia) raises two interesting points:

1) The author of the Handbook recommends interpreting everything that is being said in the court and not simply those matters which are directed at the defendant or witness. This seems to be fair, because clearly an interpreter should be able to create an environment for the defendant or witness which would be equivalent to that of a native speaker. Sadly, however, in real practice there are still judges who will not allow this, and direct the interpreter to only "interpret what I want interpreted".

2) It is advisable to have a brief conversation with the client prior to the interpreting session so as to get used to the dialect spoken by the client. This is preferred practice also, but some judges and legal counsel take exception to this. It is to be hoped that an awareness on the part of legal practitioners will rectify these unfortunate situations.

The most interesting sub-heading is 'Legal Liability of the Interpreter for Negligence.' There is not much written about this subject elsewhere so I was interested to find out the potential legal consequences of 'a slip of the tongue.' It seems that freelancers like myself should take out professional liability insurance. I suppose this applies to whatever sort of interpreting you do.

Seeking clarification

According to Miriam Shlesinger,

> *interlingual interpretation is also intercultural mediation. Whenever the source language includes a culture-bound referent, the interpreter must decide whether to explain it or make do with either a foreignism or an approximate target language equivalent. In court interpretation, this predicament is aggravated both by formal constraints and by the split-second nature of the decision entailed. For example, when an American attorney questioned an Israeli policeman about "the winter of 1986", the former was referring to the period beginning in November 1986*

*(by which time winter sets in in the area
where he lives) and lasting until about
April 1987, whereas the latter assumed
this referred to the period beginning in
January 1986 and lasting through March
of the year, in line with Israeli climate. A
rendering of "the winter of 1986" as "the
winter of 1985" would have prevented the
misunderstanding but the interpreter, de-
terred by the stricture of "faithfulness"
and "accuracy" in translation, refrained
from exercising latitude in this case." The
interpreters often discussed the legitimacy
of explicitation when referring to names
of Jewish holidays, figures in Jewish history, names of places in Israel and the
like. Although unanimous in their view
that this would facilitate understanding
by English-speaking attorneys and witnesses, they differed as to the "legal man-
date" they had to accommodate to their
listeners' ignorance of culture-bound ref-
erents.*

"Interpreters often do offer unsolicited explanations since a nonsensical answer on the part of the witness or defendant casts doubt on the quality of the interpreter's interpretation." (Berk-Seligson 1985:10:22-23)
In other words, the dilemma centres on the leeway the interpreter has in averting the risk of sounding "unprofes-
sional."

Miriam Shlesinger says:

*despite the growing realization of the interpret-
er's often decisive role in according due process
to a language-handicapped defendant, few legal
systems provide specific guidelines as to the leeway the interpreter has in performing his professional duties. Whatever the cause of the inter-*

preter's uneasiness about his role definition - failure to accommodate to his audience as he understands this obligation or the need to avoid jeopardizing his own professional reputation - a discussion of these difficulties between the bench and the interpreters will prove beneficial.

Ruth Morris comments that:

> *In striving to achieve the optimum accuracy vital for legal proceedings, interpreters may wish to clarify material. By indicating such problems to the court, they draw attention to their presence as supernumerary participants in the proceedings. If, instead, they clarify material with the speaker, they are taking an initiative to which they are not strictly speaking entitled. The third option, to venture an educated guess, is non-intrusive and more in line with the supposed neutral position of the court interpreter, but is likely to have negative effects if the guess is incorrect.*

However,

> *the effect of clarification procedures for interpretation purposes may be to unwittingly assist a witness to improve presentation of an answer, thereby giving a more positive impression through the interpretation than in the original.*

Identification of speakers

Morris continues:

> *Harris (1991) reports that the French-German interpreter at a German war crimes trial used the technique of beginning each interpretation with an identify-*

ing formula such as "The presiding judge is asking you ..." "The witness's answer is that ..." At the Demjanjuk trial the English-language simultaneous interpreters were required for the record to give the name of the speaker before each utterance, but to do so without recourse to the third person. On occasion when forced to render an entire sequence of questions and answers, the court interpreter did have recourse to formulae involving reported speech, although the required practice was to use the first person.

Morris also discusses keeping a record of the original as well as the interpreted version:

However accurate the interpreted version of proceedings is believed to be, it is of the utmost importance that an electronic and accurate written record of all original material, including that not in the language of the court plus interpreted versions of questions, be made and preserved. To do so requires the use of a microphone even in the case of whispered interpretation.

In some cases where the interpreter may unjustly be blamed for misunderstanding, the recording may also serve to protect him. For greater flexibility, the interpreter should wear an on-body radio microphone such as one attached to her clothing (jacket lapel), to avoid having to face in a certain direction or speak in a certain way.

Explanations

According to Roseann González (González, Vásquez and Mikkelson 1991):

It is important for the interpreter to know when it is appropriate to intervene in order to ensure that communication is taking place and the record of testimony is accurate. As a general rule, stepping out of the role of interpreter and taking on the role of expert should be regarded as a measure of last resort, to be undertaken with greatest caution. The interpreter should under no circumstances act as an expert on matters outside the realm of interpreting; like any professional, the interpreter should refrain from commenting or intervening in matters that are not within his or her area of expertise. There are times, though, when the interpreter, because of linguistic knowledge, is the only one who knows something in the interchange is amiss. For example, if the witness uses the Spanish term "pie" (foot) to mean the entire leg, as is common among rural Latin Americans, the interpreter may step out of the interpreting role and say: "Your Honor, the interpreter would like to clarify that it is common for rural Latin Americans to use the word "foot" to designate the entire leg."

Protocol: If communication is breaking down and the interpreter can easily resolve the issue, and if the term in question is an essential part of an answer that others could not possibly understand without an explanation, then intervention is warranted. But if it is apparent that the attorney is able to clarify the situation through follow-up questions, the interpreter should not interfere.

Quality of the interpretation

Morris (1989) points out: "Court interpretation is a special exercise with requirements differing from those applicable to a standard conference interpretation situation. Anderson (1976: 220) writes: "We should expect maximal attention to faithful interpretation - even to reproduction of intonation and gestural signs". Saint-Aubin (in Roberts 1981: 129)[24] elaborates this point, arguing that the judge bases himself primarily on the interpretation in deciding whether or not a witness is lying: "To some extent, the interpreter must be an actor." Morris continues:

> *The quality of the interpretation is crucial. The purpose of the l978 introduction of federal legislation in the United States regulating the provision of court interpretation was to ensure that only certified (and therefore supposedly competent) interpreters would work in U.S. courts. However, as has been found even in a country like the Federal Republic of Germany, where court interpreting has been stringently regulated for a considerable time, problems inevitably arise when "rare" languages have to be covered. Moreover, certification systems are not watertight: an interpreter may be certified and competent to work with two languages, but not from a third. He may nevertheless proceed to do so, with the inevitable negative results from the point of view of quality[25].*

> *Interpretation in court should never be provided other than by linguistically competent, skilled and experienced impartial interpreters and all interpreted material should always be recorded for subsequent checking. If these conditions are*

---

[24] Translation: R.Morris. Somewhat less clearly, Cronheim and Schwartz (1976: 310) write: "Whichever method is used, it is then up to the jury to assess the credibility of the witness by watching the interaction between the interpreter and the person testifying."

[25] For example, at the Fort Lauderdale proceedings against Feodor Federenko, a Treblinka death-camp guard, an interpreter certified to work in U.S. courts from and into Spanish was engaged to work from and into Hebrew. The 1978 Court Interpreters Act (Section 1827 (d)) stipulates that "when no certified interpreter is reasonably available, as determined by the presiding judicial officer, the services of an otherwise competent interpreter" shall be utilized.

not satisfied, proceedings may be distorted and justice perverted.

Berk-Seligson's (1990) seminal work on the Spanish-English courtroom in the United States, l985, (consecutive mode) shows that even minor shifts in interpretation involving such aspects as the degree of "powerfulness" of testimony are liable to affect jurors' perception of a witness' credibility.

Two Australian lawyers, Kathy Laster and Veronica Taylor (1993), one of whom has interpreted legal proceedings, complain that judges underestimate the sophistication of courtroom dialogue and the pre-requisites for court interpreting. They argue that non-English speaking protagonists' relatives or friends should not be permitted to interpret in legal settings.

Ruth Morris (1993) observes the 'generally low calibre' of court interpreting and attempts to dissuade judges and legal practitioners from "the belief that no better standards can be achieved". In her opinion, courts evade financial and administrative responsibility for the provision of competent interpreting by leaving its arrangement to parties to the courts' proceedings. Morris contends that courts are

> *fearful of the consequences for the judicial system of recognizing a genuine right to [interpreting, which] would involve the recognition of a duty for the courts to provide accurate [interpreting] in a range of languages, therby imposing on the system financial costs and the burden of administrative arrangements which it is unwilling to bear.*

She urges lawyers to

> *press for an improvement in [interpreting] standards, on all fronts: the quality, training and knowledge of those engaged to perform [court/legal interpreting; court interpreters']*

235

working conditions; and arrangements for .....
monitoring, electronic regording and, sometimes,
bilingual transcripts of all [source language] and
[target] language material for subsequent ap-
peals.

In her opinion: "Without such improvements, lawyers are handicapping themselves, their clients and the [judicial] system."

Margaret O'Toole agrees with Laster & Taylor, and Morris, that Australia's criteria for court interpreting are not stringent: she points out them that the Australian judiciary has no official role in training, testing or selecting court interpreters. The legislative and executive branches of government have the role and responsibility of providing and allocating funds and facilities for the administration of justice, including court interpreting.

The majority of interpreters used in Australia's courts is employed or retained by a federal, State or Territorial Department of Immigration and/or an Ethnic Affairs Commission. A substantial proportion of those interpreters is accredited or recognized by the National Accreditation Authority for Translators and Interpreters (NAATI) which, since its establishment in 1977, has been financed by Australia's governments. Through governmental cost sharing arrangements the taxpayer funds, directly and indirectly, most court interpreting in Australia.[26]

Self-evidently, pre-requisites for accurate court interpreting include specialised knowledge of two or more judicial systems, high levels of literacy in English and a second language and mastery in both languages of the wide range of linguistic registers used by courtroom protagonists. Ordinarily, those attributes attract remu-

---

[26] For an overview of court interpreting arrangements in Australia, see Commonwealth Attorney-General's Department , 1991. *Access to interpreters in the Australian legal system Report.* Chapters 2 and 5. Canberra: AGPS.

neration which exceeds the fees paid by Australia's governments to court interpreters. As the then Chief Justice of the High Court of Australia explained:

> *No doubt demands on the public purse.... limit the funds available [for facilities for the administration of justice]. If the limitation is severe the administration of justice suffers.*

Since the nineteen sixties, common lawyers have complained that "expert" interpreters, "readily available" in New South Wales' courts, gratuitously alter the meaning and impact of evidence, jeopardising both non-English and English speaking parties' rights to natural justice. In 1991, the Commonwealth Attorney-General's Department acknowledged complaints that: "People of non-English speaking background are likely to be greatly disadvantaged in using an interpreter because of .... the present low standard of court interpreting..."[27]

In New South Wales, *ad hoc* applications to trial judges, challenging the accuracy of audible court interpreting, are not uncommon. Appeals to the Supreme Court of New South Wales alleging a miscarriage of justice resulting from inaccurate interpreting are relatively infrequent but consume public funds, allocated for the administration of justice, and scarce judicial resources.[28]

Australia's judges do have power to control proceedings in their own courtrooms, including the power to control the behaviour of interpreters. Subject to legislation, modifying the operation of Australian common law,

---

[27] An explanation may be that insufficiently qualified court interpreters are being used, i.e. interpreters without NAATI Accreditation at a miminum of Level 3 (first professional level), that is to say "interpreters" who are not accredited at all but have merely been "Recognized" and cannot, therefore, be considered to be professional interpreters.

[28] In *Saraya v The Queen* (1994) 70 A Crim.R 515, the Supreme Court of New South Wales, Court of Criminal Appeal, upheld a limited-English speaker's appeal against his conviction for a serious crime after a five day jury trial in the District Court of New South Wales, because consecutive interpreting of questions to and oral evidence given by the accused was inaccurate.

trial judges also have a discretion to permit or to refuse to allow a witness to give evidence in a signed or non-English spoken language through an interpreter. In practice, unless a party fortuitously detects and considers it advantageous to complain of a specific interpreting error, a court may not be aware of inaccurate interpreting. Few of the non-English languages spoken audibly by courtroom protagonists are understood by judges or legal practitioners. Unless a party adduces evidence exposing biased or inaccurate interpreting, judges rarely have reliable means of determining complaints about interpreters.

Monitoring

Ruth Morris and Miriam Shlesinger are both of the view that quality control is needed in the form of monitoring. Court proceedings are generally based on the interpreter's words, not the speaker's, and the records kept also reflect the interpreter's words and not the speaker's. In fact, the interpreter's words are quoted as if they were literally those of the speaker and often no record whatsoever is kept of the original foreign-language material. Shlesinger says:

> On the face of it, any steps taken by us, as courtroom interpreters, to draw attention to possible flaws in our own performance are self-defeating, if not downright foolish. I maintain, however, that efforts on our part to stress the need for quality control will in fact complement the campaign which many of us have been waging to end the "open admissions" policy into our ranks - for reasons having nothing to do with unionism. As we know, there are many countries in which some of those currently filling the role of courtroom interpreter are not fully qualified, the interpreter is seen as an imposition and interpreting is regarded as a sideline available to anyone professing to know two languages.

As matters now stand, any breakdown of communications resulting from an error, omission, etc. in the interpretation may or may not be detected, depending on the chance observation and intervention of one of the parties present, none of whom is expressly charged with monitoring the interpreting. Thus serious flaws may be noted and corrected, but they may equally well go unheeded. While the former situation is awkward for the interpreter, the latter is potentially damaging to the defendant.

Paradoxical though it may seem, pointing out the limitations of the service we provide and drawing attention to factors which may hinder our own performance is in our own best interests. Considering that interpreters are often regarded as capable of rendering just about anything from any language into any language under any physical circumstances ("You're a professional, aren't you?") we can help formulate the ground rules and point out those situations in which errors or omissions are most liable to occur, so that these situations never snowball into an obstruction of due process.

Far be it from me to imply that courtroom interpreters are inadequate or that someone must continually be breathing down every interpreter's neck if they are to do their work properly. Anything but ! Wherever the courtroom interpreters are trained, experienced and working under proper conditions, the product is - by and large - incredibly good. But even under such circumstances, let alone others, there is much to be said in favor of measures for monitoring the interpretation.

She also writes:

some means should be expressly provided to min-
imize omissions and inaccuracies of whatever
sort, regardless of their cause.....Like everyone
else, interpreters vary in their reactions to criti-
cism, professional or otherwise, and some may
even resent the notion of having their work re-
viewed or controlled, no matter how sound the
rationale. And yet the salutary results of moni-
toring - however we courtroom interpreters may
look at it - must surely take precedence over the
psyche of the 'monitoree'.

Needless to say, a distinction must be made be-
tween those situations in which the courtroom in-
terpreter is properly trained and qualified, and
those in which he is not. The need for monitoring
is especially acute wherever the training and ac-
creditation of courtroom interpreters is lacking,
or where non-certified interpreters continue to
work in a system which introduced more strin-
gent requirements after they had begun working.
All other things being equal, though, quality con-
trol becomes increasingly critical as the profes-
sional standard declines. It would be a mistake,
however, to assume that monitoring is entirely
dispensable even in those systems where the in-
terpreters are of the highest calibre.

When a witness gives an answer indicating non-
comprehension, his *non-sequitur* indicates that something in the interpretation needs to be set right. Sometimes the Presiding Judge says: "There seems to be something wrong with the translation. Was the figure X or Y ?"
However, since the person giving the reply is unaware of
the fact that the interpreted version was not equivalent to
the original, anything less than an obvious *non sequitur* is
not likely to raise suspicion. For example: Question:
"Were there any officers higher than you?" (Back transla-

tion of the interpreted version: "Were any of the officers hired by you?") Answer: "No." As it turned out, no officers had been hired by the defendant, but there were several who were higher than he. Figures are often inadvertently misquoted, e.g. interpreting 29,000 as 92,000 when working at high speed.

In simultaneous of course there will be two interpreters who can consult one another and jot down helpful words or corrections for one another.

The record is a useful reference but, since this is *ex post facto* it will only be useful in case of any necessary corrections if clarification can be made at a later stage in the trial or cited in case of appeal. (As explained above, for this purpose it is essential to maintain a record of the original as well as the interpretation (including chuchotage).)

Obviously the more the bench is aware of the interpreters' needs, the more it is likely to project the awareness to the litigants and encourage their cooperation with the interpreters. The consecutive interpreter is of course in a far better position to request clarification or repetition than the simultaneous interpreter. One of the expert witnesses in the Demjanjuk trial, a graphologist, referred alternately to "ink lines" and "inclines". When she became aware of potential confusion due to this homophony, the consecutive interpreter into Hebrew asked the witness which of the two she was referring to. However, the simultaneous interpreters when caught in a similar predicament had no choice but to guess at the speaker's intention.

While the above rather haphazard techniques may on occasion prevent misunderstandings which might have gone undetected and could have led to a miscarriage of justice, the following measures would provide for maximum safeguard:

1. A pre-trial discussion in chambers to clarify interpretation procedure;

2. An unobstructed view of the participants and of any exhibits (maps, charts, slides, etc.);

3. Provision of a red light or buzzer to give the simultaneous interpreter technical means of alerting the bench and/or speaker to any difficulty, acoustic, technical or linguistic;

4. The recording of all interpretation whether simultaneous, consecutive or whispering (chuchotage);

5. A distinction through change of font or colour being made in the record to indicate which is original and which is interpretation.

6. All interpretation, regardless of mode, must be monitored.

Ideally, interpretation teams for any given language combination would include an additional interpreter whose expressly designated role would be to monitor the interpretation, probably on a rotation basis."Although involving greater costs and more complicated technical arrangements, the weighting of justice vs. practicability is a matter for the legislator's conscience." Ruth Morris says that the ideal court interpretation situation would be:

Competent, experienced court interpreters working with a complete view of the courtroom and all the participants; interpreters to work in teams of two and only into their mother tongue; excellent courtroom acoustics and electronics; disciplined speakers who never interrupt or speak over each other and who at all times observe a reasonable rate of delivery of around 100 w.p.m.; arrangements to provide interpretation at lawyer-client private consultations (for exam-

ple, by a third interpreter seated at the defence table, who might also act as monitor of the simultaneous interpretation); the advance provision to the interpreters of copies of all material referred to in the proceedings and, in particular, of any documents cited; an arrangement for the indication by the interpreters to clients and the bench of problems with particular material; a device for indicating when the interpreters are providing their versions, in order to prevent participants from speaking during the interpretation of a previous utterance; and appropriate monitoring arrangements during the proceedings proper, so that a neutral third party can indicate errors which have or may have occurred and either correct them or arrange for immediate clarification of the disputed material. Lastly, all material uttered at the trial, whether original or interpreted, would be electronically recorded and transcribed, and the transcript would then be checked by a third party against the original recording.

Standards

In Australia, only NAATI accredited interpreters (former Level 3, 4 or 5) should be used in Courts, Level 3 being the first professional level and level 4 being preferable. The use of interpreters below that level of accreditation is unacceptable, particularly since *ipso facto* they are not professional interpreters.

Difficulties arise when interpretation in a rare language is required, for which there are no accredited interpreters available. While NAATI has conducted tests or approved academic courses leading to NAATI accreditation in many languages, where accredited interpreters are not available in "rarer" languages, "recognized" persons have to be used, i.e. insufficiently qualified interpreters[29], which results in a most unsatisfactory situation. It is open to question which is worse: to have no interpreter at all or to have an interpreter who is incompetent.

Unfortunately NAATI does not hold accreditation tests specifically for Court Interpretation, nor are courses available in this country specifically for this type of interpretation and including some rudiments of court procedure.

The USA appears to be the only country where court interpreters are tested on objective and subjective criteria, formulated by bilingual judges, practising conference and court interpreters, linguists and testing experts, with the object of satisfying the United States Government's Constitutional obligation to afford "due process" to non-English speakers.

It is a legal principle in Australia, I believe, that unless a trial appears to be fair, as well as being fair in fact, it is not a fair trial. In the eyes of bilingual observers, however, the normal standard of court interpretation in many parts of the world today, including Australia, is such that this condition is not met.

Contracts

It is of course important for the court interpreter to have a written agreement with his employer concerning fees, working hours and conditions. International conference interpretation contracts cannot be used because of the difficulty of knowing beforehand how long the trial will last or what the actual hours and amount of work will be for the various languages, particularly as last-minute changes regarding witnesses' language requirements may arise in the course of cross-examination.

Lack of Status and recognition

---

[29] National Accreditation Authority for Translators and Interpreters (NAATI), Canberra A.C.T.: "Candidates' Manual"

It is not lack of interest that prevents conference interpreters from turning to court interpreting - on the contrary it is often considered more rewarding and sometimes more demanding, involving greater responsibility - but unfortunately the fees paid for court interpreting are insignificant compared to those paid for conference interpreting.

It is to be hoped that the fees and status of court interpreters will improve in view of the crucial role they have to play in society. Ruth Morris states, as a result of her research on interpretation at the Demjanjuk trial in 1987-88, that:

> *the use of appropriate interpreting techniques by competent interpreters can put the language-handicapped participant on a nearly equal footing with the native speaker of the language of the legal proceedings. The cooperation of practising lawyers is vital in order to achieve universal acceptance of the need for high-calibre interpreters. Certain modifications of practice may also be required such as making case papers available to interpreters in advance and improving acoustics. However, until the authorities are willing to consider interpreters as a valuable resource and treat them accordingly in terms of both fees and conditions, the quality of interpreting in the courts will tend to remain low. Similarly, unless the legal profession calls for higher standards and accepts that good interpreters can provide high-calibre language services not only in the European Court of Justice but in other legal settings also, miscarriages of justice will remain a very real possibility because of incompetent performances by unqualified individuals used as interpreters by the courts. There is a need for interpreters and lawyers to examine the situation in each country and for specific solutions to be developed in order to ensure that linguistic and*

therefore human rights are respected. Unless this is done, whether blind or not, justice will certainly be very hard of hearing in the case of the language-handicapped participant.

The more one delves into the subject of court/legal interpretation, the more one realizes how infinitely complex it is - much more complex than I have been able to represent. It is clear that interpreters of the highest calibre, discipline and awareness of court procedures are required, qualified and trained in this specialization and fully aware of the expectations of courts and judges.

Let us hope that the days are over when court cleaners were recruited at short notice to serve as interpreters in Australian courts.[30] Speaking of democracy, Churchill is reputed to have said "It's a terrible system but it's the best there is." Geoffrey Robertson comments that this also applies to the adversarial system of law; it probably applies similarly to the system of interpretation used in courts.

---

[30] *Courrier-Mail*, Brisbane, 2 March 1989: Court case concerning Sicilian "benefactor" Antonino Costantino. The newspaper report said:"Costantino finally appeared after two earlier interpreters, including a former court cleaner, were found wanting on Wednesday and Thursday."...."An Immigration, Local Government and Ethnic Affairs Department spokesman, Mr. Doug Callaghan, said yesterday the commission had asked for an Italian interpreter at l p.m. on Wednesday. "We couldn't find anybody at such short notice, which led the court to recruit the cleaner," Mr. Callaghan said.

"A court official gave her $29.75 for her appearance yesterday but Mrs. Cannizzaro refused to take it until told she had to. "I was scared and frightened I would make a mistake that would get me in big trouble," she said."

15

THE UNITED NATIONS, ITS SPECIALIZED AGENCIES, INTERNATIONAL ORGANIZATIONS AND THE EUROPEAN UNION

The United Nations includes the following agencies and programmes established by the UN:

- United Nations Children's Fund (UNICEF);

- United Nations Relief and Works Agency for Palestine Refugees in the Near East (UNRWA);

- Office of the United Nations High Commissioner for refugees (UNHCR);

- International Trade Centre (UNCTAD/WTO/ITC);

- United Nations Conference on Trade and development (UNCTAD);

- United Nations Development Programme (UNDP);

- United Nations Institute for Training and Research (UNITAR);

- United Nations Population Fund (UNFPA);

- United Nations Disaster Relief Office (UNDRO);

- United Nations Environment Programme (UNEP);

- United Nations University (UNU);

- International Research and Training Institute for the Advancement of Women (INSTRAW);

- UN Centre for Human Settlements (Habitat) (UNCHS (Habitat));
- United Nations Drug Control Programme (UNDCP).
  (See also Appendix A)

Regional Commissions include:

- Economic Commission for Europe (ECE);

- Economic and Social Commission for Asia and the Pacific (ESCAP);

- Economic Commission for Latin America and the Caribbean (ECLAC);

- Economic Commission for Africa (ECA);

- Economic and Social Commission for Western Asia (ESCWA).

The United Nations was founded in 1945 as the successor to the League of Nations. Its aim was to foster international peace, security and cooperation. One hundred and ninety one countries are members. All have a seat in the General Assembly, which meets annually, but only five (China, France, the Russian Federation, United Kingdom and United States) are permanent members of the Security Council (each with the power of veto), which functions continuously and is responsible for maintaining international peace and security; an additional ten members are elected by the General Assembly to serve on the Security Council for two-year terms. The main UN headquarters are in New York; the European Office is in Geneva, Switzerland. The International Court of Justice is based in The Hague.

Specialized Agencies of the UN

The specialised agencies of the UN are largely concerned with setting standards and regulating activity in areas of their speciality and with taking steps to extend advances in research and technology. Australia takes a prominent part in their technical activites and at their meetings. The following are Specialized Agencies:

- Food and Agriculture Organization (FAO, Rome);

- International Fund for Agricultural Development (IFAD, Rome);

- International Civil Aviation Authority (ICAO, Montreal)

- International Labour Organization (ILO, Geneva);

- International Maritime Organisation (IMO, London);

- International Telecommunication Union (ITU, Geneva)

- United Nations Educational, Scientific and Cultural Organisation (UNESCO, Paris);

- United Nations Industrial Development Organisation (UNIDO, Vienna),;

- Universal Postal Union (UPU, Berne);

- World Health Organization (WHO, Geneva);

- World Intellectual Property Organisation (WIPO, Geneva);

- World Meteorological Organisation (WMO, Geneva);

- World Trade Organization (WTO), formerly GATT (General Agreement on Tarifs and Trade).

- The International Atomic Energy Agency (IAEA, Vienna), is an autonomous international organisation which conducts its activities in accordance with the principles of the UN Charter.

International Economic Cooperation

Some of the major bodies dealing with international economic and social issues in which Australia takes part are:

- United Nations Development Programme (UNDP);

- United Nations Population Fund (UNFPA);

- United Nations Children's Fund (UNICEF);

- UN Conferenceon Trade and Development (UNCTAD);

- World Trade Organization (WTO);

- International Monetary Fund (IMF);

- The International Bank for Reconstruction and Development (IBRD, a member of the World Bank group of institutions).

The Asian Development Bank (ADB, Manila) was set up in 1965 to foster economic growth and cooperation in Asia and the Far East, including the South Pacific. There are forty-seven members of the bank - thirty-two regional (including Australia) and fifteen non-regional.

The working languages of UN are English, French, Spanish and Russian, as well as Chinese and Arabic.

The following international organizations recruit interpreters, permanent or free-lance or both:

Africa:
- African Development Bank, Abidjan: English, French
- Economic Commission for Africa, Addis Ababa:
  English, French, Spanish rarely
- UN Centre for Human Settlements (Habitat), Nairobi:
- English, Arabic, Spanish, French, Russian
- Organisation of African Unity, Addis Abeba: English, Arabic, French

- UNEP (UN Environment Programme), Nairobi: English, Arabic, Spanish, French, Russian

Americas:

- Inter-American Development Bank, Washington: English, Spanish, French, Portuguese
- ECLA (Economic Commission for Latin America), Santiago: English, Spanish, French
- IMF (International Monetary Fund), Washington: German, English, Arabic, Chinese, Spanish, French, Portuguese
- INTELSAT (International Telecommunications Satellite Organization), Washington: English, Spanish, French
- ICAO (International Civil Aviation Organization), Montreal: English,Spanish, French, Russian (also Arabic and Chinese)
- Organization of American States (OAS), Washington: English, Spanish, French, Portuguese
- UN (United Nations), New York: English, Arabic, Spanish, French, Russian, Chinese
- PAHO (Pan American Health Organization), Washington: English, Spanish (also French and Portuguese)

Asia:

- ESCAP (Economic and Social Commission for Asia and the Pacific), Bangkok: English, Chinese, French, Russian
- SPC (South Pacific Community), Nouméa: English, French

Europe:
- IAEA (International Atomic Energy Agency), Vienna: English, Arabic, Chinese, Spanish, French, Russian
- ILO (International Labour Organization), Geneva: English, French, German, Spanish, Arabic, Chinese, Japanese, Russian
- European Commission, Brussels: English, German, Danish, Spanish, French, Greek, Italian, Dutch, Portuguese.[31]
- CERN (European Organization for Nuclear Research), Geneva: English, French
- CE (Council of Europe), Strasbourg: English, French (also German, Spanish, Italian, Dutch)
- WCO (World Customs Organisation), Brussels: English, French (sometimes Spanish, Russian)
- CICR (International Red Cross Committee), Geneva: French (German, English, Arabic, Spanish, Farsi)

---

[31] Candidates must have four languages: one active and three passive. Two passive languages only may be acceptable if the interpreter can do the *retour* into another language. N.B. For the Spanish and Portuguese booths, preference is given to a Spanish or Portuguese accent.

- CJEU (Court of Justice of the European Union), Luxembourg: German, English, Danish, Spanish, French, Greek, Italian, Dutch, Portuguese[32].
- EUROCONTROL, Brussels: German, English, French, Greek, Portuguese, Turkish (also Spanish and Italian)
- FAO (UN Food and Agriculture Organization) and World Food Programme (WFP), Rome: English, Arabic, Chinese, Spanish, French, Russian
- IFAD (International Fund for Agricultural Development), Rome: English, Arabic, Spanish, French
- WTO (World Trade Organization), Geneva: English, Spanish, French
- OECD (Organization for Economic Cooperation and Development), Paris: English, French
- IMO (International Maritime Organization), London: English, Arabic, Chinese, Spanish, French, Russian
- WMO (World Meteorological Organization), Geneva: English, Arabic, Chinese, Spanish, French, Russian
- WIPO (World Intellectual Property Organization), Geneva: English, Arabic, Chinese, Spanish, French, Russian
- WHO (World Health Organization), Geneva: English, Arabic, Chinese, Spanish, French, Russian

---

[32] Recruitment based on four languages, i.e. candidates must have three passive languages in addition to mother tongue. Interpreters with law background given preference.

- WTO (World Tourism Organization), Madrid: English, Spanish, French, Russian
- UN (United Nations), Geneva, Vienna: English, Arabic, Chinese, Spanish, French, Russian
- UNOID (United Nations Organization for Industrial Development), Vienna: English, Arabic, Chinese, Spanish, French, Russian
- NATO (North Atlantic Treaty Organization), Brussels: English, French
- EP (European Parliament), Luxembourg, Brussels, Strasbourg:German,English,Danish, Spanish, French, Greek, Italian, Dutch, Portuguese[33].
- WEU (Western European Union), London, Paris: English French (occasionally German, Spanish, Italian, Dutch)
- ITU (International Telecommunications Union), Geneva: English, Arabic, Chinese, Spanish, French, Russian
- UPU (Universal Postal Union), Berne: English, Arabic, Spanish, Portuguese, Russian

This is not an exhaustive list; also the languages used by these organizations may change.

Australia and the UN

The Department of Foreign Affairs and Trade publishes *Australia in Brief*, reference papers and fact sheets on a wide range of subjects. For more information contact: International Public Affairs Branch, Department of Foreign Affairs and Trade, Canberra, A.C.T. 2600 or the state offices of the Department of Foreign Affairs and

---

[33] Four languages are necessary for recruitment (one active and three passive) unless the interpreter has among her passive languages one of the more "exotic" languages such as Danish or Greek. With regard to the Spanish booth, preference is given to a Spanish accent.

Trade in Sydney, Melbourne, Adelaide, Perth, Brisbane and Hobart.

So you want a job at United Nations?

The Chief Interpreter at the European Office of the United Nations says that a diploma from any Interpretation School or University, or proof of working at another international organization does not exempt candidates from the UN interpretation test. However brilliant the degree, experience is also required before the candidate can hope to pass the UN interpretation test. He also insists that the United Nations does not encourage "bilingualism" (that is, working in two booths, but with only two (A) languages).

Information about United Nations competitive examinations for interpreters may be obtained from the UN Information Centre in Sydney[34]. Examinations are held in New York, Geneva and other locations depending on the number of candidates. Candidates selected are subject to rotation and may be called upon to serve in Africa, Asia, Europe or Latin America, according to the needs of the UN.

If you are successful in obtaining work as an interpreter at UN, you become a custodian of international public trust and as such have to undertake an oath to give allegiance to no national government, i.e. not to accept instructions from any government.

Languages

English is definitely a must. English is in daily use in the European Community, the OECD, the Council of Europe, the Western European Union, NATO as well as the United Nations family.

Arabic is increasingly important in large international organizations, particularly in the UN family. In

---

[34] United Nations Information Centre, Suite 1, 2nd floor, 125 York Street, Sydney. Mail: GPO Box 4045, Sydney 2001.

fact, looked at from a global viewpoint, an interpreter is unlikely to be able to become established professionally without one of the following active languages (in alphabetical order): Arabic, English, French, German, Italian, Japanese, Russian or Spanish. Chinese is increasingly important as the years go by. Japanese is still in great demand not only in the Pacific Region but also now in the United States and Europe. Greek, Dutch, Italian and Danish are used within the framework of the European Union. Portuguese is not only an official EU language, but is used in an increasing number of other meetings.

The European Union

The EU has its headquarters in Brussels. Members: Austria, Belgium, Denmark, Finland, France, Germany, Greece, Ireland, Italy, Luxembourg, The Netherlands, Portugal, Spain, Sweden and United Kingdom. Other associated bodies: The European Commission (its executive), based in Brussels, the Council of Ministers of member states, the European Parliament which meets in Luxembourg and Strasbourg, and the European Court of Justice also in Luxembourg. For European Union vocabulary, try EURODICAUTOM (www2.echo.lu).

The European Commission has a Joint Interpreting and Conference Service (JICS) which has recently been considerably streamlined. It is by far the largest interpreting service in the world and provides conference interpretation and technical and organizational knowhow for the European Commission, the Council of the European Union (usually known as the "Council of Ministers"), the Economic and Social Committee, the Committee of the Regions, the European Investment Bank and other bodies of the European Union, except for the European Parliament and the Court of Justice.

Early in 1997 the European Commission approached the Thematic Network Project in the Area of Languages (SOCRATES-ERASMUS Programme) about the possibility of launching a European pilot project for the joint development of a university programme at advanced level (Master type) in Conference Interpreting to remedy the shortage of highly qualified conference interpreters, specifically with language combinations including less widely used and less taught languages. In April of that year a pilot project proposal was circulated among higher education institutions specializing in the training of conference interpreters, inviting them to submit expressions of interest. These were also made available on the Thematic Network Project's website. The Interpreting Service of the European Parliament also became involved. The coordination of the pilot project was finally entrusted to the University of Westminster chaired by Ingeborg Smallwood. Full details on this subject and regarding the SOCRATES-ERASMUS Programme are available on the Internet (European Union website homepage : http://europa.eu.int/comm/scic/index_en.htm).

The EU is the biggest employer of interpreters with 130,000 interpreter-days a year. There are currently twenty-seven member states using twenty-one languages. All staff interpreters are under pressure to add another language to their language combination. One can imagine the size of meeting rooms necessary to house twenty-one interpreting booths. For up-to-date information please consult their website indicated above.

16

NAATI, AIIC, TAALS and AUSIT

National Accreditation Authority for Translators and Interpreters (NAATI)

NAATI[35] was established in Canberra in 1977 by the Commonwealth Government, located within the Department of Immigration but in 1983 it was re-established as an independent body, partly and jointly funded by the Commonwealth, the States and the Territories, and incorporated as a public company limited by guarantee. From the beginning, NAATI was charged with the tasks of:

a) establishing and monitoring the standards to meet all of Australia's interpreting and translating needs;

b) developing the means by which practitioners can be accredited at various levels;

c) developing and implementing a national system of registration and/or licensing;

d) fostering the development of a professional association; and

e) promoting the profession.

---

[35] **National Office:**17A 2 King Street Deakin ACT 2600 Ph: +61 2 6260 3035 Fax: +61 2 6260 3036 Office hours: 9:00am - 5:00pm Monday - Friday. E-mail: <info@naati.com.au> Website: www.naati.com.au
Addresses of NAATI offices in N.S.W., N.T., Qld., S.A., Tas., Vic., and W.A. may be obtained from Head Office.

How to obtain accreditation

There are three ways to obtain accreditation with NAATI:

1. by passing a NAATI accreditation examination (the pass mark is 70% at the basic professional level and 80% at the Advanced and Senior levels);

2. by successful completion of a NAATI approved course of studies in interpreting or translation at an Australian tertiary institution;

3. on the basis of specialized qualifications in interpretation/translation obtained from a recognized tertiary education institution overseas, or of membership of a recognized international professional association such as AIIC (International Association of Conference Interpreters), which are judged by the Authority to be equivalent to the standards required for accreditation in Australia.

Designation of practitioners accredited by NAATI are:

- Paraprofessional translator, paraprofessional interpreter (formerly Level 2);

- Translator, Interpreter (formerly Level 3);

- Advanced Translator, Conference Interpreter (formerly Level 4);[36] and

- Advanced Translator (Senior), Conference Interpreter (Senior) (formerly Level 5)[37]

For up to date information concerning NAATI and NAATI accreditation please consult website: www.naati.com.au

---

[36] This would correspond to a beginner Conference Interpreter who has just terminated a qualifying university course in conference interpretation.

[37] AIIC members are accredited at this level, which is the highest.

The International Association of Conference Interpreters (AIIC)

AIIC[38] was founded in Paris on 11 November 1953. It has 2973 members in 103 countries, covering 51 languages. Approximately 250 members are permanently employed by international organizations, the rest are free-lance. Membership consists of active, associate and honorary members.

AIIC has consultative status with the United Nations, the Council of Europe, the European Union and the OECD as well as with the International Standardization Organization regarding international standards for interpretation booths and electronic simultaneous interpreting equipment.

Members are bound by a Code of Professional Ethics, in particular by the strictest secrecy which must be observed towards all persons and with regard to all information disclosed in the course of the practice of the profession at any gathering not open to the public. Members must also refrain from deriving any personal gain whatsoever from confidential information they may acquire in the exercise of their duties as conference interpreters. Members of the Association are bound not to accept any assignment for which they are not qualified: acceptance of an assignment implies a moral undertaking to work with all due professionalism.

AIIC has an impressive list of publications, many of which are available upon request from the secretariat (see website www.aiic.net). Among these is a booklet of advice to students wishing to become conference interpreters, including a list of interpreting schools. AIIC is also working with UNESCO, WIPO and ILO to achieve an international convention on the definition and recogni-

---

[38] 46 avenue Blanc, Geneva 1202, Switzerland. Tel. 41 22 908 1540. Email: info@aiic.net Website: www.aiic.net

tion of conference interpreters; a working party is in the process of drafting the outline of such a convention. The directory is on the Internet and can be accessed freely. Only members of the Association however may use the directory search machine (by means of a password provided by the Secretariat). The extranet of the website also contains fora for discussion among members of committees or working groups or for members sharing a particular interest.

Structure

The Assembly is the supreme body of the Association and is made up of all AIIC members. It meets once every three years to define general policy. The Committee on Admissions and Language Classification is elected by the Assembly and directly accountable to it.

The Council (twenty-seven members) meets at least once a year and is composed of the bureau of five including the President and Treasurer of the Association together with representatives of the twenty-two Regions.

There are a number of committees and working groups, including:

- The Technical and Health Committee, which gathers information on the simultaneous interpretation equipment and booths used at conference venues and cooperates with the International Organisation for Standardization (ISO) on standards for fixed and mobile booths and equipment and has published the *Guidelines for Technicians*. The Committee also advises architects and planners on interpretation facilities and researches health aspects of the profession.

- The Training Committee's main task is to encourage interpreting schools to adopt similar standards, and admission and graduation criteria. This committee publishes a list of schools classified according to the extent to which they conform to AIIC criteria for training conference interpreters. It also organises lectures and seminars to help members update their knowledge and improve their skills.

- The Research Committee carries out research into interpretation and linguistics, and maintains an up-to-date bibliography of research on language, interpretation and related fields.

There are also committees dealing with insurance, court and legal interpretation, disputes, staff interpreters and statistics, as well as a Budget Committee, a Disciplinary Committee and a Solidarity Fund.

The Secretariat, based in Geneva, carries out the administrative work of the association and is responsible for all official AIIC publications.

Sectors

Sectors are formed by members who have specific common interests.

- The Agreement Sector for those members working for the international organizations with which AIIC has concluded an agreement. These are the United Nations organizations, the European Union institutions, OECD, NATO, International Trade Secretariats, Interpol and the Customs Co-operation Council, who are all major employers of interpreters. Council mandates a negotiating delegation to prepare an agreement with the relevant organizations. Once formally approved by Council, the implementation of the agreement in each institution is monitored by a professional delegation.

- The Private Market Sector (PMS), for those who work for a wide range of clients in the private sector including professional associations, business corporations,

trade unions, political parties, government depart-
ments, non-governmental organizations (NGO's), academic institutions and so on. Conferences and meetings in this sector cover the medical, technical, legal,
commercial, industrial and other fields. PMS meetings are open to all AIIC members and candidates, are
held twice a year and are hosted by different AIIC Regions. A PMS meeting was held in Sydney in January
1999. The sector elects a standing committee and
regularly reviews working conditions and market
trends. In recent years, PMS has sponsored ground-
breaking work on interpretation for TV and on the
copyright aspects of interpretation.

The sectors hold their own meetings to discuss
matters of interest to them and report directly to Council.

Regions

A region is a country, part of a country or group of
countries in which members reside and work. There are
twenty-three regions. Members elect a regional bureau
consisting of a council member, a secretary and a treasurer. The candidate proposed by the region for council
member is then formally elected by the assembly.

The geographical definition of the Asia-Pacific
Region is that adopted by ESCAP. It comprises 121 members covering seventeen languages, domiciled in Australia
(21), Cambodia, China, Fiji, Hong Kong, India, Indonesia,
Japan, Korea, Malaysia, Nepal, New Caledonia, New Zealand, Singapore, Taiwan and Thailand.

How to join

Once you have worked 150 days in compliance
with the conditions set out in the Code of Ethics and Professional Standards, you will doubtless have worked with
a number of AIIC members and can ask for their sponsorship. They will need to be members of at least five years'
standing and have the right language combination. In

agreeing to act as sponsor, the member guarantees that to the best of his knowledge, the candidate has the necessary professional experience and respects the rules of the Association. The AIIC rules for sponsorship of language combinations are quite complicated but are set out clearly in the application form that the Secretariat sends upon request. Once the application form is complete, the Committee on Admissions and Language Combinations (CACL) will publish the candidate's name on the AIIC website and on a list appearing in the *AIIC Bulletin*. If the application is not challenged within 60 days of publication, the candidate automatically becomes a full member. Membership of AIIC does not preclude membership of national professional associations.

The main purpose of AIIC has always been to ensure quality - to make membership a guarantee of quality. Its goals also include setting standards for the exercise of conference interpretation, defending the interests of its members and representing the profession.

The American Association of Language Specialists (TAALS)

TAALS[39] represents language specialists in the Americas working at the international level, either at conferences or in permanent organizations. It was founded in Washington D.C. in 1957 and today has a membership of around 130 interpreters and translators, based in Argentina, Brazil, Canada, Guatemala, Mexico, Peru, United States, Uruguay and Venezuela as well as in Europe, Asia and Africa. Some members are permanently employed by international organizations, government agencies and universities; the others work on a free-lance basis.

---

[39] Suite 9, 1000 Connecticut Avenue, N.W., Washington D.C. 20036. Tel. (301) 986-1542 Washington, (212) 865-0183 New York, (416) 977-8588 Canada. Website: http://www.taals.net

How to join

Applications for membership are accepted up to August 15 and new members are admitted by a two-thirds majority at the annual Assembly.

Classifications

Interpreters are rated as follows:

A - Principal active language(s) into which they interpret and which they speak as a native;

B - Other active language(s) into which they interpret regardless of difficulties of terminology or idiom

B* - Other active language(s) into which they interpret consecutively only; and

C - Language(s) from which they interpret regardless of difficulties of terminology or idiom.

The Australian Institute of Interpreters and Translators (AUSIT)

The Professional Development Board of NAATI created AUSIT[40] in October 1987 feeling there was a need for a national professional association for interpreters and translators in this country. The first Annual General Meeting was held in June 1988 where the Constitution was adopted.

AUSIT has a branch in each State and Territory[41]. All NAATI-accredited interpreters and translators at former levels 3, 4 and 5 may become full members. The Australia-wide membership of 750 includes 25 conference interpreters at Levels 4 and 5 according to infor-

---

[40] National Office: P.O.Box 193, Surrey Hills, Vic. 3127. Tel. 1800 284 181, e-mail: admin@ausit.org website: www.ausit.org

[41] Email addresses of State and Territory branches may be obtained from the National Office

mation received from their secretariat, although the Institute is mainly concerned with community interpreters at former Level 3. For up-to-date information please consult website.

17

PROTOCOL & ETIQUETTE

Protocol

Most world leaders bring their own interpreter with them. The diplomatic corps of most Western countries rely on a team of civil service staff interpreters. The former President of AIIC, Gisela Siebourg, was interpreter to Chancellor Kohl of Germany and could generally be seen standing behind him in official photographs. Similarly, Christopher Thiéry could generally be seen behind M. Mitterand, or M. Rocard, of France. Unfortunately this is not the case in Australia.

The *tête-à-tête*

You may be the only interpreter, in which case you should sit between the two speakers. Do not be shy and hover in the background - you will only regret it later if you cannot hear properly. It is important to choose carefully where you sit before the discussion begins; you may ask the participants where they would prefer you to sit. It is also a good idea before the meeting begins to ascertain discreetly how much interpreting is needed (unless you have worked for them before). They may not need you to interpret every word and find that irritating. Perhaps they prefer to signal to you if they have not understood something. There is no relaxing however : you must follow every word and be ready to jump in and explain whenever necessary.

Always have a notepad and pen available to jot down figures and dates.

Rather than consecutive, in this situation a form of simultaneous is generally used as it saves time and enables the listener to understand almost as quickly as if they were both speaking the same language, so that the interpreter's presence is often forgotten altogether (the greatest compliment!).

If the visitor brings his own interpreter with him, each interpreter interprets what is said by his own Minister. The two interpreter colleagues often help one another out especially in case of misunderstandings or problems of any sort and there must be no hesitation for reasons of politeness in stepping in courteously to rectify any error or misunderstanding.

Two-delegation discussion

Sometimes two delegations sit opposite one another at a rectangular table. The interpreters sit at the table in the centre, next to the delegation leaders. In this way they can hear all that is said and interpret it in consecutive or simultaneously, addressing those seated opposite. If, on the other hand, there is only one delegate requiring interpretation, the interpreter sits next to that person or just behind his chair and a quiet whisper is all that is needed.

After dinner speeches

These often come at the end of a hard day when we are not at our best. However they are important for the image of our profession and generally give rise to much admiration from our audience (although they are generally not difficult), provided we carry out the task graciously and with elegance and humour. You will find that once you stand up and there is a general hush, your adrenalin starts flowing and you are capable of unexpected oratory brilliance. Those who do after dinner speeches well enjoy the experience. These are always done standing. Once again, be sure to have a notepad and pen handy and to stand where you can hear the speaker without effort. Feel free to stop the speaker after a few sentences, when you feel he has come to a convenient break. If there is a written text, it is up to the interpreter to obtain a copy beforehand. If the speech is addressed to an audience which does not understand the language being used, the interpreter should interpret simultaneously into the microphone. There is nothing more boring for an audience than to have to listen to the same speech twice particularly if the first time is in a language they do not understand. It is advisable to drink only water until the speeches are over. After that it is up to you.

Press conferences

This may be the most important part of the visit for the foreign Statesman. It is increasingly common for press conferences to be interpreted from the booth in simultaneous, which is the ideal situation. When this is not so, however, and consecutive is used, the interpreter sits next to the person giving the press conference and works both ways according to linguistic needs. The question and answer part of the session is sometimes a challenge because those asking the questions may not be accustomed to speaking in public or through an interpreter and may be difficult to follow or have very pronounced local accents. This is where the interpreter's acting talents come into play; he has to switch from one role to the other and keep the rhythm going, imitating as closely as possible the tone and attitude of the questioner.

Interpreting at the dinner-table

Seating is often a problem because the seating arrangements are based on strict protocol and sometimes the interpreter is given a chair behind the visiting statesman, so that it is difficult to hear the conversation that is taking place at the table. Unfortunately this is often the case in Parliament House in Canberra. However, when working at the Embassies, where there is a greater realization of the need for interpretation, a seat is generally provided for the interpreter at the table next to the Statesman, which makes his work more efficient. (It is often difficult, though, to find a moment to take a mouthful of food before your plate is whisked away.)

Cocktail parties, visits and excursions

Always arrive at the reception or the departure point before the Minister, you must be there waiting for him when he arrives. Wherever your Statesman goes (except for the toilet!), you must always be one step behind and stick to him like a Siamese twin. You may never leave a Reception before he does. You must always be there when you are needed and be invisible the rest of the time. It is useful if possible ahead of time to find out the linguistic requirements of those waiting to speak to the Statesman. Be ready to jump into action when required, if necessary thrusting your way through the crowd of people surrounding him.

Dress

Your aim should be to avoid being noticed. For the same reason, you should dab your nose if necessary but not blow it in public - better to disappear for a few seconds to blow your nose in private.

Patience

You will be sure to spend a lot of time waiting in corridors. Sometimes you are only there to reassure the visiting Statesman, maybe you will not be needed to interpret at all. Sometimes your presence is merely for the sake of prestige. Be patient. Above all, be vigilant. Just when you thought you could relax, someone may turn to you for a word or a quick explanation. Be sure to have a copy of the programme in your pocket, and to know it by heart so that whatever happens, you know where your next assignment is taking place in case you are seated in a car at the back of the procession and there is a traffic hold-up.

Familiarity

Beware of the Australian habit of using first names. It is safer to say *Mr. So-and-so* when interpreting; Australian familiarity is a shock to more formal nationalities, particularly in an official setting such as Parliament House.

Introductions

The easy way to remember who to introduce first is to stand beside the most senior person and to introduce the others to him or her.

Dignity

We must remember the dignity of our profession at all times. Naturally displayed dignity together with conscientiousness and professionalism are the best way we can serve our profession.

Trygve Lie, the first Secretary General of the United Nations said: "The world today depends in the first instance on the politicians and in the second on their interpreters."

Etiquette in different countries

Rules of etiquette vary enormously between countries, depending on climate, history and tradition.

When you are invited to dinner at someone's home in Europe, take flowers for your hostess. But not chrysanthemums. Chrysanthemums are the flowers of the dead; on 1st November (All Saints' Day) families visit cemeteries and deposit chrysanthemums on their dear ones' graves. In Asia, avoid white flowers, especially carnations or gifts with white floral motifs as these too are associated with bereavement.

Greetings

Hand-shaking between men is the rule in France. You must say goodmorning and good-bye to each person either with a peck on each cheek (man to woman and woman-to-woman) or a hand-shake (men, or women to men). It is customary to remove your glove before shaking hands. Hand-kissing (men to women) is also prevalent in France.

In Switzerland and Luxemburg you kiss three times on the cheek, in France the older generation prefer twice, the younger three times, but this may vary from place to place.

In Spain and Italy men often embrace one another rather than shake hands.

Table manners

There are a lot of differences to remember. For example whereas in England it is polite to keep your hands under the table when not using them to eat, in France this is considered very impolite - hands should always be above the table (you may rest your wrists on the table edge) to show, I believe, in medieval times, that you were not hiding a weapon. (Nowadays it may be to show your hands are not up to mischief under the table...) If you are in England you will drink your soup from the wide side of the spoon because you are a *grandboutien*, whereas in France you use the pointed end of the spoon because the French are *petitboutiens*. The problem is that in England soupspoons are round and not oval which really complicates matters for French visitors. Similarly, you may be a *grandboutien* or a *petitboutien* depending on which end of your boiled egg you attack.

It is not polite to cut your bread roll with a knife, you should break it with your hands. People do not put butter on the bread accompanying their meal. In France it is often considered an insult to the cook or the chef to add salt or pepper to your food at the table, in fact in some famous French restaurants the Chef has been known to come out of the kitchen to complain ! (He prides himself on the fact that the food he serves is absolutely perfect as it is.)

In Spain it is common to dunk your bread in your breakfast hot chocolate or café au lait, but this is 'not done' in England .

In Italy where people are superstitious you should never pass the salt to someone, they might think you wished them ill. Whatever you do, do not have thirteen guests at the table; it is not worth the risk of inviting fourteen in case one of them does not turn up. A plate piled high with spaghetti is often served first in Italy, as an entrée *before* the main course. Cheese is often served at the beginning of the meal in Spain, also nowadays in New Zealand I am told where cheese and wine often start the meal. In France the cheese comes before the dessert. The French find it very peculiar that the British go from salty main dish to sweet dessert and then back to salty cheese to finish. In Britain of course port used to go with the cheese; while the gentlemen were savouring their port, the ladies retired to powder their noses and talk gossip - leaving the gentlemen free to tell uncensored jokes without being inhibited by the presence of the ladies. In France port is taken in the late afternoon or as an *apéritif* before, not after, dinner.

Dress during conferences overseas

The shorts worn by adult Australian males are generally worn only by boys up to the age of about 12 in many other countries, except when on holiday by the beach. Do not be too casual. If you don't dress well you are perceived to be showing disrespect to those you meet. On the other hand it is unwise and inappropriate to dress to a high western standard in India, China, Africa or South America because this increases your chances of being robbed, mugged or kidnapped. In hot climates, cotton is preferable to any synthetic fabric however elegant.

Etiquette in Asia

The first rule is never to assume that what is polite or appropriate in Australia applies in other societes. The second is to learn about local customs from guide books or tourist information provided on the plane. The third is to be unfailingly polite and courteous and keep smiling whatever difficulties there may be (even when you thought you were opening your taxi door and discover you were holding it open for a resident). You must never shout, lose your temper or try to intimidate. He who loses his temper also loses face. And cannot be trusted.

Avoid touching children on the head. The head is the highest part of the body symbolically as well as physically. Similarly, pointing with the feet, the lowest parts of the body, is grossly insulting. One should sit with one's feet respectfully tucked to one side.

The left hand does not exist outside the western world. In other words, you never touch anyone or any foodstuff with it. Never use your left hand to give or receive and never crook your finger to call someone - this is extremely impolite.

When visiting a temple, dress properly: no shorts or revealing clothing. Shoes must be taken off before entering a room containing a Buddha image - all Buddha images at any time or place must be treated with extreme respect. It is a good idea for ladies to carry a large scarf in their handbag with which to drape themselves as appropriate.

Handshaking is customary in Indonesia for men and women on introduction and greeting and smiling is a national characteristic in Thailand, the Philippines and Indonesia.

Gifts

Alcohol and pig products are not a good idea in many countries. Ties and cuff-links are not commonly worn in Asia.

A final word: when you are next off to Beijing for a conference and you pack a few stuffed koalas and kangaroos as gifts, remember to remove the "Made in China" label from underneath....

18

CHAMPAGNE

Although they are hidden away in booths and often taken for granted, interpreters know they have a huge responsibility. They love their profession. They put up with impossible conditions: nervous speakers who speak too fast for good interpretation to be possible, not having the document being discussed, long tiring travel, uncomfortable hotels in far-flung places, unpleasant climates, and occasionally bad-tempered critical delegates looking for a scapegoat for their own failings.

They put up with all this in order to do what they enjoy. They are constantly in quest of a chance to do a good job, in spite of the odds. They would like a chance to do better than the speaker, to be clearer, more concise...

While the translator, searching through his dictionaries, is also creating something new from something old, translation does not touch his inner depths like simultaneous interpretation does. We are also "hooked" by the magnetism of the unknown, the challenge of not knowing what the speaker will say next, the spirit of adventure. A word or an expression that you have never used before, which you picked up fifteen years ago in a book or listening to someone speak, will suddenly rise to the surface of the compost in your brain and reach your lips because it is needed. Such a rediscovery fills the interpreter with jubilation and reverence but only he knows about it and he would be too embarrassed ever to mention it to anyone.

I am told an Irishman once said: "How do I know what I think until I hear what I say?" We would change that to say: "... until I hear what my interpreter says."

Given that most world leaders and top scientists speak no language other than their own, it really is a miracle that eight people can make it possible for hundreds of world specialists in a given field to understand one another and even argue, without registering the fact that interpreters are present.

John Coleman-Holmes (1971) maintains that it is rare to find an interpreter who is stupid or boring. At longish conferences in under-developed countries it is the interpreters who keep the delegates amused and happy after work by their witty stories. The delegates want to get away from their colleagues, whose conversation they know by heart and which bores them to tears, and are delighted to join a group of interpreters going off to investigate the best local restaurants. "Let us not be bashful", says Coleman-Holmes:

> *Let us face up to the fact that we have charm and social graces and are much in demand at dinner tables because of our travel tales and amusing anecdotes. In fact, interpreters have many virtues, being usually disciplined, well-organized and capable of a surprising degree of team-spirit in people who are often free-lance, individually recruited and of most diverse origin.*

The disastrous unexpected

Then there is the challenge of the unfair unexpected when someone near the speaker coughs and you miss the key word, or a nervous speaker exceeds the speed limit, or reads at high speed from a written text. There may be sudden interference in your earphones just when you are straining to follow an involved argument, documents you do not have being read out or quoted from, impossible accents which obliterate the message.

But all this frustration disappears in a warm feeling of satisfaction when you get a good, clear speaker and you know you have done a good job.

The satisfaction is even greater when you know you have contributed to peace, to the signing of an agreement banning chemical weapons or nuclear armaments, or to the eradication of smallpox, especially when many years later you recognize your own words in an international agreement, charter or regulations.

As Karla Dejean said (1981), simultaneous interpreting is like tightrope walking between thought and speech, risking a fall at every step yet never ceasing to give the impression that it is easy.

Lady Kerr (1988) refers to the "champagne of interpreting" - "champagne is the air one breathes", the privileged contacts with well-known art experts, musicians, famous scientists and architects.

> *The great Jean Herbert said to me once: 'When you study a subject at a university, you have perhaps three professors. If you are lucky, one of them will be good. When you attend an international conference on any subject, the speakers come from a range of countries and each is there because he is in the forefront of his field. Some will be better than others, but the likelihood is that most will be good. If you work as a freelance interpreter you will be in contact with the front line of new ideas and new knowledge in many diverse fields.' In his Interpreter's Handbook Herbert wrote:*

> *'It is no great paradox for an interpreter to regard the meetings he attends as so many courses in a vast itinerant international university, where the most highly qualified specialists participate in turn, in his presence, in discussing*

various topics of interest of the day - and pay him generously for kindly coming to listen to them.'

How can one describe the pleasure when on a good day an interpreter feels he is on the crest of a wave, doing a good job and doing something creative, finding expressions in utter freedom with no-one to contradict him or suggest alternatives (like a reviser does to a translator!). Just this once you truly feel on the same wavelength as the speaker, just this once you are rethinking his speech and discretely touching it up, your spirit is lifting you ever up and up, you are using words you haven't heard for years, specialized words that have risen from the dark depths of your mind, words you didn't know were there, yet now when you need them you hear yourself pronouncing them. Just this once you have full mastery, you are on top of the situation. You are also in the theatre, standing in front of the stage, and the row upon row of listeners are waiting for your every word, pausing with you when you take a breath, following your every intonation. It is heady, it is stimulating, it is intoxicating. Every interpreter has known such moments. One cannot speak of them, of course. There is no common measure between the omnipotence described above, the poetry of the moment, the feeling of eternity, and the banality of the subject being discussed. The subject deserves to be interpreted faithfully of course but it is not of a level to trigger the finer feelings of a human being, aspects of eternity. And yet it does do that. This is grotesque and that is why we prefer not to talk of it.

So we shall say no more.

19

THE LAST WORD
(WE GENERALLY HAVE IT)

Noam Chomsky, the American linguist who founded transformational-generative grammar (an original and highly influential system of linguistic analysis), believes there is only one human language, with many variations. He maintains that there is a language organ somewhere in the brain, which has not yet been discovered by brain scanners and which nobody has ever seen. His colleague, Elizabeth Bates, says that humans are animals who want passionately to communicate about objects; any two-year old of your acquaintance will corroborate this: they continually point things out, not because they want it, but because they want you to say "Yes, that is a dog." For the Australian Aborigines, according to Bruce Chatwin in "Songlines", objects don't exist until they have a name.

Chomsky believes we all have an innate ability to learn language - even the child of deaf parents will learn sign language as his first language, in the same way as a spoken language. The first language or mother tongue sets up circuits in the brain between the ages of 2 and 13; no other language learnt later will ever be so good - there will always be glitches and gaps. The majority of people have language ability in the left hemisphere of the brain though it is thought that some Asian languages such as Japanese use the right hemisphere.

Dr. Joseph Greenberg of Stanford University, U.S.A, also believes that:

in the beginning there was one people, perhaps no more than 2,000 strong, who had acquired an amazing gift, the faculty for complex language. Favored by the blessings of speech, their numbers grew and from their cradle in the northeast of Africa, they spread far and wide throughout the continent...As humans spread across the globe, they separated from one another again and again, gradually breaking into many different genetic and linguistic groups. [42]

Dr. Greenberg has grouped most of the world's languages into a small number of clusters based on their similarities. Though controversial, his language classifications roughly coincide with clusters of genetically similar people and point to a close relationship between genetic and linguistic evolution.

Some 6,000 - 7,000 languages are said to be spoken on earth today (if you include dialects), but it is estimated that 3,000 will die over the next 100 years; when a language that has never been written down dies, it is as if it had never existed. Languages are precious because of the history and culture that they represent.

About sixty languages are spoken in Europe, which is far less than the number spoken, for example, in India. It is said that in Europe the diversity of languages and cultures is the basis of their cohesion, contrary to the situation in America.

The Assertiveness of Minority Languages

The strange thing is that the more lifestyle becomes global and westernization takes over via television

[42] Dr. Joseph H. Greenberg has spent many years classifying the world's languages and has recently published the first of two volumes on Eurasiatic, his proposed super-family that includes a swathe of languages spoken from Portugal to Japan. (Report by Nicholas Wade, *Science Times (The New York Times)* 1 February, 2000.)

and computers, the more minority languages become important and minority groups insist upon their language and culture, their dances, their music. As economic, political and social integration progress and governments have to abandon their sovereignty because of the European Commission, Council or Court of Justice, nations increasingly insist upon using their own language as if it were their last link with their culture and history. It is as if someone has pushed the "panic button". In spite of the considerable expense involved, in spite of technical difficulties (there were seventeen booths in one room in a recent Bonn World Climate Summit, technicians had to maintain systems in twelve conference rooms, eight tonnes of simultaneous interpretation equipment were required for the preparatory meeting and a few months later 13 tonnes of equipment were required for the UN Summit) governments, parliaments and public opinion maintain that it is a human right for delegations (or at least those of the wealthier nations) to be free to express themselves and listen to the debate in their own language and also to receive conference documents in their own language.

Artificial languages such as Esperanto, Occitan and Interlingua have never received support so their use has never been studied effectively. If someone makes the enormous effort required to learn a new language, they want to gain access at the same time to a new culture, based on history and literature, in order to widen their horizons.

Naisbitt and Aburdene (1992) point out that:

> *Language is the pathway to culture. If the inhabitants of a Third World country sense that an outside culture is gaining undue influence, they will feel their values are threatened and may respond with cultural nationalism, vigorously asserting their language and/or religion, just as*

they would counter a political or military invasion with renewed political nationalism.

In Quimper, Brittany, "Diwan" (the "Seed") has now opened its doors in the former St. Anne private secondary school because of the large number of pupils wishing to be taught in "Breton".

The Scots now have their own Parliament and use their own language, there is an increasing amount of Welsh being taught and spoken. Naisbitt and Aburdene (1992) say:

Castilian is Spain's official language. But not in Catalonia, an autonomous region of 6 million people, where Catalan has been proclaimed the official language and is in the midst of a major revival. Nearly 70% of the people speak Catalan and 85 % understand it. Catalan newspapers, magazines, books, and folk traditions were outlawed during the reign of Franco, but are now flourishing again. Language is the basic characteristic of Catalonia's personality and the personality of its people. For centuries, Catalonia and its capital, Barcelona, have been known as the economic heart of Spain, representing 20 to 25% of the Spanish economy.

Joan Brossa, a Catalan poet, says:

Without my language I have no culture, and culture is the best weapon man has against oppression. Generalissimo Franco and his fascists knew this well. They tried to steal our language from us but they failed. Now I think the worst moments for us have passed. It is Franco who is dead, and not Catalonia.

Publishers like Edicions 62, Editorial Empuries and Editorial Laia are three of the seventy five firms in the Guild of Catalan Language

283

Editors. Edicions 62 publishes translations of William Faulkner, Graham Greene, F. Scott Fitzgerald as well as Catalan translations of science fiction; there are 21 radio stations broadcasting in Catalan as well as three television stations at least several hours a day. On Sundays at noon people gather spontaneously in front of the Barcelona Gothic Cathedral and on Sunday evenings Catalans gather on the Plaza Sant Jaume to participate in traditional dances.

Today's Catalan renaissance grows out of centuries of tradition. Catalans have been allied with Spain since the days of Christopher Columbus. But after losing their independence to Philip V in the 18th century, they sought greater autonomy, often with language as a unifying force. The literary Renaixensa of the 1850's and 1860's celebrated the language in poetry and festival, encouraging linguistic nationalism.

Catalonia today represents probably the best balance further between individuality and nationality, the most positive model for maintaining individual identity while participating in the collective. An old Catalan proverb states: "A country that defends its language defends itself." Another minority people in Spain, the Basques, are more liable to commit bomb outrages in their nationalist cause.

The more humanity sees itself as inhabiting a single planet, the greater the need for each culture on that globe to own a unique heritage. Each nation's history, language and tradition are unique. So in a curiously paradoxical way, the more alike we become, the more we will stress our uniqueness.

One need only consider how long it took the Americans to agree on English as their language. And how happy the Swiss are with four official languages, a system which works perfectly (and helps: the more languages you know, the easier it is to learn a new language). Many agree that tolerance and understanding are intimately connected with knowledge of other languages.

In Beijing, since 1996 the twice-weekly ritual of briefing foreign journalists by a spokesman from China's foreign ministry takes place in Chinese. Doing away with English interpretation coincided with other measures to encourage the study of Chinese abroad. The state-run *China Daily* which publishes in English and will presumably continue to do so, reported that more than 1,000 institutions of higher learning in sixty countries have established Chinese language programmes, in response to "China's increasing role in the world." The Foreign Ministry's Shen Guofang announced that the decision to dispense with English translation is "irreversible" but allowed that reporters who experience "insurmountable difficulties" may still ask questions in English. If Mr. Shen is feeling generous, he may even answer in English.

As for hastening the day when Chinese will rival English as the world's *lingua franca*, China is placing its faith in cyberspace and in Chinese proficiency with computers.

> *It is inevitable that in time the majority of Internet users will be Chinese. And when that happens, we will see the Chinese language being widely used in electronic communication.* (Naisbitt and Aburdene 1992)

According to the Xinhua news agency, one million people use the Internet in China, compared with 50 million people elsewhere, the vast majority of them in English.

It is clear from what is happening in the European Union that increasingly countries are asserting their linguistic identity: as economic groupings form, we are not moving towards the use of one common language in Europe or in the world.

Singapore is often said to be the most competitive nation in the world. The population of Singapore is composed of three races: a majority of Chinese, Malays and Indians. Among the Chinese, many very different Chinese dialects were spoken, mainly from South China, such as Hokkien, Cantonese, Teochew, Hainan and Hakka, to quote the most widespread. Because of trade and tourism, English was gradually taking over but the Government of Singapore in order to increase the country's competitivity decided that the official language would be Mandarin. This was done in order to assist general comprehension among the Chinese of different origins and also to facilitate trade with the emerging enormous market of China. At that time the very popular Prime Minister Lee Kwan Yew, whose mother tongue was English, in spite of his advanced years, started to study Mandarin daily and was soon making his speeches in Mandarin. Today the majority of the Chinese population of Singapore communicates in Mandarin, even at home within the family. Children sometimes have difficulty understanding their own dialect which they hear only from their grandparents. This goes to show that the economic success of a nation is not merely a matter of chance.

Television and dialect

I have heard it said that dialects are tending to disappear in Italy because of television. People hear pure Italian on their television and radio receivers and that is how young people now speak. They are increasingly embarrassed to hear their parents and grandparents using the old dialects...

The Paradox: Will American-Asian-English nevertheless prevail ?

According to *Le Courrier australien* (a monthly French-language newspaper published in Sydney) and Sydney S. Culbert of Washington University, English is spoken by 508 million people and is the official language of forty-five countries, whereas French is spoken in thirty countries by 129 million people. Spanish is spoken by 392 million in twenty countries. English is spoken by 8.6 per cent of the earth's population.

At international meetings over the last few years, Viet Nam, Cambodia, Burundi and several other former French-speaking countries have taken to using English, as well as all the former Soviet bloc. (At least they think it is English. Sometimes it is not easy to understand. If you hear "unanimous" with the "an" pronounced as if it were "ane" the meaning doesn't always strike instantaneously). In 1996 Algeria, formerly French-speaking, adopted English as the first language to be taught in schools (the first cultural language being Arabic). English is spoken in 185 member countries of the United Nations and used by the delegates of those countries at UN meetings.

"If English was good enough for Jesus Christ, it's good enough for me" said an American congressman in 1988, in testimony to the United States Joint National Committee on Languages, investigating whether American students should study foreign languages.

Dr. David Crystal (1997) believes

in the fundamental value of multilingualism, as an amazing world resource which presents us with different perspectives and insights, and thus enables us to reach a more profound understanding of the human mind and spirit. In my ideal world, everyone would be at least bilingual .....

He also believes

287

in the fundamental value of a common language, as an amazing world resource which presents us with unprecedented possibilities for mutual understanding, and ... fresh opportunities for international co-operation. In my ideal world, everyone would have fluent command of a single world language.

According to Dr. Crystal, bilingualism is the norm: three quarters of the world population are naturally bilingual, using one language for outside contacts and internationally, and the other for inside, that is, culture and within the family. Dr Crystal learnt Welsh as a second language.

Even if 500 million people in twelve countries speak English as their first language, this is a lot fewer than the 800 million or so who speak Mandarin, but it must not be forgotten that another 400 million speak English as a second language. Several hundred million more have some knowledge of English which has official or semi-official status in some sixty countries. Eighty per cent of Internet use is in English.

According to Naisbitt and Aburdene (1992):

- 250 million Chinese - more than the entire population of the United States - study English.

- In eighty-nine countries English is either a common second language or widely studied.

- In Hong Kong, nine out of every ten secondary school students study English.

- In France, state-run secondary schools require students to study four years of English or German; most - at least 85 per cent - choose English.

- In Japan, secondary students are required to take six years of English before graduation.

- Language study is compulsory for Soviet children; most study English.

- In Norway, Sweden and Denmark, English is compulsory. Within Europe, the Netherlands has the highest concentration of English proficiency outside Britain. Since Portugal entered the European Union, the demand for English classes has replaced the demand for French.

- There are 1300 English language schools in Tokyo; 100 new schools open each year. Berlitz offers both British and American English at 250 language schools in twenty-six countries. Worldwide, 80 to 90 per cent of Berlitz students study English.

It is obvious that English is the only candidate for global language. Whether you look at the film industry, science and engineering, international travel, air traffic control, sea safety or international organizations this becomes patently clear. Even pop music: 99 per cent of the 557 pop groups in the *Penguin Encyclopedia of Popular Music* work entirely or mostly in English. English is also the language spoken by Bill Gates; the protocols first developed for carrying data over the Internet were based on the English alphabet.

Chinese uses between 4,000 and 6,000 characters and each character can take a dozen strokes of the pen. Imagine the complexity of typing even the basic 2000 characters of the simplified Chinese alphabet on a normal-sized keyboard. Japanese uses somewhat fewer of these *kanji* - around 2,000 - but relies on three other alphabets in parallel: the Roman and two phonetic alphabets known as *kana*. If you want to type in Chinese, Korean, or Japanese you have to superimpose one character on top of another. There appear to be two software possibilities for Chinese: Union Way and Chinese Star. Using the Union Way system, the Big 5 code is the Chinese system code page with traditional Chinese characters commonly used by Microsoft C-Windows and most application programmes developed in Taiwan; it has about 13,000 Chinese characters. The GB code is the Chinese system code page with simplified characters commonly used by Microsoft P-Windows and most application programmes developed in mainland China: it has about 6,700 Chinese characters. For Korean, KSC is the commonly used code page by Microsoft K-Windows and most application programmes developed in Korean; it has about 5,400 Korean characters.

When we refer to "English", are we talking about English English, American English, Indian English, Asian English or any of the thousand or more other brands ? Dr. Crystal fears the emergence of a "world standard spoken English" - a kind of super-national variety which is neither British nor American nor Australian nor anything but a sort of amalgam of all these and more. You can sense this is already in existence if you listen to the kind of English that is increasingly spoken at international conferences... It has become a jargon of its own and one sometimes feels that if someone used a genuine English-English expression no-one would understand.

The world-wide use of English is not the result of its so-called simplicity, but rather of the economic and political power of present-day America. Some may say that if everyone speaks English there will be greater understanding but French- and Spanish-speakers, for example, fear that, however hard they work to learn English, they will never speak it as well as those who have it as their mother-tongue, so that they will always be in a position of inferiority. If, however, an effort is made to teach children English from a very early age, this is equivalent to condemning to death their mother-tongue and the culture that went with it. Children of all nations will adopt English joyfully because it is the vehicle of all that attracts them in American culture, giving them the feeling they are wealthy "cool dudes".

The issues of language dominance and death can be intensely political and raise nationalist passions. Some nations have even taken official measures to protect what they see as the purity and integrity of their languages. People all over the world are fiercely proud of their language. The myth of Babel ("Babylon" in Hebrew) wrongly presents the multitude of human languages as a curse, whereas it is in fact an element of freedom. What potential for tyrants if they had but one language, a single code of thought and communication to manipulate and control? Bilingualism and literacy are important weapons in the fight against such tyranny especially among peoples of the Third World, many of whose mother tongues are still only rarely written.

There is a widespread fear that computers will at some time in the future take over all information processing and speak the language of their inventors. Of the 3,000 languages currently in use on earth (discounting dialects), many will decline and perhaps even disappear completely. By 1992, in a report to the European Commission, André Danzin had already sounded the alarm.

He pointed out that natural languages react like human beings. They evolve according to the pressure put upon them by their environment like the various species of animals and plants. They too are subject to Darwinian selection. When printing began in the Maghreb, Arabic was chosen to be the printed language, although the use of Berber was more widespread. As a result, Berber declined and became no more than a dialect while Arabic became an international language and is to this day one of the working languages of the United Nations. Similarly, in the days of the great Alexandria Library, the Greeks wanted a language adapted to scientific thought - it was the time of the emergence of the sciences of mechanics, astronomy and medecine. They created the words and linguistic mechanisms needed to deal with the new knowledge. As a result, in spite of the power of Latin, Greek spread throughout the Roman Empire and became the vehicle and intellectual tool of philosophy, science and technical subjects.

According to Danzin, three forces are at work which will shape the linguistic landscape of the future. First, the dematerialisation of work. Only one and a half centuries ago, 90 per cent of work in fields or factories was mainly muscular. Today more than 70 per cent of people work on the basis of the written word. All they do is process and exchange information on paper or on a computer screen. Their working tool is language. Naturally this is becoming more and more mechanized in the form of word processing and will no doubt remain the preserve of rich countries so only those speaking a relatively small number of languages will have access to them.

The second force concerning the future of language is that in all scientific, technical, commercial or financial communication, all ambiguity must be removed. This goes against natural language which has always left some leeway. It is the existence of ambiguity or flexibility that makes conversation possible between two people of different opinions: one wishing to convince the other of his view or prove that the other's arguments are not founded. Without some vagueness, negotiation is not possible. Vagueness is also part of literature, its power of evocation, its call on the imagination. But if you are selling a nuclear power station to a foreign country you also have to provide explanations of how to set it up, how to use it, how to carry out maintenance etc., representing tons of paper or large amounts of information to be stored in computer memory. There cannot be a single vague word, there cannot be any ambiguity. This is the first time in history that it has become necessary to remove from language all possible ambiguity. It is easy to understand what a shock this is to writers of literature.

French is a very clear, precise language which passes the test for accuracy. French computer experts also attach great importance to spelling: old-fashioned spelling with the cedilla and all the French subtleties make it possible to identify each word in a sentence without any risk of error; simplification is a source of homonyms and confusion.

The third revolution concerns the ability of machines to turn written words into sound and vice-versa. This technique is already of great assistance to the blind. Some languages of South-East Asia will gain in importance because that is where these techniques will be developed; Anglo-American will retain its importance because of their lion's share of the market. According to André Danzin, the survival of other European languages is not at all sure unless governments continue to work together with this in view and are ready to make considerable financial investment.

Another problem is the bastardization of the English language, as well as most other world languages. Language is evolving all the time and new words are being invented every day to describe an enzyme, an electronic component or a new computer concept. These are generally transposed as such in all languages without translation.

So, "are we heading towards one simplified Americanized form of English?" asks André Danzin. This is reminiscent of what is happening in agriculture, for example, where one type of wheat or tomato may be found preferable from the marketing or storage point of view, or one type of cattle found to be preferable for the meat market, and other varieties are left to disappear gradually. The world is concerned about this and many international conferences have been held on the subject of biodiversity. But not so much attention seems to be paid to language diversity. The extent to which languages will be used in the future will not depend on the extent of nations' territory as in the past but rather on their mastery of information - in other words, language.

Various committees working on the future protection of nine European languages estimated the cost at some 840 million ecus (or 5.6 billion French francs of that time) over a four year period. This problem of protecting European languages in the future is now of concern all over the world. The Dutch do not want their language to disappear, the Germans are already taking action; in Great Britain and Canada there is much discussion as to what should be done. Writers and language purists object to their language being subjected to machines and therefore to change and simplification. A suggestion has been made that in non-English-speaking European countries the State should subsidize the distribution of dictionaries, free of charge, to make them freely available and prevent too many liberties being taken with their language.

André Danzin chaired a Committee on this subject in Luxembourg; one of the members of the Committee was Professor Sture Allén, President of the Jury of the Nobel Prize for Literature. When the subject of changing languages to adapt them for computer use came up, he was outraged. "Be careful ! If you mutilate a language for technical and scientific purposes you are heading towards considerably impoverishing human communication. We should be doing the very opposite, enforcing greater respect for language by perfecting the machines. It's just too bad if that makes them more expensive or slower. The main thing is not to mutilate our languages", he said.

Danzin quotes the case of a spell-check system he encountered in Canada. It is for French word-processing and was created in California by American-English speakers. The programme contains several errors. It is however commercialized by a company with considerable marketing power and is widely sold. Thus there exists an incorrect French spell-check system, conceived by Americans, yet which may be sold all over the world including in France. This is a serious matter: not only cultural identity is at stake.

Professional communication increasingly takes place through the intermediary of data banks. If these are only in English, small French, Italian, German businesses will not have access to them. One cannot force everyone to speak English. The result will be a minority group which will not have access to the professional information they need to compete in a competitive world.

The balance of power will no doubt move away from European languages and over to Asian and American-English and later to Chinese, since these are the languages of the countries developing electronic machines. This is not unlike what happened at the time of the Renaissance when the world's centre of gravity switched to the West because they knew how to make use of gunpowder, the compass and paper - all discovered by the Chinese but not taken advantage of by them.

European Language Portfolio

The year 2001 being the European Year of Languages, the Modern Languages Division of the Council of Europe, Strasbourg, France, piloted the European Language Portfolio. For information, visit their website: http://www.eurolang2001.org/eyl/EN/Learning/Learnin gCoE5_EN.htm or contact Joseph Sheils and Johanna Panthier, Modern Languages Division DG IV, Education, Culture and heritage, Youth and Sport, Council of Europe, 67075, Strasbourg, France, Tel. +33 (0)3 8841 3248. Fax +33 (0)3 8841 2788/06. E-mail: <Joseph.Sheils@coe.int> or Johanna.Panthier@coe.int.

European Language Council (*Conseil Européen pour les Langues*)

This is an independent European association the main aim of which is the quantitative and qualitative improvement of knowledge of the languages and cultures of the European Union and beyond. Membership is open to all institutions of higher education in Europe and all national and international associations with a special interest in the area of languages. The ELC plays a key role in policy-making at a European level; individually, institutions are not in a position to respond to the challenges of a multilingual and multicultural Europe. The objective of the ELC is to create the framework and conditions necessary for common policy development and provide a platform for the launching of joint projects.

French National Institute for Oriental Languages and Civilisation (INALCO)(*Institut National des langues et Civilisations Orientales*)

This organization provides instruction in the languages, geography, history and politics of Eastern and Central Europe, Asia, Oceania/Australasia, Africa and the native Americas. In total more than eighty languages and civilisations are covered with additional professional vocational training also provided.

Intergovernmental Agency for French-speaking Communities (The Francophone Agency) (*Agence Intergouvernementale de la Francophonie*

This international organization was founded by the Niamey Convention of 1970 on the initiative of three African heads of state: Léopold Sédar Senghor[43] of Senegal (also first honorary President of the Linguasphere Observatory), Habib Bourguiba of Tunisia and Hamani Diori of Niger. It currently includes 52 national states and governments who, united by the bond of sharing the French language, wish, through multilateral co-operation, to use that bond in the service of peace, intercultural dialogue and development. The Agency is the only intergovernmental representative of the French speaking world. The

---

[43]) Léopold Sédar Senghor, President of the Republic of Senegal from 1963 to 1980, member of the "Académie française". A distinguished poet, he was also a professional politician of great skill who guided his nation to independence and proved to be an able and effective leader for the following two decades. He was also a very gentle, kind and wise man.

Linguasphere Observatory received support from the Agency during the early years of its development, including the publication of "*Les Langues de France et des Pays et Régions Limitrophes au 20e siècle*" (1993).

Concerned with the protection of the French language, they are now also planning a French-speaking economic cooperative based on consensus, and aim to defend the common position of the "French-speaking bloc" in various international political and economic fora. The French-speaking group of countries hopes to play a part in all future discussions of the World Trade Organization as well as the International Monetary Fund, the World Bank and even the United Nations. They are also working on various proposals to lighten the burden of debt born by the poorer French-speaking countries.

Linguasphere Register

The Linguasphere Register of the World's Languages and Speech Communities is the first attempt at a comprehensive and transnational classification of the modern languages and dialects of the world and of the communities of humankind. Compiled over several decades by David Dalby[44], the Register classifies all known

---

[44] Dr. David Dalby, Linguasphere Observatory, London School of Oriental and African Studies and University of Wales, Cardiff, was Director and creator in 1983 of a bilingual (English/French) organization called "Language Watch" (Observatoire Linguistique) in the hamlet of Cressenville, Normandy, France, where he lived at the time. He is of dual British and French nationality and has published on German, French, English and African languages (including his *Language Map of Africa* in 1977, one of the most complex language maps every compiled). Emeritus Reader in African languages in the University of London, he was also the first Hans Wolff Visiting Professor in Linguistics at Indiana University and was the Director of the International African Institute (IAI) in London.

Language Watch has now become Linguasphere and has prepared a computerized World Language Survey; it also runs an international information service on questions relating to language and language use. The two-volume *Linguasphere Register of the World's Languages and Speech Communities* (in hard copy and also in updateable electronic format) can be obtained via the website of the Linguasphere Press (www.linguasphere.net). It is based on a system of digital classification (the linguasphere key) for the ready identifica-

languages and dialects on the basis of their closest linguistic relationships and includes a theoretical and practical discussion and presentation of the linguasphere.

It was first established in 1983 to promote research and education in multilingualism; it serves as the framework for an integrated database on the languages of the world. Using the present website (http://www.linguasphere.org/observatory.html), the updating and enlargement of the Register will be developed as a transnational and inter-institutional project, "Exploring the Linguasphere", the results of which will be placed at the disposal of UNESCO's Linguapax programme in its preparation of a series of regular reports on the state of languages in the world. It will also provide a framework for the integrated global mapping of language and communication around the globe.

In Paris on 25 September 1997 the first pre-publication copy of the "Linguasphere Register" was presented to Sr. Federico Mayor, Director General of UNESCO, by the Director of the Observatory and by the Chairman of the Observatory's Research Council, in response to Dr. Federico Mayor's call (Bilbao, 1996) for the preparation of a detailed linguistic map of the world

Work on a French language version of the Linguasphere Register, the *Répertoire des Langues du Monde* has already benefited from the support of the Agence de la Francophonie and further francophone support is being sought to enable the entire Register and Linguasphere Mapbase to be published also in French.

---

tion and location of the world's languages and peoples, within a unique index of over 70,000 linguistic and ethnic names.

The Linguasphere Observatory (*Observatoire Linguistique*)

The Linguasphere Observatory is a transnational research institute devoted to the worldwide study and promotion of multilingualism. It is an independant non-profit organization, successively designed, developed and co-ordinated in Quebec, Normandy and Wales since 1983 with no governmental, political, religious or commercial affiliations.

Since 1997, the present LinguasphereWebsite: <http://www.linguasphere.org/observatory.html> has become the institutional focus of the Linguasphere Observatory, providing a unique research base and viewing platform in cyberspace. From this vantage-point the collective and individual development of the world's languages and the linguistic impact of the communications revolution are being carefully observed and described with increasing emphasis on the welfare and education of each of the world's speech communities, regardless of their size. Their motto is: "*Dans la galaxie des langues, la voix de chaque personne est une étoile*" in French, "In the galaxy of languages, each person's voice is a star" in English and "*Seren yw llais pob un yng ngalaeth yr ieithoedd*" in Welsh.

Terralingua

An international non-profit organization concerned about the future of the world's cultural and biological diversity. They report two main aims: preserving the world's linguistic diversity and investigating connections between biological and cultural diversity. Their website (see<http://www.linguasphere.org/links.html) includes an extensive internet index of resources on preserving linguistic diversity, language endangerment, survival and revitalization.

THE VERY LAST WORD (We generally have that, too)

It seems to be generally accepted that by the end of the next century, everyone will be speaking American-Asian-English or Chinese peppered with American-English words. Perhaps by then French, Dutch, Spanish, Italian, etc. will still exist but as old-fashioned dialects. If that is so, we still have a few years before us during which interpretation will be required.

We must remember that we are in rapidly changing times; this applies particularly to the interpreting profession and the "upheaving" effects modern technology has on our profession each new year.

One thing is clear: in the conference world today, those who need us most are those who are not in a position to pay.

Another is that there is a proliferation of interpreter schools, turning out many outstanding young interpreters each year all over the world, who then find it difficult to get a foot in the interpreting booth door. Yet a conference organizer who recently enquired about the cost of hiring simultaneous interpretation equipment was amazed when I mentioned human beings were required as well. He expected just to have to switch the equipment on for interpretation to pour out of the earphones in all required languages.

Clearly, as times change, so must the interpreting profession. If we are able to adapt to new requirements, there seems no doubt that skilled interpreters will be needed so long as international conferences are held particularly for the exchange of scientific information on recent discoveries, medical research and new technologies. So long as some conference delegates - at least those from the wealthier countries contributing to the budgets of the international organizations - retain the right to speak and listen in their own tongue, we shall continue to be needed. If interpreting and translating were merely a matter of word exchange, computers and translation machines would have taken over our work before now. But it is not, as I hope I have made clear.

So long as there is a Tower of Babel, the yellow parrot has an important part to play. Long live the Yellow Parrot !

Appendix A

THE UNITED NATIONS SYSTEM

Major Funding Programmes

- United Nations Development Programme (UNDP)

- United Nations Children's Fund (UNICEF)

- United Nations Fund for Population Activities (UNFPA)

- World Food Programme (WFP)

Developmental Bodies

- World Food Council (WFC)

- Economic Commission for Africa (ECA)

- Economic Commission for Europe (ECE)

- Economic Commission for Latin America and the Caribbean (ECLAC)

- Economic and Social Commission for Asia and the Pacific (ESCAP)

- Economic and Social Commission for Western Asia (ESCWA)

- United Nations Conference on Trade and Development (UNCTAD)

- International Trade Centre UNCTAD, WTO (ITC)

- United Nations Environment Programme (UNEP)

- Department of Technical Cooperation for Development of the UN Secretariat (DTCD)

- Centre for Social Development and Humanitarian Affairs (CSDHA)

- Department of International Economic and Social Affairs (DIESA)

Humanitarian Assistance

- United Nations Disaster Relief Office (UNDRO)

- Office of the United Nations High Commissioner for Refugees (UNHCR)

- United Nations Relief and Works Agency for Palestinean Refugees in the Near East (UNRWA)

Research and training institutions

- United Nations University (UNU)

- United Nations Institute for Training and Research (UNITAR)

- United Nations Research Institute for Social Development (UNRISD)

- United Nations Social Defence Research Institute (UNSDRI)

- International Research and Training Centre for the Advancement of Women (INSTRAW)

- United Nations Centre on Transnational Corporations (UNCTC)

- United Nations Centre for Human Settlements (Habitat) (UNCHS (Habitat))

- United Nations Institute for Disarmament Research (UNIDIR)

Multilateral Financial Institutions
- International Monetary Fund (IMF)
- International Bank for Reconstruction and Development (IBRD)
- International Development Association (IDA)
- International Finance Corporation (IFC)
- Multilateral Investment Guarantee Agency (MIGA)
- African Development Bank (AfDB)
- Asian Development Bank (AsDB)
- Inter-American Development Bank (IDB)

International Institutions related to the UN System
- Consultative Group on International Agricultural Research (CGIAR) (13 international agricultural research centres)

Appendix B

HOW TO IRRITATE YOUR DELEGATES WITHOUT REALLY TRYING

Are you an expert ?[45]

To play this exciting game, add up your DAV[46] figures and extrapolate.

1. Breathe heavily and/or gasp for breath from time to time. If possible, throw in an audible yawn, groan or sniff. (DAV 5)

2. Rustle papers close to the microphone. This can have a delightfully nerve-racking effect if continued uninterruptedly and accompanied by clicking noises (use of pens, metal bracelets and/or knitting needles recommended).
(DAV 5)

3. Do not use the cough button for asides in the booth. Always switch your mike off altogether. Hearing the original from time to time has a pleasingly bewildering effect on delegates, especially in the middle of a sentence.
(DAV 3)

4. Make sure your door is open whenever a group of colleagues outside is enjoying a delegate's latest howler. This may disturb you somewhat but the slight discomfort is well worth while in view of the high intrinsic DAV of this exercice. (DAV 4.75)

5. If there is a bright central light in your booth, do not switch it off when films or slides are shown. Why should you ? (DAV 3)

---

[45] With thanks to *AIIC Bulletin*.
[46] Delegate Annoyance Value.

6. Female interpreters should rummage in their hand-bags as soon as they're settled in the booth. (Note: DAV can be enhanced by your colleague temporarily purloining whatever you were looking for as soon as you have found it, so that rummaging can begin again immediately.) Alternatively, electronic watches may be worn or pocket calculators carried that beep into the mike unexpectedly. Laptop or notebook PC's may also be effective for this purpose.

(DAV 5)

7. Old hotel bills, theatre tickets, shopping lists etc. should be ripped into small pieces in front of the mike.

(DAV 2)

8. Always insist on being invited to all conference parties and social occasions but never attend any of them. On no account apologise for your absence, either before or after the event. (DAV 4)

9. If you have to mingle with delegates socially, make sure you talk down at them, or better still, ignore them altogether. Winning the race to the buffet is of the essence.

(DAV 5)

10. When doing consecutive, seize every opportunity to interrupt and correct speakers. (Anything goes in this exercice; the important thing being to make them feel small. Sometimes, a mere hint of a superior sneer will do the trick.) (DAV 10)

REFERENCES AND BIBLIOGRAPHY
References

AIIC, 1992. *Communicate,* No.l, Autumn.

AIIC Training Committee. *Advice to students wishing to become conference interpreters.*

Altman, Janet. 1989. "Overcoming Babel: the role of the conference interpreter in the communication process" in: *Babel: The cultural and linguistic barriers between nations.* Edited by Rainer Kölmel and Jerry Payne, Aberdeen: Aberdeen University Press.

Andronikof, Prince. 1968. "Introduction" in *L'Interprète dans les conférences internationales.* D. Seleskovitch, Paris: Minard.

Arnaud, Vincent G. 1950. *Los intérpretes en el descubrimiento, la conquista y la colonización en el Rio de la Plata.* Buenos Aires.

Beisel, A. 1989. AIIC, Technical and Health Committee Report. Article entitled "All Ears" by Ingrid Kurz. November.

Bertone, Laura. 1985. Article in AIIC *Bulletin* , XIII, (2), October.

Bleicher, Josef. 1980.*Contemporary Hermeneutics, Hermeneutics as method, Philosophy and Critique*, London: Routledge & Kegel Paul.

Bourgain, G. 1991. A Genève, retour de Nuremberg. AIIC *Bulletin* No.4, December .

Bowen, David and Margareta. 1985. Article in META.30 (1): 74-77, March.

Bros-Brann, Eliane. 1996. Article in AIIC *Bulletin*, September.

307

Chernov. 1978. *Teoria i praktika sinkhronavo piriboda*, Moscow.

Coleman-Holmes, John. 1971. *Mâcher du Coton*. Paris: Entre-temps.

Colombus, Christoph. 1970. *Das Bordbuch 1492. Leben und Fahrten des Entdeckers der Welt in Dokumenten und Aufzeichnungen.* Edited and revised by Robert Grün. Tübingen: Horst Erdmann Verlag.

Commission of the European Communities. *Short courses for student Interpreters*. Joint Service Interpretation-Conferences.

Cooper, Anna. 1983.The Alexander technique - a Contribution to Health, A.I.I.C.*Bulletin*,XI(3), September.

Cortés, Hernán. 1946. *Cartas y relaciones*. Emecé: Buenos Aires

Crystal, David. 1997. *English as a Global Language*. Cambridge: Cambridge University Press.

Danzin, André. 1992a. European Linguistic Infrastructure. Report. 1992b. Pour une politique de promotion des industries de la langue et des industries de l'information basées sur l'informatisation du français. Report to the Conseil Supérieur de la Langue Française. 1993. *La croissance autrement*. Paris: Éditions européennes thermique et industrie.

Déjean Le Féal, Karla. 1981. L'enseignement des méthodes d'interprétation. University of Ottawa Quarterly. 1982. *Why impromptu speech is easy to understand.* Abo Akademi Foundation Publication No. 78. Abo Akademi. 1985a. Machine translation and the print media. *Studies on editology*. No.16:283-294 1985b. *Simultaneous Interpretation from and into Asian languages*.Seoul: Graduate School of Interpretation and Translation, Hankuk University of Foreign Studies. 1987. *Simultaneous interpretation from and into Asian languages.* V(1):2-5.1988. A look into the black box. *Fremdsprachen.*

No.4:237-240. 1990. Some thoughts on the evaluation of simultaneous interpretation. *Interpreting yesterday, today and tomorrow*. American Translators' Association. Vol. IV.1991. "La Liberté en interprétation" in *La Liberté en Traduction*. Paris: Didier Erudition. Aptitudes et Connaissances nécessaires aux Études d'Interprétation". *Le Françaisdans le Monde*. Comment un interprète de conférence perfectionne ses langues actives et passives. *Les Nouveaux Cahiers d'Allemand*. 92(1):7-19.

de Juan, Marcela. 1977. *La China que ayer viví y la China que hoy entreví*. Part of the *La Vida Vivida* series. Barcelona: Luis de Caralt Editor S.A.

Dickson, Paul. 1992. *Dickson's Word Treasury, A Connoisseur's Collection of Old and New, Weird and Wonderful, Useful and Outlandish Words*. New York: John Wiley & Sons.

Forum. 1991. University of Queensland. No.8, June. 1994. University of Queensland. No.20, June.

Garcia-Landa, Mariano. 1985.MML (Mariano's mailing list), 2(1&2), July.

Gile, Daniel. Les Petits Lexiques Informatisés: Quelques Réflexions. *AIIC Bulletin*.

González, Roseann Dueñas, Victoria F. Vásquez and Holly Mikkelson. 1991.*Fundamentals of Court Interpretation - Theory, Policy and Practice*. Durham: Carolina Academic Press.

Handy, Charles B. 1989. *The age of unreason*. London: Hutchinson Business.

Harris, Brian. 1981. "Observations on a Cause Célèbre: Court Interpreting at the Lischka Trial" in *L'interprétation auprès des tribunaux*. Edited by Roda P. Roberts. Ottawa: University of Ottawa Press.

Herbert, Jean. 1952. *The Interpreter's Handbook*. Georg: Université de Genève.

Keiser, Walter. 1975. Memorandum on the Selection and Training of Conference Interpreters and Interpretation Services at Scientific Meetings. December. 1992. Articles in *AIIC Bulletin*.

Kerr, Anne. 1988. *Lanterns Over Pinchgut*. Sydney, Macmillan.

Kolmer, Herbert. 1983. Our Working Environment. Notes for the International AIIC Symposium on"Intercultural Communication in a Changing World", Brussels, 14 and 15 January 1987. Article in *Oesterreichische Hochschulzeitung*, Journal of Austrian Universities and Academies, Vienna. June.What price an interpreter's ears? *AIIC Bulletin*, pp.44 & 45.

Kurz, Ingrid. *All ears*. Technical and Health Committee, AIIC.

Kurz, Irene. 1992. Luis de Torres. *AIIC Bulletin*. XX(4), 30 December.

Laster, Kathy and Veronica Taylor. 1993. *Interpreters and the Legal System*, Annandale NSW: The Federation Press.

Longley, Pat. 1988. Are Conference Interpreters really necessary? *Conferences & Exhibitions*. January.

Luther, Martin (1483-1546). *Sendbrief des Dolmetchens*

McCallion, Michael. 1988. *The voice book*. Faber and Faber.

Mackintosh, Jennifer, 1983. Relay Interpretation: an exploratory study." M.A. thesis. University of London.

Mansilla, L.V. 1870. Letters in *La Tribuna*. May to September.1966. *Una excursión a los indios ranqueles*. Buenos Aires: Kapelusz.

Melero, Francisca. A glossary in need is a friend indeed. *AIIC Bulletin*

Morris, Ruth. 1993. Images of the Interpreter: A Study of Language-Switching in the Legal Process. PhD thesis. Department of Law, Lancaster University.

Naisbitt, John and Patricia Aburdene. 1992.*Megatrends 2000: Ten new directions for the 1990s*. New York: Morrow

Nida, Eugene. 1960. Article in *Babel*. 6 (2).1964. Toward a science of translating. Leiden: E.J.Brill.

Paneth, Eva. 1956. *Conference interpreting*, London University.1958. *L'interprète*. No.4:2.

Robinson, Ludmilla. 1994. Handbook for legal interpreters. North Ryde, NSW: The Law Book Company.

Roditi, Edouard. *Interpreting: Its History in a Nutshell*, Washington D.C.: NRCTI publication, Georgetown University.

Sayeg, Yuki. 1992. Note-taking for beginners. *Forum*. No. 12, July.

Seleskovitch, Danica. 1968. *L'interprète dans les Conférences Internationales*. Chapter VI, "Le problème de la langue d'expression".Paris, Editions Minard, Lettres Modernes.1974. *Langage, langues et mémoire, Etude de la prise de notes en interprétation consécutive*.1977. Take care of the Sense and the Sounds will take care of themselves (Lewis Carroll) or Why Interpreting is not Tantamount to translating Languages. *AIIC Bulletin*. V(3):76-86 and articles in various issues of *AIIC Bulletin*.

Sen Nishiyama. Translation and Interpretation in Japan. META. XXVIII(1).

Shlesinger, Miriam. 1990. "The Next Step: Quality Control for Courtroom Interpreting" in *Proceedings, Twelfth World Congress of the International Federation of Translators (FIT)*. Edited by Mladen Jovanovic. Belgrade. Prevodilac.Article in *Parallèles*. Cahiers de l'Ecole de Traduction et d'Interprétation, University of Geneva, Switzerland. No.11.

Sierra, Emilio Manuel. 1988. El primer intérprete blanco en el Río de la Plata. *Babel.* 34:3.

Skunke, M.-F. 1993.A propos du quarantième anniversaire de la naissance de l'AIIC. *AIIC Bulletin.*XXI (3), l5 September.

Spinoza, Benedict de. l670. *Tractacus theologicus-politicus.* Chapter 7. Amsterdam.

Tench,Watkin.1996. 1788: *A Narrative of the Expedition to Botany Bay and a Complete Account of the Settlement at Port Jackson.* Edited and Introduced by Tim Flannery Melbourne: Text Publishing.

Tusa, Ann and John. 1983.*The Nuremberg Trial.* Macmillan.

van Emde Boas, M. 1957. *L'interprète.* No.4, 1958. *L'interprète.* No.l.

Wade, Nicholas. 2000. Article in the "Science Times" section, *New York Times.* February 1.

Further reading

1. Interpretation
Ilg, Gérard. 1959. *L'enseignement de l'interprétation à l'Université de Genève.* Geneva: École d'Interprètes.

International Standard IEC 914: Conference systems - Electrical and audio requirements, available from International Electrotechnical Commission, Geneva.

International Standard ISO 2603 - Booths for simultaneous interpretation - General characteristics and equipment, available from ISO (International Standards Organization), Geneva.
International Standard ISO 4043: Booths for simultaneous interpretation - Mobile booths - General characteristics and equipment. ISO, Geneva.

Longley, Patricia. 1968. *Conference Interpreting*. London: Pitman.

Moggio-Ortiz, Evelyn. *The Interpreters: A Historical Perspective*. Video-cassette.
Researched and directed by Evelyn Moggio-Ortiz. Traces the history of interpreting up to the present day at United Nations, New York. Starts with the challenging Danny Kaye peroration delivered specifically for the delectation of the simultaneous interpreters. There are interviews in all six official languages of the United Nations: English, French, Spanish, Russian, Chinese and Arabic. Available in all six languages with subtitles whenever someone speaks in one of the other five, in NTSC, VHS or PAL/SECAM, from AIIC, Geneva.

Plant, D. *The student interpreter's work book*. Trieste: Edizioni Lint.

Rozan, J.-F. 1974. *La prise de notes en interprétation consécutive*. Geneva: Georg.

Setton, Robin. 1999. *Simultaneous interpretation. A cognitive-pragmatic analysis.*Philadelphia: John Benjamins.

van Hoff, Henri. *Théorie et Pratique de l'Interprétation*. Munich: Max Hueber Verlag.

Liaison interpreting

Gentile, Adolfo, Uldis Ozolins and Mary Vasilakakos. 1996. *Liaison interpreting*. Melbourne: Melbourne University Press.

2. Parliamentary, meeting and conference procedures
Carr, Cecil E., and Alan R.Foyster. 1962. *Take the Chair*. Perth, WA: Australian Rostrum Council
Citrine, Walter McLennan. 1982. *Citrine's ABC of chairmanship*. London: NCLC.

Demeter, George. 1969. *Dementer's manual of parliamentary law and procedure for the legal conduct of*

313

business in all deliberative assemblies. Blue book ed., rev., expanded and updated. Boston: Boston, Little, Brown.

Rigg, John. 1920. *How to conduct a meeting, standing orders and rules of debate.* London: Allan & Unwin.

3. Terminology

Anderson, Ralph J.B. 1972. *French-English glossary of French legal terms in European treaties: Selected legal terms in French texts of European Community treaties, conventions, agreements and related documents and of Council of Europe conventions, agreements and related documents, explained in the light of the law of France.* Prepared by R.J.B. Anderson and R.J. Deckers. London: Sweet & Maxwell.

Buttress, F.A. 1966. *World List of Abbreviations.* London: Hill.

*Conference Terminology: a manual for conference members and interpreters in English, French, Spanish, Russian, Italian German and Hungarian.*1962. 2nd ed. Glossaria Interpretum series. Amsterdam: Elsevier.

Greiser, Josef. 1955. *Lexikon der Abkürzungen aus dem Finanz- imd Steuerrecht.* Osnabrück: Fromm

Haensch, Günther. 1965. *Dictionary of International Relations and Politics; systematic and alphabetical in four languages: German, English/American, French, Spanish.* New York: Elsevier.

Hipgrave, Richard. 1985. *Computing Terms and Acronyms*: A dictionary. London: The Library Association.
Union des associations internationales (ed.). 1985. *International organization abbreviations and addresses.* London: K.G.Saur.

Longley, Dennis, and Michael Shain . 1987. Data and computer security - Dictionary of standards, concepts and terms. New York: Stockton Press.

WIPO. 1980. WIPO glossary of terms of the law of copyright and neighbouring rights. Geneva: WIPO.

4. Public Speaking

Bryant, Donald Cross, and Karl Wallace. 1962. *Oral communication: A short course in speaking*. New York: Appleton-Century-Crofts.

Doriac, A. and Gaston Dujarric. 1953. Toasts, allocutions et discours modèles pour toutes les circonstances de la vie privée et publique, précédés d'un Traité sur l'art de parler en public. New edition. Paris: A. Michel

Hamilton, William Gerard. 1946. *Parlamentarische Logik, Taktik, und Rhetorik*. Zurich: Societas-Verlag.

McCall, R., and H. Cohen. 1963. *Fundamentals of speech: The theory and practice of oral communication*. New York: Macmillan.

Vital speeches of the Day. Bimonthly. New York: City News.

5. Oral communication

Büchmann Georg. 1971. "Geflügelte Worte". München.

Genest Emile. 1954. Dictionnaire des citations: Dictionnaire des phrases, vers et mots célèbres employés dans le langage courant avec précision de l'origine. Paris: Nathan.

Ilg, Gerard. 1960. *Proverbes français: suivis d'équivalents en allemand, anglais,espagnol, italien, neérlandais*. Glossaria Interpretum series. Amsterdam: Elsevier.
Johnson, Albert. 1954. *Common English Proverbs*. London: Longmans Green. 1963. Common English quotations. London: Longmans Green.

Jones, Hugh Percy (ed.) 1923. *Dictionary of Foreign Phrases and Classical Quotations: Comprising 14,000 idioms, proverbs, maxims, mottoes, technical words and terms, and press allusions from the works of the great writers in Latin, French, Italian, Greek, German, Spanish, Portuguese, alphabetically arranged, with English translations and equivalents.* Edinburgh: John Grant.

Partridge, Eric. 1978. *A dictionary of clichés.* 5th ed. London: Routledge & Paul.
Roget, Peter Mark. 1977. *Roget's thesaurus of English words and phrases.* New ed., revised and modernised by Robert A. Dutch. London: Longman.

Vinay, Jean Paul, and Jean Louis Darbeinet: *Stylistique comparée du français et de l'anglais.* Paris: Didier

6.Court Interpreting

Bennett, John. 1981."Training of Court Interpreters: an ideal and a realistic view", in *L'interprétation auprès des tribunaux.* Edited by Roda P. Roberts. pp.179-182. Ottawa: Editions de l'Université d'Ottawa.

Berk-Seligson, Susan. 1990. *The bilingual courtroom: Court interpreters in the judicial process.* Chicago: University of Chicago Press.

Bowen, Jan. 1994. *The Macquarie Easy Guide to Australian Law.* 2nd ed. Sydney: Macquarie Library.

Carr, Sylvana (ed.) 1984. *Manual for Court Interpreters.* 4 vols. Vancouver: Vancouver Community College. 1988. "Towards a Court Interpreting System in a Multicultural Society: English-Speaking British Columbia", in *Language at Crossroads.* Edited by Deanna L.Hammond.pp.417-422. Proceedings of the 29th Annual Conference of ATA.
Chisolm, Richard, and Garth Nettheim. 1997.*Understanding Law.* 5th Edition. Sydney: Butterworths.

Colin, Joan, and Ruth Morris. 1996. *Interpreters and the legal process.* Winchester: Waterside Press.

Commonwealth Attorney-General's Department. 1991. *Access to Interpreters in the   Australian Legal System.*

Report. Canberra: Commonwealth Attorney-General's Department

Driesen, Christiane J. 1988. "Paradoxes de l'interprétation auprès des tribunaux" in *Proceedings XIth World Congress of FIT, Translation, Our Future*. Edited by Paul Nekeman. Maastricht: Euroterm. 1990. "Initiation à l'interprétation juridique" in *Proceedings, 12th World Congress of FIT*. Edited by Mladen Jovanovic. Belgrade: Prevodilac.

Gibbs, Sir Harry. 1988. *Interpreters and the law*. 28 July.

Keating Kathleen.1981. *A Handbook for Court Interpreters*.Vancouver: Vancouver Community College

Krauthammer Sarah. 1986. "On the Recognition of the Court Interpreter as a Professional" in *Building Bridges*. Edited by Karl Kummer. Proceedings of the 27th Annual Conference of ATA. Medford, N.J.: Learned Information.

Leeth J. *The court interpreter examination*. Washington, D.C. National Resource Centre for Translation and Interpretation, Georgetown University.

Morris Ruth. 1988. "Court Interpreting", ITI *News*, Institute of Translation and Interpreting, London.3(1): 9-131996. With Joan Colin. *Interpreters and the Legal Process*. Waterside Press, Winchester. 1989a. Court interpretation: The Trial of Ivan John Demjanjuk - A case study, *The Interpreters' Newsletter*, Trieste University School of Interpretation and Translation, No.2:27-37 1989b Court Interpretation and the Record of Legal Proceedings: Eichman v. Demjanjuk. *Parallèles*. Cahiers de l'Ecole de Traduction et d'Interprétation, Université de Genève, No.11:9 – 28 1990a. "Interpretation at the Demjanjuk trial" in *Interpreting - yesterday, today and tomorrow*. Edited by Bowen and Bowen. American Translators' Association Scholarly Monograph Series, Bowen & Bowen, Vol.IV(101-107), State University of New York at Binghamton. 1990b. "Court interpreter: record or participant? in *Proceedings, XIIth World Congress of FIT* (International Translators' Federation),(724-729). Jovanovic, Mladen (ed.), Prevodilac: Belgrade. 1993a. "Nobs and Yobs - the provision of interpreters for legal proceedings involving high-status foreigners and others", *Proceedings, XIIIth World Congres of FIT* .(International Translators' Federation). Edited by C. Picken. pp. 356-366.. 1993b. The interlingual interpreter - cypher or intelligent participant? Or, The interpreter's turn... *International journal for the semiotics of law* VI(18): 271-291. 1995a.The moral dilemmas of court interpreting. *The Translator*, l(l):25-46 1995b. Pragmatism, precept and passions: The attitude of English-language legal systems to non-English speakers in *Translation and the law*. Edited by M. Morris. American Translators' Association Scholarly Monograph Series, Vol.VIII(263-279). Philadelphia: John Benjamins 1997. *Great Mischiefs - A historical look at language legislation in Great Britain, in Language Legislation and Linguistic Rights*. Philadelphia: John Benjamins

O'Barr, William .1982. *Language Power and Strategies in the Courtroom*. New York: Academic Press

Repa, Jindra. l981. A training program for court interpreters. Montreal:META.26(4):394-396.

Roberts Roda P. (ed.) (1981a) *L'interprétation auprès des tribunaux: Actes du mini-colloque tenu les 10 et 11 avril 1980 à l'Université d'Ottawa*. Ottawa: Editions de l'Université d'Ottawa. 1981b. "Training Programs for Court Interpreters in Canada" in *L'interprétation auprès des tribunaux*. Edited by Roda P. Roberts, pp.183-188.Ottawa: Editions de l'Université d'Ottawa.

Shlesinger, Miriam. 1988. Effects of interpreter-dependence on intercultural communication in the courtroom., paper read at the TRANSIF (Translation in Finland) Seminar on Empirical Research in Intercultural Studies and Translation, Savonlinna, 22-24 September.

Tayler, Marilyn R., Roda P. Roberts and Ellie de la Bandera. 1988. "Legal Interpretation Education: The New Jersey Legal Interpretation Project", in Deanna L. Hammond (ed.), *Language at Crossroads*. Edited by Deanna L. Hammond. pp.389-398. Proceedings of the 29th Annual Conference of ATA.

Trabing Eta. 1980. *Manual for Judiciary Interpreters (English-Spanish)*. Houston: Agri-search International

Walker, Anne Graffam. 1986a. Context, transcripts and appellate readers. *Justice Quarterly* 3(4):409. 1986b. The "verbatim" record: A surprise or two. *Court Call* 1-3.)1988. Court reporting: Another Kind of Interpretation MS. 1990. "Language at work in the law, The customs, conventions and appellate consequences of court reporting" in *Language in the Judicial Process*. Edited by Judith N. Levi and Anne Graffam Walker. pp. 203-244. New York: Plenum Press.

Zazueta Fernando Rochin O. 1975 Attorney's guide to the use of court interpreters, with an English-Spanish glossary of criminal law terms. *University of California at Davis law review*. No. 8: 471 - 522.

Spender, Lynne (ed.). 1997. *The law handbook*. 6th ed. Redfern, NSW: Redfern Legal Centre.

7. The future of languages

Le Cornec, Jacques. 1990. Rapport sur les moyens modernes du soutien du français, *Revue*. No. 155, October - November-December.

DANNY KAYE

Speech made by Danny Kaye, Regional Director for the World, reporting to the Board of UNICEF and interpreted into French, Spanish and Russian :

"Thank you very much. Ladies and Gentlemen:

"I had no method of making a Report about six hundred and forty-three million children received four thousand one hundred and eighty seven litres translated insofar as the insufficient quarts dedicated to the incredible kind of leader quality which of course has not had the vitamin-ized process of our milk distribution. But in a sense that has not yet come to the attention of those, and so we feel, more or less, that they have, and we should continue on the basis of not so much insofar as we can, but that they can in a sense realize their true value.

I'd like to see what the interpreters are going to make of that."

CPSIA information can be obtained at www.ICGtesting.com
Printed in the USA
LVOW011613311011

252875LV00014B/76/P